THE ASSASSINATION OF JOHN F. KENNEDY

A Complete Book of Facts

THE ASSASSINATION OF JOHN F. KENNEDY

A Complete Book of Facts

James P. Duffy
and Vincent L. Ricci

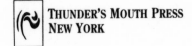

THUNDER'S MOUTH PRESS
NEW YORK

To Bob Urban

Copyright © 1992 by James P. Duffy and Vincent L. Ricci
All rights reserved.

1 2 3 4 5 6 7 8 9 10 / 98 97 96 95 94 93 92

Published by
Thunder's Mouth Press
54 Greene Street, Suite 4S
New York, NY 10013

Library of Congress Cataloging-in-Publication Data
Duffy, James P., 1941-
    The assassination of John F. Kennedy: a complete book of facts /
James P. Duffy, Vincent L. Ricci. — 1st ed.
        p.   cm.
    Includes bibliographic references.
    Includes filmography: p.
    ISBN 1-56025-042-9 : $14.95
    1. Kennedy, John F. (John Fitzgerald), 1917-1963—Assassination.
I. Ricci, Vincent L. II Title.
E842.9.D77 1992
364.1'524'0973—dc20
                           92-17536
                              CIP

Editorial production and text design by Thumb Print
Cover design by Mike Stromberg
Printed in the United States of America

Distributed by
Publishers Group West
4065 Hollis Street
Emeryville, CA 94608
(800) 788-3123

ACKNOWLEDGMENTS

The authors would like to thank the following people, whose assistance made this book both more accurate and more complete than it would otherwise have been: At Thunder's Mouth Press, Joan Fucillo, acting managing editor; Barbara Elovic, managing editor; and Marian Cole, editorial assistant; and, at Thumb Print editorial and design services, editors James Waller and Marian Appellof and designers Jay Anning and Areta Buk.

CONTENTS

LIST OF ILLUSTRATIONS

LIST OF ILLUSTRATIONS

INTRODUCTION

It has been called the most infamous crime of the century, possibly of our entire history. The assassination of President John F. Kennedy on November 22, 1963, as he rode in a motorcade in Dallas, Texas, has created more controversy than any other single event in American history. Speculation about exactly what happened and who was involved began only brief minutes after the president's car sped from the scene of the shooting and raced to a nearby hospital.

In this volume we have sought to gather accurate information about all the people, places, events, facts, objects, and theories associated directly or indirectly with the young president's death. We feel that presenting these elements in a reference-book format will help the reader better understand the controversies that continue to envelop this tragic incident, which has left an indelible impression on every American old enough to realize what happened that terrible day.

A word about the entries: It was necessary to set guidelines on what was to be included in and excluded from the book and to set a limit on the extent of information presented in any given entry. Without such guidelines this work could have stretched on for years and resulted in several volumes rather than the single-volume, accessible source we envisioned.

To keep the book accessible, each entry has been made as concise as possible, although some entries are necessarily longer and more comprehensive than others. As we watched the book grow in size—with more and more potential entries—some topics were selectively excluded. The result is a volume containing many subjects directly related to the assassination and its aftermath and a lesser number that are more peripherally related to the president's death. So many hundreds of articles and books, containing so many speculations connecting those directly involved with those only marginally—or quite theoretically—implicated, that we had to establish cut-off points. In some cases we have followed up on connections because they appeared relevant; at other times we did not, feeling they were not germane to this book.

We expect that not all readers will agree with our decisions. Some will insist that we should have included an entry on this or that topic, or that there are entries on topics that have no business being here. But ultimately we had to make the decision to include only those entries we believed would best help our readers understand more than they presently do about the assassination of President John F. Kennedy and the controversies engulfing the event. We think that we have included an entry on every topic appropriate to this ambitious goal. In the interest of improving further editions of this book, we shall be glad to hear from readers who want to suggest other topics they feel warrant inclusion. Those who do send suggestions are reminded that we are the arbiters of the book's contents. Readers with recommendations are invited to write to us in care of the publisher, Thunder's Mouth Press, at 54 Greene Street, Suite 4S, New York, NY 10013.

James P. Duffy
Vincent L. Ricci

How to Use This Book

The Assassination of John F. Kennedy: A Complete Book of Facts includes a number of reference-book elements designed to help the reader find his or her way about in the great mass of material relating to the assassination. First, entries are alphabetically arranged. Almost all entries make mention of other topics that are treated separately in their own entries. A dagger (†) is used to indicate that a particular topic is given separate, full treatment in the alphabetical listing. The dagger precedes the first mention of that topic; note that the dagger comes directly before the word under which that topic is alphabetized. For example, on first mention in a given entry, the name Jack Ruby appears with the dagger in front of Ruby, like so: Jack †Ruby.

In addition to the numerous full entries, the book includes a number of what are called "blind" entries, which simply direct the reader to other places where information on a given topic is to be found. For example, "AM/LASH" was the code name for CIA operative Rolando Cubela, so the blind entry for AM/LASH directs the reader to see CUBELA, ROLANDO.

Almost every full entry is followed by a "source" line to let readers know which book or books we depended upon most heavily in compiling the information in that entry and to tell readers where they can go most easily to find out more information on that topic. The source line is indicated by a book icon that looks like this: 📖. In deciding which sources to list at the ends of entries, we chose the most readily available books: Almost all the books mentioned in the source lines are in print as of this writing. (A much more complete bibliography follows at the end of the book, as does an annotated list of some of the motion pictures and television shows that have been made about the assassination.) In the source lines, book titles are somewhat abbreviated. A key showing the full titles, authors, and publication information follows on the next page.

KEY TO SOURCES

Assassination Tapes: George O'Toole. *The Assassination Tapes: An Electronic Probe into the Murder of John F. Kennedy and the Dallas Coverup.* New York: Penthouse Press, 1975.

Best Evidence: David S. Lifton. *Best Evidence: Disguise and Deception in the Assassination of John F. Kennedy.* New York: Carroll & Graf, 1988.

Conspiracy: Anthony Summers. *Conspiracy.* New York: Paragon House, 1989.

Conspiracy of Silence: Charles A. Crenshaw. *JFK: Conspiracy of Silence.* New York: Signet, 1992.

Contract on America: David E. Scheim. *Contract on America: The Mafia Murder of President John F. Kennedy.* New York: Zebra Books, 1988.

Coup d'Etat: Michael L. Canfield and Alan J. Weberman. *Coup d'Etat in America: The CIA and the Assassination of John F. Kennedy.* New York: The Third Press, 1975.

Crossfire: Jim Marrs. *Crossfire: The Plot That Killed Kennedy.* New York: Carroll & Graf, 1989.

Death of a President: William Manchester. *The Death of a President: November 20–November 25, 1963.* 25th anniversary ed. New York: Harper & Row, 1988.

Fatal Hour: G. Robert Blakey and Richard N. Billings. *Fatal Hour: The Assassination of President Kennedy by Organized Crime.* New York: Berkley, 1992.

Final Disclosure: David W. Belin. *Final Disclosure: The Full Truth About the Assassination of President Kennedy.* New York: Charles Scribner's Sons, 1988.

Heritage of Stone: Jim Garrison. *Heritage of Stone.* New York: Berkley, 1972.

High Treason: Robert J. Groden and Harrison Edward Livingstone. *High Treason: The Assassination of President Kennedy and the New Evidence of Conspiracy.* New York: Berkley, 1990.

High Treason 2: Harrison Edward Livingstone. *High Treason 2: The Great Cover-up: The Assassination of President John F. Kennedy.* New York: Carroll & Graf, 1992.

Mafia Kingfish: John H. Davis. *Mafia Kingfish: Carlos Marcello and the Assassination of John F. Kennedy.* New York: McGraw-Hill, 1989.

Mortal Error: Bonar Menninger. *Mortal Error: The Shot That Killed JFK.* New York: St. Martin's Press, 1992.

On the Trail of the Assassins: Jim Garrison. *On the Trail of the Assassins.* New York, Warner, 1991.

Plausible Denial: Mark Lane. *Plausible Denial: Was the CIA Involved in the Assassination of JFK?* New York: Thunder's Mouth Press, 1991.

Reasonable Doubt: Henry Hurt. *Reasonable Doubt: An Investigation into the Assassination of John F. Kennedy.* New York: Henry Holt, 1985.

Ruby Cover-up: Seth Kantor. *The Ruby Cover-up.* New York: Zebra Books, 1992.

Rush to Judgment: Mark Lane. *Rush to Judgment.* New York: Thunder's Mouth Press, 1991.

Texas Connection: Craig I. Zirbel. *The Texas Connection: The Assassination of President John F. Kennedy.* Scottsdale, Ariz.: The Texas Connection Company, 1991.

Warren Report: The Warren Commission Report (many editions).

THE ASSASSINATION OF JOHN F. KENNEDY

A Complete Book of Facts

ABADIE, WILLIAM

A onetime employee of Jack †Ruby, the man who shot and killed Lee Harvey †Oswald, Abadie repaired jukeboxes and slot machines for Ruby's gambling operations. He also briefly doubled as a bookmaker in one of Ruby's clubs. On December 6, 1963, William Abadie told FBI agents that Ruby was well connected with local racketeers and corrupt police officials in both Dallas and Fort Worth. He also claimed to have seen local police officers hanging out in one of Ruby's bars while patrons were engaging in illegal gambling activities.

📖 *Contract on America*

ABRAMS, GUS W.

Abrams is reportedly one of three †hoboes found near the scene of the assassination and taken in for questioning by the Dallas police almost immediately after. Initially charged with vagrancy, all three were later released. There has been confusion about their identities, what they were doing in the railroad yard behind the †Grassy Knoll, and why they were released so quickly.

📖 *High Treason 2*

"ABRAMS, DR. MORRIS"

This is the fictitious name that researcher David S. †Lifton assigned to a doctor who examined President Kennedy's autopsy report together with drawings of the wounds made by Dr. James J. †Humes of †Bethesda Naval Hospital. Abrams reportedly voiced the opinion that for some inexplicable reason the president's brain had been cut prior to the autopsy.

See also AUTOPSY CONTROVERSY.

📖 *Best Evidence*

ABT, JOHN

An attorney with offices in New York City, Abt was noted for his defense of Smith Act violators in the late 1940s and early 1950s. Following his arrest, Lee Harvey †Oswald attempted unsuccessfully to contact Abt, who was away from his home on the weekend following the assassination.

📖 *Conspiracy*

ACCESSORIES AFTER THE FACT

Written by Sylvia †Meagher and first published by
Bobbs-Merrill in 1967, *Accessories after the Fact: The
Warren Commission, the Authorities, and the Report* is
an in-depth critique of the †Warren Report. In
Accessories, Meagher charges that the Warren Report
contains important inaccuracies, omissions,
misleading statements, and untrue statements. The
book is a highly regarded resource that is frequently
quoted by critics of the Warren Commission Report.

ACOUSTICAL EVIDENCE

Police departments routinely tape-record the
conversations that take place over their radio
networks. The †Dallas police dispatch tape recorded on
November 22, 1963, was used by the †Warren
Commission and the †Dallas police to pinpoint the
locations and review the movements of all officers
during the presidential motorcade and immediately
following the assassination. It then lay untouched for
sixteen years, until Mary †Ferrell brought it to the
attention of investigators from the †House Select
Committee on Assassinations. The tape was analyzed
by several acoustics experts from †Bolt Beranek and
Newman and by Mark †Weiss.

Using highly sophisticated, state-of-the-art acoustical equipment, experts concluded that four shots were fired in †Dealey Plaza, not three as the Warren Commission postulated, and that the third shot was fired from the area of the †Grassy Knoll. Before the House Assassinations Committee adjourned, the members asked the Justice Department to pursue some of the leads it had developed. The Justice Department requested the National Science Foundation to verify the acoustical evidence on the dispatch tape. The Foundation's findings disputed the earlier hypothesis and have been used to discredit the conclusion that four shots were fired.

See also ARNOLD, GORDON; ASCHKENASY, ERNEST; BARGER, DR. JAMES; BELL LABORATORY; COMMITTEE ON BALLISTICS ACOUSTICS; GRASSY KNOLL WITNESSES; MCLAIN, H. B.; OVERPASS WITNESSES; PELLICANO, ANTHONY.

📖 *Conspiracy*

ACOUSTICAL SOCIETY OF AMERICA

The †House Select Committee on Assassinations solicited recommendations from the Acoustical Society—a nonprofit professional association of acousticians—for experts who could interpret what were presumably gunshots on an audio tape copied from the November 22, 1963, †Dallas Police dispatch tape. The Society recommended the firm of †Bolt Beranek and Newman of Cambridge, Massachusetts, and Mark †Weiss, a computer scientist.

📖 *Contract on America*

ACLU
See AMERICAN CIVIL LIBERTIES UNION.

ADAMCIK, JOHN
John Adamcik is one of three Dallas police detectives (the others being Richard Stovall and Gus †Rose) who investigated Buell Wesley †Frazier and searched the home of Ruth †Paine, where they confiscated Lee Harvey †Oswald's possessions. Adamcik provoked a minor conflict when in his testimony before the †Warren Commission he disavowed any understanding of the Russian language. This statement directly contradicted the police report submitted to the Commission, which declared that he "understands a little Russian." Adamcik is no longer a member of the Dallas Police; his whereabouts are unknown.

📖 *Assassination Tapes*

ADAMS, VICTORIA
Adams, a †Texas School Book Depository Building

employee when the assassination occurred, was
interviewed by both federal agents and the †Warren
Commission counsel. She was on the fourth floor of the
Depository when she heard the gunshots that
presumably killed the president and wounded Texas
governor John †Connally. According to her statements,
she rushed to the stairs, descended swiftly to the first
floor, and ran outside. If her account of the sequence is
accurate, she should have been in the stairwell at the
same time Lee Harvey †Oswald is alleged by the
Warren Commission to have been fleeing from his
sixth-floor †sniper's nest to the sanctuary of a second-
floor cafeteria, where he was seen by Police Officer
Marrion L. †Baker. Adams claimed she saw or heard
no one on the stairs.

In a session with the Warren Commission counsel,
Adams volunteered the opinion that the shots she
heard came from below her fourth-floor window and to
the right, not from above and the left, where Oswald
allegedly fired the fatal bullet.

Adams added another unsolicited piece of
information that has fueled the controversies
surrounding the shooting scene. She recalled that
when she reached the street minutes after the
assassination, she and coworker Mrs. Avery †Davis
saw a man at the corner of Houston and Elm streets

questioning people much in the manner of a police officer. Later, after viewing Jack †Ruby on television, she said he "looked very similar" to the man at Houston and Elm. However, other persuasive testimony places Ruby at the *Dallas Morning News* offices at the time.

📖 *Best Evidence*; *Rush to Judgment*

AIR FORCE ONE

Air Force One was a customized Boeing 707 familiar to most Americans through the media. Although the plane was maintained and flown by select U.S. Air Force personnel, it appeared on the exterior identical to a commercial 707 except for the legend "United States of America" painted in large white letters above the windows on either side. The craft was officially designated #26000 and bore the †Secret Service code name "Angel."

The presidential party had come to Dallas's Love Field on the plane, and, following the assassination, *Air Force One* was used to transport the coffin presumably containing President Kennedy's body, as well as Jacqueline †Kennedy, President and Mrs. Lyndon B. †Johnson, and members of both presidential staffs, from Dallas to †Andrews Air Force Base outside Washington, D.C. President Johnson was sworn into office aboard the plane before it left Dallas. Controversy has surrounded this flight almost from the moment it touched down at Andrews. The fact that it was one-half hour late led to speculation that the president's body was either tampered with during the flight or was removed from the coffin, spirited from the plane at Andrews, secretly placed aboard a nearby Army helicopter, and flown somewhere else to afford members of the conspiracy an opportunity to alter Kennedy's wounds before the autopsy. A second possibility is that the president's body was removed from *Air Force One* while it was still at Love Field before departing Dallas.

See also AUTOPSY CONTROVERSY; BODY BAG CONTROVERSY; COFFIN CONTROVERSY.

📖 *Best Evidence*

AIR FORCE TWO

This, as well as Secret Service code name "Angel Two," is the name given to any of a number of aircraft made available to the vice president for official trips. Unlike †*Air Force One*, no single airplane is specifically dedicated to the vice president's use. The *Air Force Two* designation applies to whatever plane the vice president is flying aboard at the moment. The name itself was coined by members of the vice president's

press corps. Researcher David S. †Lifton raised, then
rejected, the possibility that President Kennedy's body
could secretly have been transported to Washington
from Dallas aboard *Air Force Two*.
📖 *Best Evidence*

AKIN, DR. GENE C.

Dr. Akin, an anesthesiologist, was one of sixteen
doctors at Dallas's †Parkland Memorial Hospital who
rushed to the emergency room area as the dying
president's limousine sped to the hospital. Dr. Akin
was one of several doctors who testified to the †Warren
Commission that the wound in the rear of the
president's head, officially designated the entry wound
for the bullet that penetrated his brain, was actually
an exit wound.
See also PARKLAND MEMORIAL HOSPITAL STAFF.
📖 *Best Evidence*; *High Treason*

ALBA, ADRIAN

Adrian Alba owned and operated the †Crescent City
Garage on Magazine Street in New Orleans, not far
from the famed French Quarter. The garage had
contracted with federal government agencies to garage
and service official vehicles, including some assigned
to the †Federal Bureau of Investigation and the †Secret

Service. Next door was the †William Reily Coffee Company, where from early May until mid-July 1963, Lee Harvey †Oswald worked as a machinery oiler. Oswald became friendly with Alba, sometimes spending his spare time in the garage browsing through Alba's gun magazines and talking about his firearms collection. Oswald asked Alba about ordering guns by mail, and Alba claims he helped Oswald repair the sling on a †Mannlicher-Carcano rifle, the kind of rifle Oswald allegedly used to shoot Kennedy.

Alba, a quiet man who shunned publicity about his friendship with Oswald, related a curious anecdote to researcher Anthony Summers. According to Alba, one day in the early summer of 1963, a man who showed him FBI credentials appeared at the garage and requested a car. The man was given a green Studebaker. The next day Alba saw what seemed to be the same Studebaker stop at the curb in front of the Reily Coffee Company. He saw Oswald approach the car and bend down to look in the window. A hand reached out the window holding what appeared to be a large envelope, which Oswald accepted and slipped inside his shirt. A few days later the car returned and Oswald once again met it; this time he held a brief conversation with the driver. Several days later the agent dropped the Studebaker off at the garage.

Another strange story involving the Crescent City Garage concerns a report, allegedly made by an employee of Alba's, that on the morning of the assassination a man claiming to be a friend of Alba's showed up at the garage asking whether he could look at Alba's gun magazines. Alba was out, but the man was permitted to go through the magazines. After the assassination, federal agents reportedly discovered that a coupon had been cut out of an issue of *American Rifleman*—and that the torn edges of this clipping matched those of the coupon Oswald allegedly used to order the Mannlicher-Carcano rifle. Curiously, Oswald's coupon had appeared in the magazine's February 1963 issue, whereas the altered *American Rifleman* in Alba's stack of magazines was the June 1963 issue.

See also AMERICAN RIFLEMAN ADVERTISEMENT; 544 CAMP STREET.

📖 *Conspiracy; Reasonable Doubt*

ALDERSON, DR. LAWRENCE

A longtime resident of Houston, Dr. Alderson, a dentist, claims that FBI agents placed him under surveillance shortly after the assassination, and finally questioned him in December 1963. Although there is no known official record of this interview,

Alderson says the subject of their questions was his friendship with Jean †Souetre, a Frenchman who had once attempted the assassination of Charles de Gaulle. Alderson knew Souetre in the early 1950s while he was a lieutenant in the U.S. Army stationed in France, and Souetre was a captain in the French air force.

Alderson told the FBI agents he hadn't seen Souetre since leaving France, but that the two had continued to exchange Christmas greetings each year. The dentist claims that during the interview, the agents indicated that Souetre had been traced to Dallas the day before the assassination, but that they had lost him there. They were trying to determine how the Frenchman had left Dallas, and whether anyone had helped him leave. In 1983, when a reporter asked Souetre about his relationship with Alderson, Souetre denied knowing him, despite the fact that Alderson has a photograph of the two men, taken while they were both in France.
📖 *Reasonable Doubt*

ALEMAN, JOSÉ
A prominent and wealthy figure in Miami's Cuban exile community, Aleman allegedly told the †House

Select Committee on Assassinations that an organized crime figure told him, in September 1962, that President Kennedy was "going to be hit" because of harassment by his brother, Attorney General Robert F. †Kennedy, of Teamsters president Jimmy †Hoffa.

Aleman claimed he met Florida †Mafia boss Santos †Trafficante at the Scott-Bryant Motel in Miami Beach to discuss a $1.5 million loan from the Teamsters Union. According to Aleman, during the meeting Trafficante railed against the Kennedys and said the president was going to get what was coming to him. Thinking Trafficante meant Kennedy would lose the next election, Aleman said he disagreed, that Kennedy would be reelected. Trafficante allegedly replied, "No, José, he is going to be hit."

Aleman insisted that he told the FBI about the threat on the president's life voiced by Trafficante, but nothing was ever done about it. Aleman claimed that FBI agents questioned him hours after the assassination, but the Bureau denied this.

Aleman appeared before the House Select Committee on Assassinations in 1978. Expressing abject fear for his life, he changed his story slightly, testifying that Trafficante was talking about Kennedy losing the next election. Under immunity from prosecution, Trafficante admitted meeting Aleman at the motel in September, but denied predicting Kennedy's death.

See also MARCELLO, CARLOS; ROSELLI, JOHNNY.

📖 *Conspiracy; Contract on America*

ALEXANDER, WILLIAM F.

Alexander was an assistant district attorney for Dallas County when Kennedy was shot. From the time Lee Harvey †Oswald was arrested until his murder by Jack †Ruby, Alexander was outspoken about Oswald's guilt and his alleged ties to an international communist conspiracy. Alexander is also believed by many to have been the source of rumors circulated among reporters in Dallas shortly after the assassination hinting that Oswald was a paid informer for the †Federal Bureau of Investigation.

Later appointed an assistant U.S. attorney for Dallas federal district, Alexander was quoted as saying, fourteen years after the assassination, that there was a "real possibility" Oswald was on his way to meet an accomplice when he shot and killed Dallas police officer J. D. †Tippit.

See also RIGHT-WING EXTREMISTS.

📖 *Assassination Tapes; High Treason*

ALIASES USED BY OSWALD

Lee Harvey †Oswald is known to have used at least two aliases during the time he lived in Dallas before the assassination. When Oswald was arrested, he was carrying a forged Selective Service card identifying him as Alek James Hidell. Some researchers believe the card was planted on Oswald. The †Mannlicher-Carcano rifle allegedly found in the †Texas School Book Depository Building following the assassination had been ordered from †Klein's Sporting Goods Company by a person identified only as A. Hidell and had been shipped to a post office box rented by Oswald. Oswald also placed a separate order for a .38 caliber Smith & Wesson revolver using the name A. J. Hidell. (Some researchers have postulated that Oswald may have taken the name Hidell from a nickname that members of his Marine Corps unit used for one of Oswald's Marine Corps buddies, John R. †Heindel.)

Oswald used the name O. H. Lee when he lived in the Dallas rooming house operated by Mrs. Earlene †Roberts. He is also reported to have used the name Leon Oswald in the †Odio Incident. Oswald used the name Osborne in the summer of 1963, when ordering materials for the †Fair Play for Cuba Committee from two printing houses in New Orleans.

📖 *Conspiracy; High Treason; Reasonable Doubt*

ALPHA 66

A militant †anti-Castro Cuban exile group with headquarters in Florida and Dallas, Alpha 66 made headlines around the world in the early 1960s for its gunboat raids on Cuban ports. Soviet and Cuban ships were favorite targets of these raids. Because President Kennedy had publicly criticized the group's activities and called for a stop to the attacks on Cuba, many Alpha 66 members had become anti-Kennedy. Following the assassination, several individuals charged that the group was behind the murder, but no proof of its involvement could be found.

Interestingly, Antonio †Veciana, a leader of Alpha 66, claimed to have witnessed his CIA contact, known to him as Maurice †Bishop, talking to a stranger in a downtown Dallas office building lobby in either late August or early September 1963. Veciana said he thought nothing of it until he saw the man's picture displayed on television as the assassin of President Kennedy, Lee Harvey †Oswald.

See also BAY OF PIGS.

📖 *Conspiracy*

ALTGENS, JAMES W.

An Associated Press photographer, Altgens had stationed himself at a vantage point on Elm Street

across from the †Texas School Book Depository
Building to photograph the presidential motorcade as
it passed through †Dealey Plaza and headed onto the
Stemmons Freeway. Altgens captured the president on
film in a now-famous shot taken within two seconds of
the impact of the bullet that struck his head. For a
while, controversy raged around a figure visible in the
background of the photograph. A man many people
thought strongly resembled Lee Harvey †Oswald was
pictured standing in the front entrance of the Book
Depository Building. If it was, in fact, Oswald, he
could not have been on the sixth floor of the building
when the shots were fired.

The †Warren Commission discounted any
possibility that the figure was Oswald, and instead
identified the man as Billy Nolan †Lovelady, another
building employee. The man in the photo is wearing a
dark, heavy-textured shirt open halfway to the waist
over a white undershirt. Lovelady later told reporters
that he was wearing a red-and-white-striped sport
shirt that day. The identity of the man in the photo
has never been clearly established.

James Altgens told Commission investigators that
he raced up the †Grassy Knoll immediately after the
president was hit because several uniformed Dallas
police officers ran in that direction with weapons

drawn, apparently in response to the sound of gunfire from that direction. Altgens's testimony that "flesh particles flew out of the side of his [Kennedy's] head in my direction from where I was standing . . . " has been cited by many investigators to support the conclusion that the president's head wound was caused by a bullet fired from the Grassy Knoll, which was to Kennedy's right and front, not from the Texas School Book Depository Building, which was to his rear. *See also* DEALEY PLAZA WITNESSES; HEAD WOUND CONTROVERSY.

📖 *Best Evidence*; *Rush to Judgment*

ALVARADO, GILBERTO

Gilberto Alvarado was a young Nicaraguan who, two days after the assassination, visited the American Embassy in †Mexico City and told shocked diplomats he had seen Lee Harvey †Oswald at the Cuban consulate there. Alvarado said that two months earlier he had seen Oswald meet on the consulate's private patio with a thin black man who spoke fluent English. They were joined briefly by a Cuban who gave the black man a fistful of U.S. dollars, then departed.

Alvarado swore he heard the black man tell Oswald, "I want to kill the man," to which Oswald replied that he was not man enough to do the job, but that he, Oswald, would take care of it. Oswald then took the money from the black man and said, "The people are waiting for me back there." With that, both men parted company.

Although Alvarado's story was impossible to verify, it received more than a little credibility because the †Central Intelligence Agency staff in Mexico City already knew Oswald had been there, thanks to their constant surveillance of the Cuban consulate. (Some researchers believe this "Oswald" to have been an impersonator.) Researchers such as Anthony Summers, who charge that the CIA was involved in the assassination, have labeled Alvarado's story a piece of disinformation calculated to further the belief that Oswald was working for the Cuban government. ⌑ *Conspiracy*

AMBULANCE CONTROVERSY
When †*Air Force One* landed at †Andrews Air Force Base, the president's coffin was removed from the craft and placed inside a Navy ambulance for the trip to †Bethesda Naval Hospital. Jacqueline †Kennedy and Attorney General Robert F. †Kennedy, who had met the plane, also rode in the ambulance. A second ambulance reportedly joined the motorcade from the

air base to the hospital to serve as a decoy, drawing the crowd of curiosity seekers away from the ambulance bearing the president's coffin.

The motorcade reached Bethesda at approximately 6:55 P.M., Friday, November 22, 1963. Mrs. Kennedy and the president's brother alighted and entered the front door of the hospital, leaving the ambulance containing the coffin outside under guard by a group of sailors hand-picked specifically for this duty. The Military District of Washington, D.C., †Casket Team had flown by helicopter from Andrews to Bethesda,where the members loaded into a pickup truck. They waited near the front entrance to the hospital until the ambulance pulled away to drive around back to the loading dock. The truck attempted to keep pace with the ambulance, which reportedly drove at high speed, but lost sight of it and then lost its bearings. Returning to the hospital's main entrance, the truck started again for the rear of the building, where the ambulance was found waiting. The coffin was finally removed by the Casket Team. Although Bureau records purportedly indicate that FBI agents accompanied the coffin from the ambulance to the autopsy room at 7:17 P.M., the Casket Team case report puts the time the coffin was transferred at 8:00 P.M.

According to a statement that researcher David S. †Lifton attributed to Petty Officer Dennis †David, who was chief of the day for the medical school when Kennedy's body arrived, David brought with him to the loading platform "seven or eight sailors" who unloaded the coffin and brought it into the autopsy room. This does not correspond with either of the two reports, one by the FBI men at the scene (the †O'Neill and Sibert report) and the other by the Casket Team, concerning who unloaded the coffin. Adding to the controversy is a statement Lifton attributed to X-ray technician Jerrol F. †Custer that Custer witnessed Mrs. Kennedy's arrival through the front entrance of the hospital while he was carrying X rays of her husband's head to be developed. If the president's body was still in the coffin inside the ambulance in which Mrs. Kennedy arrived, it was impossible for Custer to be arranging to develop X rays of his wounds.
See also AUTOPSY CONTROVERSY; BIRD, SAMUEL R.; BODY BAG CONTROVERSY; COFFIN CONTROVERSY; LIPSEY, RICHARD A.; WEHLE, PHILIP C.
📖 *Best Evidence*

AMERICAN CIVIL LIBERTIES UNION (ACLU)
Lee Harvey †Oswald established a curious relationship with the ACLU. After reportedly attending a meeting

of the organization's Dallas chapter with Michael and Ruth †Paine, he wrote to the group's national headquarters asking how he could get in touch with "ACLU groups in my area" without mentioning that he had already attended the local meeting. Then, on November 1, 1963, he rented a post office box, naming the †Fair Play for Cuba Committee and the ACLU as authorized addressees.

When Oswald was arrested on Friday, November 22, 1963, a delegation from the ACLU visited Dallas Police Headquarters. They were assured that Oswald's rights were being protected, but were refused permission to see him. Oswald was not informed of this visit, even when, on the following afternoon, he requested that the ACLU arrange legal representation. ⌂ *Conspiracy; Death of a President*

AMERICAN FACT-FINDING COMMITTEE

On the day the president was killed, the American Fact-Finding Committee sponsored a full-page advertisement in the *Dallas Morning News* headlined "Welcome Mr. Kennedy to Dallas." Bordered in black, the ad contained a series of pointed questions and harsh statements critical of the Kennedy administration. The man who signed the ad, Bernard †Weissman, testified that he and some friends had invented the committee name when they wrote the ad.

Weissman prepared the ad with help from two other men: Joseph P. †Grinnan and Larrie H. Schmidt. There is no indication that any of the three knew either Lee Harvey †Oswald or Jack †Ruby before the assassination. According to the †Warren Commission, the money to pay for the advertisement was contributed by three Dallas businessmen: Nelson Bunker †Hunt, Edgar R. Crissey, and H. R. Bright. 📖 *Warren Report*

AMERICAN GUILD OF VARIETY ARTISTS (AGVA)

Characterized in the 1960s and 1970s by federal law enforcement agencies as a mob-influenced union, AGVA represented nightclub performers, among other entertainment workers. Two years before President Kennedy's assassination, Senator Karl Mundt, a member of the U.S. Senate Permanent Subcommittee on Investigations, labeled AGVA "purely a racket to collect money."

As a nightclub owner, Jack †Ruby had close ties with AGVA and many of its mob-connected officials. Telephone company records show that, in the days leading up to the assassination, Ruby made numerous telephone calls to AGVA. Ruby claimed he called union officers about unfair practices, asking them to stop his competitors from featuring certain types of shows that Ruby was prevented from staging in his clubs because of union rules. Observers who believe Ruby was part of a mob plot to assassinate the president associate these calls with the assassination planning.

See also MAFIA.

📖 *Contract on America*

AMERICAN RIFLEMAN ADVERTISEMENT

In early 1963, †Klein's Sporting Goods Company received a mail-order coupon clipped from an advertisement it had placed in the February issue of *American Rifleman*. The order was for the Italian-made †Mannlicher-Carcano 6.5-millimeter rifle featured in the ad. The handwriting on the coupon was that of Lee Harvey †Oswald, but the name on the order form was A. Hidell. The rifle was to be shipped to †post office box 2915, Dallas, Texas, a box rented to Oswald. The cost of the rifle was $21.45. According to Klein's records, the rifle the firm shipped in response to that coupon bore serial number C2766, the same serial number on the rifle allegedly discovered on the sixth floor of the †Texas School Book Depository Building shortly after President Kennedy was shot. Much has been made of Oswald's allegedly purchasing the rifle through the mail, and thus establishing a definite trail of possession, since he had to provide Klein's with a name and address for shipping purposes, when he simply could have walked into any of more than a dozen stores in Dallas and purchased the same weapon without having to provide even a fictitious name and address.

See also ALBA, ADRIAN; ALIASES USED BY OSWALD.

📖 *Death of a President; Reasonable Doubt*

AM/LASH

See CUBELA, ROLANDO.

AMMUNITION CLIP

An ammunition clip is a small, bluish metal spring-loaded cartridge receptacle used to load automatic and semiautomatic rifles. It permits rapid firing, which is otherwise not possible by manually loading a new cartridge into the firing chamber after each shot. Whether or not an ammunition clip for the †Mannlicher-Carcano rifle was actually found in the †Texas School Book Depository Building remains questionable.

The original inventory of articles found in what became known as the †sniper's nest, where Lee Harvey †Oswald allegedly was when he fired at Kennedy, does not list an ammunition clip despite an otherwise meticulous detailing of every item recovered along with the rifle. According to assassination researcher Sylvia †Meagher, the first reference to a clip surfaces in the †Warren Report, published in September 1964. Prior to that, no mention of an ammunition clip appears anywhere. Some researchers, seeking to explain the apparent absence of a clip, have advanced the theory that Oswald reloaded the rifle manually and that someone later added the clip to the inventory. Most experts agree that without using a clip Oswald could not possibly have fired more than one round before the president's car sped from the scene, indicating that the additional shots had to have come from a second source.

📖 *Reasonable Doubt*

ANDERSON, EUGENE D.

A U.S. Marine Corps marksmanship expert, Major Anderson was, at the time he testified before the †Warren Commission, assistant head of the Marksmanship Branch of the Marine Corps. Major Anderson testified that it was possible for Lee Harvey †Oswald to have shot the president twice within the time span of 4.8 to 5.6 seconds, the window established by the Commission between the first and second shots that hit Kennedy.

He also testified about Oswald's marksmanship record while he served in the Marine Corps. Anderson's testimony that weather conditions and a poor rifle could account for wide differences in Oswald's marksmanship scores has been challenged by Mark †Lane.
See also FIRING SEQUENCE CONTROVERSY.
📖 *Rush to Judgment*

ANDERSON, JACK

A Washington-based syndicated newspaper columnist, Jack Anderson first reported, in 1967, allegations that Fidel †Castro was behind the Kennedy assassination. Anderson's source for much of the information supporting his reports was a high-ranking mobster named Johnny †Roselli, who claimed to have worked closely with the †Central Intelligence Agency in plotting to kill Castro.

Anderson revealed to his readers that Roselli told him Jack †Ruby was ordered by the mob to kill Lee Harvey †Oswald because it was feared he would "crack and disclose information that might lead to them." They believed disclosure of mob ties to the assassination would trigger a major crackdown on the †Mafia.

G. Gordon Liddy has stated that Anderson was discussed as a target for assassination because of his exposés divulging discreditable CIA activities. Liddy claims the discussion took place during a luncheon attended by himself, E. Howard †Hunt, and a CIA agent known as Dr. Gunn.

📖 *Conspiracy; Contract on America*; *Plausible Denial*

ANDERTON, JAMES

An FBI agent, James Anderton was contacted on Monday, November 25, 1963, by Dr. Jack Harper from Dallas's Methodist Hospital. The doctor explained that his nephew, William Allen Harper, a college student, had found a fragment of what appeared to be a human bone in the grassy triangle just to the left of where the president was hit.

When the †Secret Service learned about the fragment, Anderton was told to send it directly to the White House. That order was quickly countermanded by FBI assistant director Alan Belmont, who ordered the piece of bone sent to the FBI laboratory in Washington, D.C.

See also HARPER BONE FRAGMENT.

📖 *Best Evidence*

ANDREWS, DEAN, JR.

A New Orleans attorney with reputed links to underworld figure Carlos †Marcello, Dean Adams

Andrews, Jr., testified to the †Warren Commission that
Lee Harvey †Oswald had consulted him several times
to discuss legal options open to him to reverse his less
than honorable discharge from the Marine Corps.
Andrews said that Oswald was usually accompanied
by a man who appeared to be a Mexican.

Andrews further attested that the day after the
assassination, he was called by an acquaintance
named Clay Bertrand, a name many investigators
believe to be an alias used by CIA operative Clay
†Shaw. According to Andrews, Bertrand asked him to
defend Oswald in Dallas on the charge that he had
killed the president.

The attorney later became a key figure in the
investigation of the assassination conducted by New
Orleans district attorney Jim †Garrison. When
Andrews recanted his account of the Bertrand/Shaw
incident, Garrison had him indicted for perjury and
obtained a conviction.

📖 *Conspiracy; On the Trail of the Assassins; Rush to
Judgment*

ANDREWS AIR FORCE BASE

Andrews Air Force Base, located in the Maryland
suburbs of Washington, D.C., was the scene of the
arrival at 6:05 P.M. on Friday, November 22, 1963, of

[†]*Air Force One* bearing the coffin of the fallen president. The scene took on a surrealistic character. In the harsh brilliance of television klieg lights, with the sound of helicopter rotors beating in the background, the coffin purportedly containing the president's body was removed from the Boeing 707 and placed in a waiting ambulance for the trip to [†]Bethesda Naval Hospital, where an autopsy team prepared to perform the postmortem examination.

Some investigators have expressed doubt that the coffin actually contained the president's body. They theorize that it was removed from the opposite side of the aircraft and taken aboard a nearby Army helicopter, where the wounds could have been altered before the autopsy.
See also BODY BAG CONTROVERSY; COFFIN CONTROVERSY.
📖 *Best Evidence*; *Death of a President*

"ANGEL" OR "ANGELO"
See ODIO INCIDENT.

ANGEL, DR. LAWRENCE
As curator of Physical Anthropology at the Smithsonian Institution, Dr. Lawrence Angel was among those who attempted to isolate the exact place

on the president's skull where the ⁺Harper bone fragment splintered away. Angel refused, finally, to identify it as positively coming from the back of the skull. Some investigators feel that the inability to match the fragment to a precise location on the skull is proof the head wound was altered.

📖 *Best Evidence*

ANGLETON, JAMES J.

Former chief of counterintelligence at the ⁺Central Intelligence Agency, Angleton led a faction within the Agency that refused to believe Soviet KGB defector Yuri ⁺Nosenko when he denied that the KGB had any communication with Lee Harvey ⁺Oswald. A memo allegedly signed by Angleton has also tied him to speculation that E. Howard ⁺Hunt, a CIA agent who late became a prominent Watergate figure, was in Dallas the day of the assassination. Hunt maintains he was in Washington.

📖 *Fatal Hour; Plausible Denial*

ANSON, ROBERT SAM

A television producer and political correspondent, Anson is the author of a book titled *They've Killed the President! The Search for the Murderers of John F. Kennedy*, published in 1975 by Bantam Books. In his text, Anson assesses the blame for the assassination on organized crime.

See also CONTRACT ON AMERICA.

ANTI-CASTRO CUBANS

A wave of embittered exiles fled Cuba after the success of Fidel †Castro's revolution in 1959. Many settled in Miami, which soon became a hotbed of †Central Intelligence Agency activity. CIA operative E. Howard †Hunt openly recruited disaffected refugees in the streets of Miami, and Operation Mongoose, the CIA's Miami-based plan to overthrow Castro, included many veterans of former Cuban dictator Fulgencio Batista's military.

A particularly troublesome aspect of the CIA's anti-Castro operations was that the Agency worked hand in hand with members of the †Mafia in its attempts to overthrow Castro. The Mafia's eagerness to participate in efforts to get rid of Castro resulted from its having been banned from the island by the new communist government and, hence, prevented from continuing to cash in on what had been its extremely lucrative hotel and casino business in Havana.

After the failure of the †Bay of Pigs invasion, many of the anti-Castro Cubans who had been involved in the CIA's secret war against Castro felt betrayed. Some blamed President Kennedy for the invasion's failure, thinking that he had withheld air support necessary for its success. They were even more dismayed when, in September 1963, Kennedy authorized William Attwood, his special adviser for African affairs at the United Nations, to meet with Cuba's envoy to the U.N. to discuss the possibility of negotiations.

The possible connection of anti-Castro Cubans to the assassination of President Kennedy has also been suggested by the fact that, in New Orleans, several anti-Castro organizations had their offices at [†]544 Camp Street, which also housed the offices of Guy [†]Banister and which was the address Lee Harvey [†]Oswald used on literature he distributed for the phony branch of the [†]Fair Play for Cuba Committee (a pro-Castro group) he set up in that city.
See also ALPHA 66; ARAGON, ERNEST; ARCACHA SMITH, SERGIO; BRINGUIER, CARLOS; CASTELLANOS, NESTOR; FERRIE, DAVID; HEMMING, GERRY PATRICK; MILTEER, JOSEPH; ODIO INCIDENT; OPERATION 40; SHAW, CLAY.

APPLIN, GEORGE J.
George Applin was a patron in the [†]Texas Theatre on November 22, 1963, when Lee Harvey [†]Oswald was

arrested there for the murder of Police Officer J. D.
†Tippit. Applin told the †Warren Commission that
during Oswald's arrest, he observed a man sitting in
the rear of the theater who not only appeared
uninterested in the film but also quietly watched over
the arrest while other patrons were ducking for cover.
In 1979, Applin admitted to the *Dallas Morning News*
that he later recognized Jack †Ruby as the man he had
seen in the movie house. He said he was afraid to tell
the police or the Commission what he knew in 1964
because he had read an article about the deaths of
people who were witnesses to the assassination or
connected in some way to the incident.
📖 *Crossfire*

ARAGON, ERNEST

Aragon was, according to researchers Michael L.
†Canfield and Alan J. †Weberman, a †Secret Service
agent in Miami who was assigned to investigate the
†Odio Incident and everyone involved in it.
Researchers have uncovered several glaring omissions
in his performance of this assignment. He is accused
of neglecting to pursue vigorously his investigation of
Juan, or John, Martin, a shadowy individual believed
to have been involved in running guns for †anti-Castro
Cubans. Aragon's detractors also claim he failed to

follow up on a lead provided by a long-distance operator in †Mexico City who alleged that she overheard two men discussing "the Castro plan" (the Kennedy assassination?) and one of them remarking ominously, "Bobby is next."

☐ *Coup d'Etat*

ARCACHA SMITH, SERGIO

A leader among †anti-Castro Cubans in the New Orleans area, Arcacha reportedly had close ties to underworld figure Carlos †Marcello and to Guy †Banister, a former FBI agent with links to intelligence agencies. Arcacha set up the office of the †Cuban Revolutionary Council at †544 Camp Street, though he denied being acquainted with Lee Harvey †Oswald. Arcacha was implicated in the Kennedy assassination by a female drug addict who was hospitalized near Eunice, Louisiana, after being thrown from a car during the night of November 20, 1963. According to reports attributed to Lieutenant Francis Frugé, the state police officer who handled her case, she told him the men she was with had discussed killing President Kennedy while he was in Dallas. The woman, known as Rose Cheramie, but whose real name may have been Melba Christine Marcades, said she worked for Jack †Ruby at his Dallas club. Two days later, when the

assassination actually took place, Frugé used the woman's description to identify one of the men in the car as Arcacha. The owner of a bar where Cheramie and the men had been drinking before she was dumped identified Arcacha in a photograph as one of her companions. Arcacha denied any knowledge of the incident. On September 4, 1965, Cheramie was killed on a Texas highway when an automobile ran her over after she had apparently been thrown from a car.
See also BANISTER, GUY; FERRIE, DAVID.
📖 *Conspiracy; Crossfire*

ARCE, DANNY GARCIA

Arce was one of many witnesses at the assassination scene whose perception of the direction from which the shots were fired helped to further the controversy over the †Warren Report. Arce told the FBI that he was standing in the grassy area in front of the †Texas School Book Depository Building when he heard the shots. He told law enforcement officers he thought they "came from the direction of the railroad tracks near the parking lot at the west end of the Depository Building."
See also DEALEY PLAZA WITNESSES; TEXAS SCHOOL BOOK DEPOSITORY BUILDING EMPLOYEES.
📖 *Rush to Judgment*

ARCHER, DON R.
After Jack †Ruby shot Lee Harvey †Oswald, Dallas police lieutenant Archer reportedly told Ruby that Oswald was dead and that Ruby would probably be executed for the killing. This news apparently brought a sigh of relief from Ruby.

📖 *Conspiracy; High Treason*

ARMSTRONG, ANDREW
Andrew Armstrong was working as a handyman at Jack †Ruby's †Carousel Club when President Kennedy was slain. He acknowledged being with his employer when Ruby heard that Dallas police officer J. D. †Tippit also had been killed. According to Armstrong, Ruby was distraught because, Ruby said, Tippit was a close friend. In testimony before the †House Select Committee on Assassinations, Armstrong refuted Ruby's explanation that a suspicious series of calls he made to mob figures and leaders of the †American Guild of Variety Artists in the weeks before the assassination were appeals for help because his business was being badly hurt by competitors who were violating union regulations against amateur strippers. Armstrong said, to the contrary, that business had been "picking up" at Ruby's club during the fall of 1963.

📖 *Contract on America; Rush to Judgment*

ARMSTRONG, LESLIE

Leslie Armstrong was the jury foreperson at a 1985 trial involving a libel suit brought by CIA agent E. Howard †Hunt against the publication †*Spotlight* concerning an article by Victor †Marchetti that implicated Hunt in the assassination of President Kennedy. The jury found for *Spotlight*. After the trial, Armstrong told the press she believed the evidence presented by defense attorney Mark †Lane proved that the †Central Intelligence Agency had killed Kennedy and that Hunt was involved. The trial is the centerpiece of Lane's best-selling 1991 book, †*Plausible Denial*, published by Thunder's Mouth Press.

ARNETT, GEORGE

Dallas police lieutenant George Arnett confirmed to investigators that Jack †Ruby and Police Officer J. D. †Tippit had had a long-standing friendship. Arnett theorized that Tippit's murder by Lee Harvey †Oswald may have been Ruby's true motive for shooting Oswald. *See also* WILLIAMS, HAROLD.
📖 *Rush to Judgment*

ARNOLD, CAROLYN

Mrs. Arnold was employed as the secretary to the vice president of the Texas School Book Depository when the assassination took place. Although she never testified before the †Warren Commission or the †House Select Committee on Assassinations, Arnold was interviewed extensively by the FBI. From that interview FBI agents derived that Mrs. Arnold believed that on November 22, 1963, she saw Lee Harvey †Oswald standing on the sidewalk in front of the †Texas School Book Depository Building at about 12:15 P.M., only minutes before the fatal shots were fired.

In 1978, however, Mrs. Arnold claimed she was misquoted in the FBI report of the interview, which she read long after it was given. Disavowing the report, she insisted it was a gross misrepresentation of her statements to the FBI, then went on to clarify her original version of what she saw that day: At approximately 12:15 P.M., Mrs. Arnold went to the company lunchroom for a drink of water. She saw Oswald seated in a booth, apparently eating his lunch. Although neither spoke, Arnold declares that she knew Oswald well enough, and passed sufficiently close to him, to be absolutely certain it was he. Mrs. Arnold's testimony raises considerable doubt that Oswald could have fired the rifle that killed the president. He would have had to race to the sixth floor, assassinate the president, and return in less than two minutes to the second-floor cafeteria, where he was confronted by Police Officer Marrion L. †Baker and building manager Roy †Truly only minutes after the shooting.

See also TEXAS SCHOOL BOOK DEPOSITORY BUILDING EMPLOYEES.

⌒ *Conspiracy; Crossfire; Reasonable Doubt*

ARNOLD, GORDON

One of a group that came to be called the †Grassy Knoll witnesses, Gordon Arnold was on leave following his Army basic training. He was an amateur cinematographer anxious to film the presidential motorcade from the best possible angle. Dressed in his Army uniform, Arnold first chose as his site the railroad overpass at the western end of †Dealey Plaza, which offered a clear, unobstructed view of the plaza, through which the motorcade was to pass. Arnold was prevented from entering the overpass by a well-dressed man who showed him a †Secret Service badge and ID. Official records indicate that no Secret Service agents were assigned to patrol the area on foot that day. However, a Dallas police officer and a county deputy sheriff reportedly encountered a second such "agent" on the †Grassy Knoll immediately after the shooting.

Arnold then found a suitable vantage point from

which to shoot his movie film, only a few feet in front of the stockade fence on the Grassy Knoll. Suddenly he felt a shot whiz past his left ear. He threw himself to the ground in an involuntary reaction, probably due to his recent training. Questioned by a uniformed police officer a few seconds later, Arnold insisted that the shots had come from behind him. The officer confiscated Arnold's film.

Arnold recounted the experience in a 1978 interview published in the *Dallas Morning News*. While some people discounted his story, it received tacit corroboration from then-senator Ralph †Yarborough, who was riding with Vice President Lyndon B. †Johnson two cars behind Kennedy's. Yarborough wrote the *Morning News* that he recalled that when the first shot was fired he saw a uniformed figure immediately "hit the dirt" at the spot where Arnold said he was filming. The senator remembered thinking to himself that the man's quick reaction suggested he must be a "combat veteran."

Nothing more has ever been heard of Arnold's confiscated film, and the police officer who took it and the Secret Service agent who prevented Arnold from going onto the overpass have never been identified.
📖 *Conspiracy; Contract on America; Reasonable Doubt*

ARTIME, MANUEL

A leader among †anti-Castro Cuban exiles with allegedly close ties to E. Howard †Hunt of the †Central Intelligence Agency, Artime is believed to have been deeply involved in plots to kill Fidel †Castro through an undercover Cuban CIA informant named Rolando †Cubela. At the time Kennedy was assassinated, Artime reportedly was maintaining a small force of several hundred Cubans in Nicaragua who were preparing for assassination assignments against the Castro regime. He later served as a civilian representative for Brigade 2506, which was training for the invasion of Cuba.

See also BAY OF PIGS.

📖 *Conspiracy; Fatal Hour; High Treason*

ASCHKENASY, ERNEST

Aschkenasy, an acoustics expert, was called on by the †House Select Committee on Assassinations to review earlier acoustics studies of background sounds caught on the †Dallas police dispatch tape during the assassination. When Aschkenasy, Dr. James †Barger, and Professor Mark †Weiss completed their analysis of the taped sounds of what appeared to be four gunshots recorded through the open microphone of a Dallas police officer's motorcycle radio, they concluded that there was a 95 percent or better probability that the report of the third shot came from the area of the †Grassy Knoll.

See also ACOUSTICAL EVIDENCE; BELL LABORATORY; RAMSEY REPORT.

📖 *Fatal Hour; High Treason*

THE ASSASSINATION TAPES

Written by George †O'Toole, a former CIA computer specialist, and published by Penthouse Press in 1975, this book is based on results obtained with a "psychological stress evaluator," an electronic device that measures voice stress levels to determine whether a subject is lying or telling the truth. O'Toole used the device on myriad taped interviews, press conferences, and the like, with people connected (some remotely) to the assassination and subsequent events. These included eyewitnesses, police officers at the scene, medical examiners, and members of the †Warren Commission. O'Toole also conducted additional private interviews. The book purports to prove that two conspiracies existed: one to actually murder the president and the other to frame Lee Harvey †Oswald, who the author declares was innocent.

ASSASSINATION WEAPON
See MANNLICHER-CARCANO RIFLE.

ATSUGI AIR BASE
In 1957, when Lee Harvey †Oswald was serving in the U.S. Marine Corps, one of his assignments was the radar room at Atsugi Air Base, southwest of Tokyo, Japan. During this time, he carried a military security clearance alternately reported as "confidential" and "secret." Atsugi was also a major operations center for the †Central Intelligence Agency's supersecret †U-2 spy plane program. Oswald's proximity to the CIA installation prompted speculation that he may have been recruited by the Agency while at Atsugi. Researchers have found no consistent pattern to Oswald's activities there, and remain unable to account for his strange, prolonged disappearance from the base, which was ostensibly attributed to treatment for a minor disease.
📖 *Conspiracy*

AUTOPSY CONTROVERSY
The president's autopsy was performed at †Bethesda Naval Hospital outside of Washington, D.C. Every facet of the autopsy has been controversial, including these provocative questions: Why wasn't it done in

Dallas, as Texas law requires and the Dallas medical examiner, Earl †Rose, wanted? And why was it that the men selected to perform it lacked experience in performing autopsies on gunshot victims? There is a host of conflicting theories about bullet entry and exit points, the absence of the president's brain at the autopsy, why †Secret Service men were temporarily denied entry to the autopsy room with the coffin, and why the chief of the autopsy team, Dr. James J. †Humes, burned notes made during the autopsy as well as the first draft of the autopsy report.

The official autopsy report indicated that two bullets struck the president. One, the fatal shot, entered the rear of his head and disintegrated, causing massive loss of skull bone and brain and other tissue. The second entered his back below the shoulders at a steep angle, causing a shallow superficial wound that Humes penetrated with his finger, dislodging the bullet. According to their testimony before the †Warren Commission, when the autopsy was performed, the Bethesda doctors were unaware that the hole in the front of the president's neck had been a bullet hole before Dr. Malcolm †Perry in Dallas's †Parkland Memorial Hospital used it for a †tracheotomy. Dr. Perry had identified the original hole in the president's neck as a bullet entry wound, making a persuasive case that the bullet that entered the president's neck had to come from somewhere in front of him.

See also AMBULANCE CONTROVERSY; BODY BAG CONTROVERSY; BOSWELL, DR. THORNTON; COFFIN CONTROVERSY; HEAD WOUND CONTROVERSY; SINGLE BULLET THEORY; THROAT WOUND CONTROVERSY; X-RAY CONTROVERSY.

📖 *Assassination Tapes; Best Evidence; High Treason*

AUTOPSY PARTICIPANTS

Among those who participated in or witnessed the autopsy of President Kennedy's body were the following individuals, each of whom is discussed in a separate entry in this book: Dr. Thornton Boswell, Bethesda's chief of pathology; Dr. George Burkley, chief medical officer of the White House and President Kennedy's personal physician; Dr. Robert Canada; Jerrol F. Custer; Dennis David; Dr. John Ebersole; Dr. Pierre Finck; Dr. Calvin Galloway; Dr. James J. Humes; James E. Metzler; Paul K. O'Connor; Edward Reed; Floyd A. Riebe; and Jan Gail Rudnicki. Many researchers believe that many more people were in the autopsy room, including a number of civilians who sat in the gallery overlooking it, than have been identified in official reports.

See also BAKEMAN, DR. GEORGE.

B

"BABUSHKA LADY"
See OLIVER, BETTY.

BADEN, DR. MICHAEL
A forensic pathologist, Dr. Baden chaired the Forensic
Pathology Panel assembled by the †House Select
Committee on Assassinations. After his panel
questioned the Bethesda doctors who performed the
autopsy and examined the photographs and X rays of
the president's body, Baden focused an important part
of his testimony on the location of the back wound
caused by the so-called †magic bullet. Dr. Baden
positioned the entry wound in the president's back a
full two inches below the location identified by the
autopsy team. This trajectory made the projected path
of the bullet even more extraordinary than was earlier
believed.
See also AUTOPSY CONTROVERSY; SINGLE BULLET
THEORY.
📖 *Best Evidence*

"Badgeman"

The "Badgeman" is a shadowy figure who appears in the background of a photograph taken by a witness to the assassination. Precisely when the fatal bullet shattered President Kennedy's skull, Mary †Moorman, who was standing near the curb across from the †Grassy Knoll, captured the drama in a snapshot taken with her Polaroid camera. Although it was never examined by the †Warren Commission, the photo has nevertheless held great interest for many researchers because on the Grassy Knoll in the background is the stockade fence that many believe shielded a second gunman.

Using a slide made from the original photograph, which was sold to United Press International, researchers Gary Mack and Jack †White examined blow-ups of the image, ultimately concentrating on two incongruous figures at the north end of the stockade fence. Although not clearly discernible in the fuzzy background, one figure seems to be wearing a police uniform not unlike those worn by Dallas police, while the other appears to be dressed in work clothes and a hard hat. The "uniformed" figure, dubbed "Badgeman" because of a shiny object on his chest believed to be a badge, looks to be holding a rifle that

has just been fired. A puff that could be from the
muzzle blast partially obscures his face. A 1988
British-made television documentary entitled "The
Men Who Killed Kennedy" cast "Badgeman" as Lucien
Sarti, an alleged professional killer from Corsica.
See also GRASSY KNOLL WITNESSES; SMOKE FROM
THE GRASSY KNOLL.
📖 *Crossfire; High Treason*

BAKEMAN, DR. GEORGE
A Dr. George Bakeman is listed in the autopsy report
as being among those present in the room when the
president's body was examined, but no information
exists regarding who he is.
📖 *High Treason 2*

BAKER, MRS. DONALD
See RACHLEY, VIRGIE; TEXAS SCHOOL BOOK
DEPOSITORY BUILDING EMPLOYEES.

BAKER, MARRION L.
Baker was one of several motorcycle officers escorting
the presidential motorcade through Dallas. He had
just turned off Houston Street onto Elm in front of the
†Texas School Book Depository Building when he

heard a shot. Looking up, he saw a flock of pigeons fly off the roof as if startled by the sound. He parked his motorcycle and raced into the building, followed by the building manager, Roy †Truly, who had been watching the motorcade from in front of the building. The two started to take an elevator, but both cars were locked on the fifth floor, so they used the stairs.

Through the glass window in the door of a second-floor lunchroom, Baker saw a man hurrying away from him. With Truly close at his back, Baker flung open the door and challenged the man with gun drawn. When Truly identified the man as a Book Depository employee, Officer Baker continued up the stairs to the roof. According to the report Baker filed with the FBI the following day, the man, who later was identified unequivocally by two competent witnesses as Lee Harvey †Oswald, was "drinking a Coke," which he evidently purchased from a lunchroom vending machine only moments before. The words "drinking a Coke" were deleted from the report, and any reference to the soft drink during Baker's testimony before the †Warren Commission was stricken.

The Coke has become a pivotal detail with Warren Commission critics for two reasons: first is the Commission's deletion of Baker's statement about it, and second is the testimony of another building employee, Mrs. Robert A. †Reid, that she saw Oswald drinking a Coke moments later. Critics argue that the Commission wanted knowledge of the Coke suppressed, because it was impossible for Oswald to have fired the shots that killed the president from the sixth floor, hidden his rifle behind some boxes on the other side of the floor, raced down the stairs to the second floor, purchased a Coke from the vending machine in the lunchroom, and begun drinking it before he was confronted by Baker and Truly. When Captain Will †Fritz of the Dallas police asked him about his whereabouts when the assassination happened, Oswald said he was in the second-floor lunchroom drinking a Coca-Cola.

See also TEXAS SCHOOL BOOK DEPOSITORY BUILDING EMPLOYEES.

📖 *Best Evidence*; *High Treason*

BAKER, ROBERT "BARNEY"

Robert Baker was an associate of former Teamsters boss Jimmy †Hoffa. Some investigators who seek to tie the president's homicide to the †Mafia identify Baker as a part of that link. He had strong personal reasons for hating the Kennedys. Attorney General Robert F. †Kennedy told Baker he was "underworld lice . . . the

scum of the earth." The president's brother also called him Hoffa's "ambassador of violence." Two weeks before the assassination, Jack †Ruby reportedly received a call from Baker. The following day Ruby called another Hoffa associate in Miami, then he called Baker for a second conversation. Although Baker later testified that Ruby was calling about his problems with the †American Guild of Variety Artists, skeptics find that hard to believe. Most suspect the calls were related to the increasing pressure Baker's boss, Hoffa, was receiving from the Kennedy Justice Department.
📖 *Conspiracy*

BALL, JOSEPH

A senior counsel to the †Warren Commission, Ball reportedly helped promote the case against Lee Harvey †Oswald as the †lone assassin. Along with David †Belin, he is credited with preparing "The Assassin," chapter 4 of the †Warren Report, which details the evidence of Oswald's guilt. According to assassination researcher David S. †Lifton, when Ball was asked on a Los Angeles television program about the possibility of a gunman shooting at the president from the †Grassy Knoll, he responded, "There were no people there."
📖 *Best Evidence*

BALLEN, SAMUEL

Samuel Ballen, a friend of Lee Harvey †Oswald's, provided a positive assessment of the presumed assassin's character. According to press reports issued soon after the assassination, Ballen, a petroleum economist, knew Oswald well enough to describe him as "the kind of person I could like." He also described Oswald as physically frail, and said he was an "inquiring young man" who was an independent thinker.

📖 *Plausible Denial*

BANISTER, GUY

One of the FBI agents involved in the killing of the infamous "public enemy number one" John Dillinger, Banister eventually became special agent-in-charge of the FBI's Chicago office. During World War II he reportedly worked in Naval Intelligence, returning to the FBI when the war ended. Following his retirement in the early 1950s he moved to New Orleans to accept the post of deputy chief of police. Forced to retire from that job after threatening a waiter with his gun, Banister set up a private detective agency called Guy Banister Associates.

Many researchers contend that Banister forged a link between Lee Harvey †Oswald, the American intelligence community, and [†]anti-Castro Cubans. He maintained offices at [†]544 Camp Street in New Orleans, an address shared with a number of Cuban organizations attempting to overthrow Fidel [†]Castro. An active supporter of these Cubans, he also had long-standing close ties with several intelligence agencies. The common denominator tying Oswald with Banister and the latter's shadowy activities is the 544 Camp Street address. When Oswald was arrested in New Orleans after a fight with Cubans who were angry because he was distributing pro-Castro material, he had in his possession pamphlets that came from the [†]Fair Play for Cuba Committee, whose address was given as 544 Camp Street. Since this was the address of so many anti-Castro activists, it is strange that Oswald used it for a pro-Castro group.

Guy Banister's death in 1964 was ascribed to a heart attack, although researchers Robert J. [†]Groden and Harrison Edward [†]Livingstone report that "some say" that a bullet wound was found in his body. He was never questioned by anyone from the [†]Warren Commission about his relationship with Oswald or whether he knew anything about the assassination. *See also* BRINGUIER, CARLOS; FERRIE, DAVID; MARTIN, JACK.

📖 *Conspiracy; Crossfire; High Treason*

BARGER, DR. JAMES

Dr. Barger was an acoustics scientist with the Cambridge, Massachusetts, firm of †Bolt, Beranek and Newman, which was hired by the †House Select Committee on Assassinations to examine the †Dallas police dispatch tape. Working with Mark †Weiss and Ernest †Aschkenasy, Barger created a visual presentation of the gunshots fired in †Dealey Plaza when President Kennedy was assassinated. In August 1978, Barger went to Dallas and conducted on-site tests of the sounds of rifles firing from the two critical locations: the †Texas School Book Depository Building and the †Grassy Knoll. Comparing his results with the sounds on the tape, he concluded that four shots were fired at the president: three coming from the Depository Building and one from the Grassy Knoll. *See also* ACOUSTICAL EVIDENCE; BELL LABORATORY; PELLICANO, ANTHONY; RAMSEY REPORT.
📖 *Best Evidence; Conspiracy; High Treason*

BARNES, WILLIE E.

Sergeant Barnes of the Dallas police was given two spent shells recovered from the J. D. †Tippit murder scene by Officer J. M. †Poe. For identification purposes, Barnes immediately scratched the initial B inside each shell. When asked by the †Warren Commission to

identify the shells he had been given by Poe, Barnes could not find his initial in any of the four shells the Commission showed him. This strongly suggests the possibility that the original shells were replaced, while in police custody, with shells that matched the handgun belonging to Lee Harvey †Oswald. If this is so, then someone else, not Oswald, shot Tippit.
📖 *Rush to Judgment*

BARNETT, WELCOME
Barnett, a Dallas police officer, told the †Warren Commission that a construction worker approached him shortly after the shooting and said he saw a rifle sticking out of an upper-floor window of the †Texas School Book Depository Building. Although the individual was never identified, the Commission assumed it was Howard L. †Brennan, a construction worker who gave similar testimony.
📖 *Rush to Judgment*

BARNUM, GEORGE A.
Barnum, a Coast Guard yeoman, was a member of the Military District of Washington, D.C., †Casket Team that watched as the president's coffin was taken from †*Air Force One* at †Andrews Air Force Base and placed

inside a Navy ambulance. The team, arriving at
†Bethesda Naval Hospital separately from the
ambulance, removed the coffin from the ambulance
and transferred it to the hospital's autopsy room.
Seven days later, at the urging of his superior officer,
Barnum wrote a complete description of his experience
with the death of the president.
See also AMBULANCE CONTROVERSY.
📖 *Best Evidence*

BASHOUR, DR. FOUAD A.

Although a cardiologist, Dr. Bashour assisted in the
emergency room of †Parkland Memorial Hospital when
the president's body was brought in. When, in 1979,
he was shown a copy of the official autopsy photograph
of the president's head wound, he is quoted as saying,
"Why do they cover it up? This is not the way it was."
See also PARKLAND MEMORIAL HOSPITAL STAFF.
📖 *High Treason*

BATCHELOR, CHARLES

Batchelor was assistant chief of the Dallas police at
the time of the assassination. Batchelor's activities
have come under scrutiny by some researchers. For
instance, because of the difficulty researchers have

had in establishing how Jack †Ruby was able to enter
the garage at Dallas Police Headquarters, where he
murdered Lee Harvey †Oswald, the suspicion exists
that Batchelor may have allowed Ruby into the
building. Criticism has also been directed at the fact
that Batchelor, despite failing in his responsibility to
protect the president during his visit to Dallas and
failing to protect Oswald when he was in police
custody, was later promoted to Dallas police chief.
See also DAVIS, RED; GRAVES, L. C.; VAUGHN, ROY.
  High Treason

BAXTER, DR. CHARLES R.

An assistant professor of surgery at †Parkland
Memorial Hospital, Dr. Baxter was present when the
president's body was taken into the Parkland
emergency room. He described the head wound to the
†Warren Commission as a "large gaping wound in the
back of the skull." Dr. Baxter's description of the
laceration is not only remarkably different from the
autopsy report, which placed the lethal injury higher
on the head, but is entirely consistent with an exit
wound that would have literally blown away the back
of the skull.

    Baxter characterized the wound in the front of the

president's neck as a small-caliber "entry wound." This account coincided precisely with that of the others present at the time, all of whom described the wound as having no jagged edges. Their collective observations conflict with Dr. James J. †Humes's description of the hole as having "widely gaping irregular edges." Baxter said that after the cut for a †tracheotomy, the opening measured 4 to 5 centimeters at the widest. At †Bethesda Naval Hospital, Dr. Humes placed the opening at 6.5 centimeters. These and other differences between the wounds described by the doctors and nurses at Parkland and those described at Bethesda have been cited to support allegations that Kennedy's wounds were altered to provide a basis for the theory that he was shot from behind.

See also AUTOPSY CONTROVERSY; PARKLAND MEMORIAL HOSPITAL STAFF; THROAT WOUND CONTROVERSY.

📖 *Best Evidence*; *High Treason*

BAY OF PIGS

On April 17, 1961, a force of Cuban exiles invaded Cuba in a CIA-sponsored attempt to overthrow Fidel †Castro's communist dictatorship. Planning for the operation began during the Eisenhower administration, and Kennedy approved going ahead with it after his inauguration in January 1961. The operation was an abject failure. Most of the outnumbered, outgunned invaders were killed or taken prisoner. Both the invasion force, known as Brigade 2506, and the CIA advisers who had armed and trained the troops, attributed the catastrophe to Kennedy's eleventh-hour withdrawal of promised vital air support. Some researchers feel a strong case can be made for putting blame for the president's death on ⁺anti-Castro Cubans and/or ⁺Central Intelligence Agency agents motivated by bitterness over his abdication of his commitment in the Bay of Pigs Invasion.

BECKER, EDWARD

A petty underworld fringe figure, Becker related that during a meeting with reputed New Orleans ⁺Mafia boss Carlos ⁺Marcello in the autumn of 1962, Marcello talked freely about his desire to kill both John and Robert F. ⁺Kennedy. His Sicilian-style vendetta against the Kennedys grew out of Bobby's relentless assault on the Mafia boss, particularly Marcello's April 1961 arrest and subsequent (temporary) deportation. Becker says Marcello boasted how he would ensure that the mob would escape blame for the assassination, by "setting up a nut to take the blame."

📖 *Conspiracy; Mafia Kingfish*

BELIN, DAVID

Belin was assistant counsel to the †Warren Commission. He assisted with the investigation into Lee Harvey †Oswald's guilt, and helped write "The Assassin," chapter 4 of the †Warren Report. He later served as chief counsel to the Rockefeller Commission established by President Gerald †Ford (a member of the Warren Commission) to investigate U.S. intelligence operations inside the United States.

Belin remains a strong supporter of the Warren Commission findings and regularly speaks out against its critics and the various conspiracy theories they postulate.

He is the author of two books, *November 22, 1963: You Are the Jury,* published by Quadrangle in 1973, a defense of the Warren Commission findings, and *Final Disclosure: The Full Truth About the Assassination of President Kennedy,* published by Scribner's in 1988, largely a critique of what he termed the "assassination scam" created by authors of books advancing conspiracy hypotheses.

See also BALL, JOSEPH.

📖 *Best Evidence*; *High Treason*

BELKNAP, JERRY B.

Jerry Belknap was eventually identified as the man who, shortly before the presidential motorcade arrived, collapsed near the front of the †Texas School Book Depository Building in what appeared to be a seizure. He was taken by ambulance to †Parkland Memorial Hospital, but left the hospital without receiving treatment. Some researchers find this incident suspicious, saying that it distracted the attention of at least one police officer away from the †Grassy Knoll, where other witnesses later reported seeing men heading for the fence there just before the president arrived. When investigation yielded his identity, Belknap said he had suffered seizures since a childhood accident. He claimed he left the hospital because the president was brought in soon after his own arrival and he wasn't getting any treatment.

📖 *Crossfire*; *On the Trail of the Assassins*

BELL, AUDREY

Audrey Bell was the operating room nursing

supervisor on duty at †Parkland Memorial Hospital when the president's body was brought in, yet she was never questioned by either the †Warren Commission or the †House Select Committee on Assassinations. In interviews with the *Dallas Morning News*, Bell divulged that she gave a Texas highway patrolman bullet fragments that had been removed from Governor †Connally's wrist and thigh, presumably pieces of the so-called †magic bullet that allegedly caused his wounds. She resolutely maintained as late as 1978 that she saw four or five bullet fragments, not the three placed in evidence by the Warren Commission; in her description, "the smallest was the size of the striking end of a match and the largest at least twice that big." The fragments she described are too large to account for the small amount of material missing from the magic bullet, and many researchers offer this fact to debunk the †single bullet theory. *See also* PARKLAND MEMORIAL HOSPITAL STAFF.

📖 *Best Evidence*; *Conspiracy*

BELL LABORATORY

According to the †House Select Committee on Assassinations, the †Warren Commission submitted to the Bell Telephone Acoustics & Speech Research Laboratory for analysis an audiotaped description of the assassination scene by Sam Pate, a local Dallas radio news reporter covering the president's motorcade. The †Warren Report made no mention of this tape, and some researchers question why it was never pursued further after the people at the Bell Laboratory reported "six nonvoiced noises" on the tape that many believe were gunshots.

See also ACOUSTICAL EVIDENCE; BARGER, DR. JAMES; WEISS, MARK.

📖 *High Treason*

BELMONT, ALAN
Belmont was the assistant director of the FBI at the time of the Kennedy assassination.
See HARPER BONE FRAGMENT.

BENAVIDES, DOMINGO
An auto mechanic, Domingo Benavides witnessed Dallas police officer J. D. †Tippit's killing, thus becoming involved in the controversy over Lee Harvey †Oswald's role in the assassination of President Kennedy. Shortly after 1:00 P.M., less than an hour after the assassination, Benavides was driving his pickup truck west on 10th Street in the Oak Cliff section of Dallas when he witnessed Tippit's murder. The †Warren Commission believed he used the radio in

Tippit's police car to report the shooting, but this is in some dispute. He did pick up two spent cartridge shells, which he gave to Police Officer J. M. †Poe. Benavides was never called in by police to identify Tippit's killer from a lineup, which Warren Commission senior counsel David †Belin called "a gross error." Benavides reportedly received death threats after it was widely publicized that he had witnessed the Tippit killing.

See also BENAVIDES, EDWARD; BOWLEY, T. F.; TIPPIT MURDER SCENE WITNESSES.

📖 *Crossfire; Final Disclosure; High Treason; Rush to Judgment*

BENAVIDES, EDWARD

In February 1964, Domingo Benavides's brother Edward was killed, the victim of a gunshot to the head. Some assassination researchers believe Edward so closely resembled his brother that his unknown assailant killed him in a case of mistaken identity.

See also BENAVIDES, DOMINGO; BOWLEY, T. F.

📖 *High Treason*

BENNETT, GLEN

†Secret Service agent Bennett was riding in the car

directly behind the presidential limousine when the bullets struck the president. He was sitting behind presidential aide Dave †Powers. During the return trip to Washington aboard †*Air Force One,* Bennett wrote down his impressions. He describes having seen a bullet enter the president's back "about four inches down from the right shoulder," which is consistent with the placement of holes in Kennedy's clothing. Researcher David S. †Lifton mistrusts Bennett's account as simply a fabrication to corroborate the results of the autopsy. To support this theory, he presents photographs taken at the time of the assassination showing everyone in Bennett's car facing forward except Bennett, whose head was turned to the right as he looked at the crowd of people lining the route.

📖 *Best Evidence*

BENTLEY, PAUL

Dallas policeman Bentley was one of the arresting officers when Lee Harvey †Oswald was apprehended at the †Texas Theatre as a suspect in the killing of Police Officer J. D. †Tippit. Bentley claimed he found a false identification bearing the name Alek Hidell in Oswald's wallet, which he examined on the way to

Police Headquarters following the arrest. Some researchers question the validity of this, based on the absence of the Hidell ID from the list of items contained in the preliminary record of the radio call to headquarters detailing items bearing the name Lee Harvey Oswald. Skeptics say the bogus identification was ostensibly planted on Oswald later to cement his connection with the †Mannlicher-Carcano rifle ordered from †Klein's Sporting Goods Company under the name A. Hidell.

See also ALIASES USED BY OSWALD; HILL, GERALD L. ☐ *Assassination Tapes*

BERTRAND, CLAY
See SHAW, CLAY.

BEST EVIDENCE
Published by Macmillan in 1980 and reissued by Carroll & Graf in 1988, *Best Evidence: Disguise and Deception in the Assassination of John F. Kennedy* is the work of David S. †Lifton, who spent fifteen years researching the assassination. A graduate of Cornell University with a degree in engineering physics, he was formerly a NASA computer engineer and has more recently been a consultant for television

programs dealing with the assassination. Lifton makes extensive use of statements by individuals at †Parkland Memorial Hospital and †Bethesda Naval Hospital, as well as many others, to focus on what he believes is evidence that Kennedy's wounds were altered between the time the body left Parkland and when the autopsy was performed at Bethesda. This book is the most detailed account of the medical evidence related to the assassination.

BETHELL, TOM

Bethell is a correspondent for *The American Spectator*. Claiming he participated in the assassination investigation conducted by New Orleans district attorney Jim †Garrison, Bethell wrote an article that appeared in the December 16, 1991, issue of *The National Review* exposing what he considers to be a completely false portrayal of the investigation in the movie †*JFK*. He also reveals that Garrison's lawyers and investigators were relieved when they learned of the death of David †Ferrie, one of Garrison's leading suspects, in February 1967, because it offered an opportunity for Garrison to drop the investigation. According to Bethell, Garrison's staff felt the investigation had led to nothing more than "a stream of courtroom embarrassments for his lawyers

to clean up." Of Garrison, Bethell writes, "His most striking characteristic as D.A. was a truly astounding recklessness and irresponsibility."
See also BOXLEY, BILL.

BETHESDA NAVAL HOSPITAL

The autopsy on President Kennedy's body was performed at Bethesda Naval Hospital, one of the two large military hospitals in the suburbs of Washington, D.C. (The other is †Walter Reed Army Medical Center.) According to Texas law, the president's body should not have been removed from the state—where the homicide had occurred—before an autopsy had been performed. Over strenuous objections from the Dallas medical examiner, Dr. Earl †Rose, the body was removed from Texas and flown to Washington, D.C. Before †*Air Force One*, bearing the president's coffin, landed at †Andrews Air Force Base, there was some confusion about where the body should be taken for an autopsy. It was finally decided to use Bethesda because Kennedy had been a naval officer and it had been his official hospital during his presidency.
See also AMBULANCE CONTROVERSY; AUTOPSY CONTROVERSY.
📖 *Best Evidence*

BETRAYAL

Written by former CIA employee Robert D. †Morrow
and published in 1976 by Henry Regnery Company,
Betrayal traces a tangled sequence of events
beginning with the †Bay of Pigs and culminating in
the assassination of President Kennedy. Morrow
implicates rogue elements in the Agency in the
commission and subsequent cover-up of the crime.
This book provides an intriguing insight into the
workings of the CIA. Among its shocking disclosures
is Morrow's admission that, prior to the
assassination, he purchased for the Agency three
†Mannlicher-Carcano rifles identical to the one
allegedly found in the †Texas School Book Depository
Building on November 22, 1963.
See also CENTRAL INTELLIGENCE AGENCY.

BETZNER, HUGH, JR.

Hugh Betzner, Jr., witnessed the assassination almost
immediately after snapping three photographs of the
scene near the intersection of Houston and Elm
streets. He ran through †Dealey Plaza in an effort to
keep pace with the president's limousine while he took
several more pictures. Betzner allegedly told a
sheriff's deputy that he believed at least some of the

shots were fired from the area of the picket fence on the †Grassy Knoll. He surrendered his camera and film to Deputy Eugene L. †Boone, who had the film developed and returned both the camera and the negatives to Betzner.
See also "BLACK DOG MAN"; DEALEY PLAZA WITNESSES.
📖 *Crossfire; Rush to Judgment*

BICKERS, BENNY H.
Bickers owned a nightclub a block from Jack †Ruby's †Carousel Club in Dallas. He confided to FBI investigators that Ruby was very close to the Dallas Police Department. Bickers complained that Ruby's police contacts allowed him to regularly flout laws regulating the activities and the drinking hours of such clubs.
📖 *Rush to Judgment*

BILLINGS, RICHARD N.
A staffer for the †House Select Committee on Assassinations, Billings prepared the Committee's report. Along with Committee general counsel G. Robert †Blakey, he wrote an article for *Parade* magazine discussing how the Committee concluded that organized crime was responsible for the

president's murder. The two men also coauthored *The Plot to Kill the President*, published by Times Books in 1981 and reissued as *Fatal Hour: The Assassination of President Kennedy by Organized Crime* by Berkley Books in 1992. The book also accuses organized crime of masterminding the assassination. Some researchers challenge the book, whose manuscript was approved by the †Central Intelligence Agency, as a cover-up of the CIA's involvement in killing Kennedy.
📖 *Crossfire; High Treason*

BIRD, SAMUEL R.

Army Lieutenant Bird was in charge of the Military District of Washington, D.C., †Casket Team that stood honor guard when †Secret Service agents removed the president's coffin from †*Air Force One* and placed it inside a Navy ambulance. Bird and his team were then flown to †Bethesda Naval Hospital by helicopter to meet the ambulance. Bird later suffered an injury in Vietnam that severely hampered his memory, but on December 10, 1963, he had written in his official report that the coffin was taken from the ambulance to the autopsy room at 8:00 P.M. This conflicts with the †O'Neill and Sibert report that the coffin was taken into the autopsy room at 7:17 P.M., and with autopsy chief Dr. James J. †Humes's report that he received the body at 7:35 P.M. This discrepancy in the times has fueled speculation that the president's wounds could have been altered during the unaccounted-for half hour.

See also AMBULANCE CONTROVERSY; WEHLE, PHILIP C.

📖 *Best Evidence*

"BISHOP, MAURICE"

"Maurice Bishop" is a cover name used by a CIA agent who was deeply involved in †Central Intelligence Agency activities designed to overthrow the Fidel †Castro government in Cuba. He was also the case officer for a Cuban operative named Antonio †Veciana, who swears he saw "Bishop" meet with Lee Harvey †Oswald in Dallas before the assassination. Veciana also swears that "Bishop" solicited him to pressure his cousin who worked in the Cuban Embassy in †Mexico City into accepting a bribe to confirm that he saw Oswald in the embassy. Some observers believe "Bishop" was actually David Atlee †Phillips, a CIA agent with a long and active history in Latin American affairs.

📖 *Conspiracy; High Treason*

BISSELL, RICHARD

This former deputy director of planning for the
†Central Intelligence Agency has been linked with plots
to assassinate Fidel †Castro and with the †Bay of Pigs
invasion. Following the Bay of Pigs fiasco, Kennedy
fired CIA director Allen W. †Dulles, Bissell, and others
for what he viewed as a lack of leadership. The plots
against Castro's life are believed to have been behind
Castro's reputed desire to see Kennedy dead.
See also EDWARDS, SHEFFIELD.
📖 *High Treason*

"BLACK DOG MAN"

Several photographs taken during the assassination
by Hugh †Betzner, Jr., and Philip L. †Willis show a
dark figure that is barely discernible behind a low
wall at the south end of the †Grassy Knoll. Investigators originally referred to this figure as the "Black
Dog Man" because many thought it resembled a dog
sitting on the wall. Computer enhancement later
disclosed that the figure could actually be a man
standing a short distance behind the wall, possibly
carrying a long object that some believe might be a
gun. If it was a man, he has never been identified.
See also GRASSY KNOLL WITNESSES.
📖 *Crossfire*

BLAHUT, REGIS

Blahut was the CIA's liaison with the †House Select
Committee on Assassinations. He was fired for
breaking into the safe holding the Committee's copies
of autopsy photographs. For some undisclosed reason
the break-in, which occurred in 1978, was not made
public until the following year.
📖 *High Treason*

BLAKEY, G. ROBERT

A law professor and the director of the Notre Dame
Institute on Organized Crime, Blakey was appointed
general counsel to the †House Select Committee on
Assassinations in June 1977. Blakey has come under
attack on a number of fronts from virtually every
critic of the †Warren Report. His appointment came
after the Committee investigation, which was being
conducted openly, was already under way. (He
replaced Richard †Sprague.) Blakey's first move was to
discontinue the press conferences that until then had
been keeping the American public abreast of the
Committee's findings. Blakey has been charged with
blocking the development of new evidence, firing
staffers and investigators who demonstrated too much
vigor in their work, and having close ties to the
intelligence community, especially the †Central

Intelligence Agency. Many researchers blame Blakey for underwriting the Committee's failure to investigate the assassination thoroughly.

With Richard N. †Billings as his coauthor, Blakey wrote a book based on the Committee's findings. Originally titled *The Plot to Kill the President* (Times Books, 1981) and reissued as *Fatal Hour: The Assassination of President Kennedy by Organized Crime* (Berkley Books, 1992), the book assesses the blame on organized crime. Some researchers see *Fatal Hour* as an attempt to divert attention from CIA involvement. Blakey admitted that the Agency reviewed the manuscript before it was published. ⌷ *Best Evidence*; *Crossfire*; *High Treason*; *Plausible Denial*

BLEDSOE, MARY E.

During October 1963, Mrs. Bledsoe allegedly rented a furnished room in her Dallas house to Lee Harvey †Oswald. She took an immediate dislike to him and asked him to leave within the week. On November 22, 1963, Mrs. Bledsoe was at the scene, watching the presidential motorcade. After the assassination, she boarded the same bus, driven by Cecil J. †McWatters, that Oswald supposedly took after shooting Police Officer J. D. †Tippit. She told the †Warren Commission that Oswald came on the bus looking "like a maniac." Her description of the wild-looking man on the bus does not agree with the description given by McWatters.

See also JONES, MILTON R.

📖 *Rush to Judgment*

BODY BAG CONTROVERSY

According to statements by nurses and others in the emergency room at Dallas's †Parkland Memorial Hospital, the president's body was wrapped in sheets when it was placed inside the coffin (which was lined with plastic) in preparation for the trip from Dallas to Washington. The men who removed the body from the coffin in the autopsy room at †Bethesda Naval Hospital described the body as wrapped inside a zippered, rubberized body bag similar to the military body bags widely used to send home the remains of soldiers and sailors killed in battle. This discrepancy has led many to believe that the president's wounds were altered between the time the body left Parkland and the autopsy was performed at Bethesda.

See also AMBULANCE CONTROVERSY; COFFIN CONTROVERSY; JENKINS, JAMES CURTIS; O'CONNOR, PAUL K.; RIKE, AUBREY.

📖 *Best Evidence*; *High Treason*

BOGARD, ALBERT G.

Bogard was a car salesman for Dallas's †Downtown
Lincoln-Mercury when a man calling himself Lee
†Oswald asked about a Mercury Comet. That was
November 9, 1963. Bogard said he selected a red
Comet and joined the prospective customer for a test
drive. Oswald drove unusually fast and recklessly,
according to Bogard, and finally told the salesman he
was coming into some money in two or three weeks
and would return then. When Bogard repeated this
story to the †Warren Commission, he passed an FBI
polygraph test verifying that he was telling the truth.
His story was also corroborated by other salesmen at
the dealership who saw Oswald and spoke with him
that day. The Warren Commission discounted his
testimony because Oswald was said to be elsewhere
that day. If Bogard was correct, and the man who took
the test drive was actually Oswald, then from what
source did he expect a large sum of money soon after
the assassination? If the man wasn't Oswald, who
impersonated him, and why? These questions remain
unanswered.

On February 14, 1966, in a cemetery in Hallsville,
Louisiana, Albert Bogard, age forty-one, was found
inside his car with a hose running from the exhaust
pipe into the interior. His death, although ruled a

suicide, leaves still another question open to speculation. According to one of his fellow salesmen, shortly after testifying before the Commission, Bogard was severely beaten and hospitalized, and then quietly disappeared from Dallas.

📖 *High Treason; Rush to Judgment*

BOGGS, HALE

A highly respected long-term congressman from Louisiana, Boggs was selected by President Lyndon B. †Johnson to sit on the †Warren Commission. Boggs openly faulted the FBI for using "Gestapo tactics" and seriously questioned the Warren Commission findings concerning the assassination. In 1972, the congressman's small plane disappeared while he was flying across Alaska. His body was never recovered.

📖 *Crossfire; High Treason*

BOLDEN, ABRAHAM

Bolden, the first black †Secret Service agent, was assigned to White House security until he criticized the lax security around the president and was transferred to the Chicago office. Bolden later disclosed that prior to November 1, 1963, he had come into possession of an FBI teletype hinting of a plot by four Cuban assassins to kill the president. His

attempts at further investigation led to stonewalling by the FBI with denials that the teletype ever existed. Following the assassination, Bolden called †Warren Commission counsel J. Lee †Rankin and volunteered to testify before the Commission about his foreknowledge of a planned assassination. The Commission ignored his offer, and not long after, he was arrested and jailed for allegedly attempting to sell government files. Bolden claimed that the charges were trumped up.
📖 *High Treason; Rush to Judgment*

BOLT BERANEK AND NEWMAN
This high-tech acoustics firm located in Cambridge, Massachusetts, was employed by the †House Select Committee on Assassinations to review the †Dallas police dispatch tape. In its analysis of the tape, the firm concluded that more than three shots were fired in †Dealey Plaza at the time Kennedy was shot.
See also ACOUSTICAL EVIDENCE; ASCHKENASY, ERNEST; BARGER, DR. JAMES; RAMSEY REPORT; WEISS, MARK.
📖 *Crossfire; High Treason*

BOOKHOUT, JAMES W.
FBI special agent Bookhout was present when Captain Will †Fritz of the Dallas police interrogated Lee

Harvey [†]Oswald at Police Headquarters. Bookhout reported that when Oswald was shown a photograph of himself holding a rifle resembling the [†]Mannlicher-Carcano found in the [†]Texas School Book Depository Building, he said the head in the photo might be his, "but that it was entirely possible that the Police Department had superimposed this part of the photograph over the body of someone else." Bookhout added that Oswald denied any involvement in the assassination. *See also* OSWALD, BACKYARD PHOTOGRAPH OF.
📖 *Rush to Judgment*

BOONE, EUGENE L.

Deputy Sheriff Boone and Deputy Constable Seymour [†]Weitzman were two of the officers who found the rifle on the sixth floor of the [†]Texas School Book Depository Building minutes after the assassination. Boone told the [†]Warren Commission he "thought it was a 7.65 Mauser." Boone said Captain Will [†]Fritz of the Dallas police also identified the weapon as a Mauser. Weitzman later signed an affidavit concurring with this conclusion, as did initial police reports to the press. When Boone was shown the [†]Mannlicher-Carcano rifle allegedly belonging to Lee Harvey [†]Oswald, he could not identify it as the weapon he found. The legend "Made in Italy, Cal. 6.5" is clearly

stamped on the Mannlicher-Carcano.
See also BETZNER, HUGH, JR.; CRAIG, ROGER D.;
MOONEY, LUKE; WADE, HENRY W.
📖 *Rush to Judgment*

BORING, FLOYD

Assistant chief of the †Secret Service White House
detail, Boring helped search the presidential
limousine after it was flown from Dallas to
Washington. Two metal fragments believed to have
come from the bullet that struck Governor John
†Connally were recovered during this search.
See also MAGIC BULLET; MILLS, THOMAS; PATERNI,
PAUL.
📖 *Best Evidence*

BOSWELL, DR. THORNTON

Chief of pathology at †Bethesda Naval Hospital, Boswell
was one of two doctors present when the president's
body was removed from the coffin after its arrival from
Dallas. The other was Dr. James J. †Humes. During the
autopsy, Boswell made a sketch of the wound in
Kennedy's skull, indicating the missing section as a
large rectangular area rising from the lower right rear
and extending up across the top. This representation

differs greatly from the drawing made at †Parkland Memorial Hospital at the time of the president's death, which shows the wound and missing section of skull to be considerably smaller and in the lower rear.
See also AUTOPSY CONTROVERSY; HEAD WOUND CONTROVERSY; LUNDBERG, DR. GEORGE.
📖 *Best Evidence*

BOUCK, ROBERT

When the assassination occurred, Bouck was head of the †Secret Service Protective Research Section, a position that involved him in a cloudy controversy about an item officially designated as a "missile" that presumably either fell or was removed from the president's body during the autopsy. In this case the "missile" is universally assumed to mean a bullet. Bouck signed a receipt for items given him by the president's physician, Admiral Dr. George †Burkley, on November 26, 1963. The seventh item on this receipt was identified as "one receipt from FBI for a missile recovered during examination of the body." Evidently the missile has either been lost or never clearly identified. Bouck was also the person who ordered that the †Harper bone fragment be sent to the White House after its discovery.
📖 *Best Evidence*

BOWEN, JOHN "JACK"

Bowen, a self-styled itinerant preacher, allegedly used the alias Albert Osborne. The †Warren Commission was satisfied that Osborne and Lee Harvey †Oswald shared a double bus seat during a trip to †Mexico City, where Oswald allegedly visited either the Cuban embassy or the Soviet embassy. When Oswald was arrested, he reportedly had in his wallet a library card under the name John L. Bowen. The card has since vanished. Interestingly, "Osborne" was also one of the †aliases used by Oswald.

📖 *Conspiracy; High Treason*

BOWERS, LEE, JR.

Lee Bowers, Jr., manned a railroad control tower fourteen feet above the ground and approximately fifty feet beyond the †Grassy Knoll. He reported having seen three strange vehicles driving through the area around the tower minutes before the assassination, and having noted the presence of two men standing near the fence on the knoll. Although he was occupied at the time, Bowers remembered that something like "a flash of light or smoke or something" caught his attention. He had a sense of it coming from the spot where the two men stood. Friends of Bowers claim that right after the assassination he disappeared for several days and note that when he returned, one of his fingers had been amputated. They suspect that Bowers saw more than he admitted, but feared for his life. On August 9, 1966, Bowers was killed in a mysterious car crash on a lonely stretch of Texas highway.

See also GRASSY KNOLL WITNESSES; SMOKE FROM THE GRASSY KNOLL.

📖 *Crossfire; Rush to Judgment*

BOWLES, JIM

Police Officer Bowles, who would later become Dallas county sheriff, commanded the radio division in November 1963 and prepared the †Dallas police dispatch tape for review by the †House Select Committee on Assassinations. He has reportedly said that the tape was borrowed by federal agents shortly after the assassination and later returned to him. Bowles is also quoted as stating that the police motorcycle with an open microphone that allegedly transmitted the sound of the four shots taped from the †Dealey Plaza location was actually two miles away at the time.

📖 *Final Disclosure; High Treason*

BOWLEY, T. F.

Bowley stated that he was driving west on 10th Street in the Oak Cliff section of Dallas when he saw a police

officer (J. D. †Tippit) lying on the ground next to a
police cruiser. Checking his watch, he noted the time
as 1:10 P.M. When he realized the officer was gravely
wounded, Bowley called the police on the car radio.
The official Dallas police radio log indicates Bowley's
transmission was received by 1:16 P.M. The time of the
radio call has been advanced by some researchers as
proof that Lee Harvey †Oswald did not have time to
travel the distance from his rooming house to the
Tippit murder scene and kill Officer Tippit.
See also BENAVIDES, DOMINGO; TIPPIT MURDER
SCENE WITNESSES.
📕 *Rush to Judgment*

BOWRON, DIANA
Bowron was a nurse on duty in the emergency room at
†Parkland Memorial Hospital when the president's
body was brought in; she helped remove his clothes.
She testified before the †Warren Commission that
although she clearly saw the large hole in the
president's skull, "in the back of the head," she did not
see the small bullet entry wound in the rear of the
skull described by Dr. James J. †Humes in the report
of the autopsy performed at †Bethesda Naval Hospital.
See also PARKLAND MEMORIAL HOSPITAL STAFF.
📕 *Best Evidence*

BOXLEY, BILL
Bill Boxley was the pseudonym of William Wood, an investigator who worked on the assassination investigation conducted by New Orleans district attorney Jim †Garrison. Boxley reportedly told Garrison he had once worked for the CIA. According to an article by Tom †Bethell in the December 16, 1991, issue of *The National Review*, Garrison's staff forced Boxley out when they realized he was feeding Garrison misleading information that was creating chaos in the investigation.

BRADEN, JIM
Braden was arrested in the Dal-Tex Building across from †Dealey Plaza minutes after the assassination. He said he was in the building looking for a telephone so he could call his mother to tell her what had happened. Dallas police could find no reason to hold him, and Braden was released. Investigators later identified him as Eugene Hale Brading, a suspected †Mafia courier.
📖 *Crossfire; High Treason*

BRAIN CONTROVERSY
There has been much speculation about the condition and even the alleged disappearance of the president's

brain from the body that was delivered to the autopsy room at †Bethesda Naval Hospital. According to Paul K. †O'Connor, a surgical assistant at the autopsy whose function was to remove the deceased brain so it could be placed in a hardening substance for later dissection (a routine autopsy procedure), when he removed the president's body from the body bag, there was no brain. It had apparently already been removed. The brain remains unaccounted for, and, along with other vital autopsy-related information such as X rays and photographs, is missing from the †National Archives. *See also* AUTOPSY CONTROVERSY; BODY BAG CONTROVERSY; HEAD WOUND CONTROVERSY. 📖 *Best Evidence*; *Crossfire*; *High Treason 2*

BREHM, CHARLES
Brehm was one of the spectators lining the curb on the driver's side of the president's limousine when the assassination took place. He was sufficiently close that he can be seen in the †Zapruder film cheering as the car is passing him. Brehm gave eyewitness interviews that same day to newspaper and television reporters, and was also briefly detained at the sheriff's office, where he reportedly gave police a deposition. He described seeing a portion of the president's skull fly

backward and to the left when he was hit. According
to a quote in a *Dallas Times-Herald* article, he
"seemed to think the shots came from in front of or
beside the president." Brehm was never questioned by
the †Warren Commission, and the Sheriff's
Department report no longer exists.
See also HARGIS, BOBBY W.; MARTIN, B. J.
📖 *Best Evidence*; *Rush to Judgment*

BRENNAN, HOWARD L.
Brennan, a forty-five-year-old steamfitter, was
working on a job near †Dealey Plaza when he broke for
lunch and found a place to eat while he waited for the
president's motorcade to arrive. According to
testimony, Brennan was approximately 107 feet from
the front of the †Texas School Book Depository
Building across the street when he noticed a man
standing at a sixth-floor window in the southeast
corner of the building. The sound of shots drew his
attention back to the window just as the man fired the
final shot.

Brennan's detailed description of the sniper is
credited by the †Warren Commission with leading to
Police Officer J. D. †Tippit's attempt to arrest Lee
Harvey †Oswald. Although Brennan failed to pick

Oswald out of a lineup at Police Headquarters, he later identified Oswald's corpse as the man he saw in the window. Brennan's testimony is full of discrepancies, including the fact that he said the man in the window was standing, which allowed him to estimate the man's height and weight. Photos taken seconds after the shooting show the window was raised less than halfway, suggesting that the shooter would have had to kneel.

See also EUINS, AMOS L.; MILLICAN, A. J.; SORRELS, FORREST V.; SPEAKER, SANDY; TERRY, L. R.

📖 *Assassination Tapes; Best Evidence*; *Rush to Judgment*

BREWER, E. D.

E. D. Brewer was a Dallas police motorcycle officer who initially started toward the †Grassy Knoll when the shots were fired, but was stopped by an unidentified man who said he saw someone "pull the weapon back through the window from the southeast corner of that Depository building." Brewer was one of at least three officers whose first impression was that the shots came from the Grassy Knoll, but he was distracted from his objective when a nameless bystander intervened and directed his attention to the Depository.

See also HARGIS, BOBBY W.; HAYGOOD, CLYDE A.;

TEXAS SCHOOL BOOK DEPOSITORY BUILDING.
📖 *Best Evidence*

BREWER, JOHNNY

On November 22, 1963, Johnny Brewer was at work managing a retail shoe store on Jefferson Boulevard in the Oak Cliff section of Dallas. He heard the news of the assassination on the radio and, shortly after, the announcement that a police officer had been shot not far from the store. Just as he heard police sirens approaching, a man ducked into the entranceway of his store and waited with his back to the street while the police car passed. He then stepped back out onto the sidewalk and walked away. Brewer, suspecting the man might be trying to avoid the police, followed him. Less than a hundred feet up the street, his quarry slipped into the †Texas Theatre movie house without purchasing a ticket. Brewer told this to the cashier, Julia Postal, who had been distracted because she was listening to news reports of the president's assassination on her radio. Postal called the police.

According to Brewer's testimony to the †Warren Commission, when the police arrived, the house lights in the theater were turned up and Brewer singled out Lee Harvey †Oswald as the man who had behaved so suspiciously. Brewer's story regarding how the police officers decided that Oswald was the man they wanted in connection with the shooting of Officer J. D. †Tippit differs from the stories told by other witnesses. According to the testimony of the arresting officer, M. N. †McDonald, Oswald was pointed out by an unidentified man sitting near the front of the theater. ⊓ *Conspiracy; Crossfire*

BRIGADE 2506
See BAY OF PIGS.

BRINGUIER, CARLOS
A member of the †anti-Castro Cuban exile community living in New Orleans, Bringuier recalls that Lee Harvey †Oswald approached him on August 5, 1963, explained he was a former Marine, and volunteered to help train exiles in guerrilla warfare techniques. A few days later, on August 9, Bringuier learned through an associate that the same Oswald was distributing leaflets for the pro-Castro †Fair Play for Cuba Committee (FPCC). Bringuier, with two other exiles, combed downtown New Orleans looking for Oswald. When they found him, they took his leaflets and scattered them in the air. Bringuier began shouting that he was a traitor, when police arrived

and arrested the group for disturbing the peace.

The true significance of this incident has been debated for years. Some observers think Oswald was attempting to create a cover as a pro-Castro activist because he wanted to move to Cuba. Others believe Oswald and Bringuier staged the entire episode as part of a plan to discredit pro-Castro Americans, especially FPCC.

See also BANISTER, GUY; 544 CAMP STREET.

📖 *Conspiracy; Warren Report*

BROCK, MARY

Mrs. Brock was the wife of a mechanic who worked at a service station near the scene of the murder of J. D. †Tippit. She testified to the †Warren Commission that she was visiting her husband at work on November 22, 1963, and that she saw a man she later identified as Lee Harvey †Oswald shortly after Officer Tippit was shot. She saw the man walk briskly into a nearby parking lot located behind the service station, which was on the corner of Jefferson and Crawford streets. The jacket Oswald was believed to be wearing when Tippit was killed was allegedly recovered in the same parking lot.

📖 *Warren Report*

BRONSON FILM

Six minutes before the first shot was fired at the president, Charles Bronson filmed the scene in †Dealey Plaza, panning in on the motorcade route with his 35mm home-movie camera. Officially dismissed by the FBI as containing no relevant information, the film lay neglected in a storage vault until 1978, when it was retrieved and reviewed by photographic expert Robert J. †Groden. His analysis focused on simultaneous movements in two separate sixth-floor windows of the †Texas School Book Depository Building, which he interpreted to mean that at least two, and possibly three, people could have been in that crucial area only minutes before the shooting.

See also DEALEY PLAZA WITNESSES; HUGHES, ROBERT; SELZER, ROBERT.

📖 *Conspiracy*

BROWDER, EDDIE

A pilot long suspected of having close †Mafia contacts, Browder, with Jack †Ruby, reportedly smuggled guns to Fidel †Castro's forces before the Cuban dictator deposed the Batista regime. Browder's contacts with mob figures have been traced through Norman "Roughhouse" Rothman to Santos †Trafficante.

📖 *Conspiracy*

BROWN, CHARLES W.

On November 23, 1963, Charles W. Brown drove a police cruiser to the Dallas Police Headquarters garage to collect the suspect Lee Harvey †Oswald for transfer to the Dallas County jail. The car was not in place when Oswald was escorted to the garage, necessitating a brief delay and a longer walk than Oswald's guards had anticipated. It was during that interim that Jack †Ruby shot Oswald. The reason the car was not in its designated place before the prisoner was brought to the garage has never been fully explained.

See also GRAVES, L. C.; LEAVELLE, JAMES R.; MONTGOMERY, L. D.

📖 *Rush to Judgment*

BROWN, JOE

District court judge Brown presided over Jack †Ruby's trial for the murder of Lee Harvey †Oswald, reportedly hiring a public relations consultant to polish his image during its duration. Despite the protest of Ruby's lawyers, who introduced numerous news accounts of local hostility toward Ruby, and the support of nearly one hundred Dallas citizens, Brown ruled against a defense motion to move the trial out of Dallas. Brown also refused to exclude as potential jurors anyone who had seen Ruby shoot Oswald on television. The result of the trial—a conviction and a death sentence—was reversed on appeal.

📖 *Texas Connection*

BROWN, MADELINE

Madeline Brown admits to having had an affair with Lyndon B. †Johnson for twenty years, beginning in 1948. In an interview on the television program "A Current Affair" broadcast on February 25, 1992, she revealed that after the assassination Johnson had told her that he knew about the assassination in advance. According to Ms. Brown, Johnson confided that the assassination had been the work of the CIA and Texas oil interests, two groups that wanted Kennedy dead for their own reasons.

📖 *Texas Connection*

BROWN, ORAN

Brown was a salesman working in the same Dallas Lincoln-Mercury dealership as Albert G. †Bogard, who singled out Lee Harvey †Oswald as a prospective new car customer he took for a test drive only two weeks before the assassination. Oswald is said to have told Bogard that he would have "some money coming in," so he would buy a car soon. Brown was questioned by the FBI about the incident, and he buttressed Bogard's testimony. When researcher/author Mark †Lane interviewed Brown on April 4, 1966, Brown told him he was reluctant to talk because Bogard had been severely beaten after he testified before the †Warren Commission and had then dropped from sight. During this conversation with Lane, Brown was unaware that Bogard's body had been found in Hallsville, Louisiana; his death was ruled a suicide, but the circumstances were strangely suspicious.

See also DOWNTOWN LINCOLN-MERCURY.

📖 *Rush to Judgment*

BRUNO, JERRY

Bruno was Kennedy's advance man, responsible for ensuring that the president's Texas trip, essentially a political move to win Texas votes in the 1964 election, went smoothly. Bruno claims he fought a bitter battle with Texas politicians, including Governor John †Connally, over the route of the motorcade. He describes this extensively in his book, *The Advanceman*, published by William Morrow in 1971.

📖 *Texas Connection*

BULLET #399
See MAGIC BULLET.

BULLETS FIRED, NUMBER OF
The †Warren Report stands or falls on the belief that only one person, Lee Harvey †Oswald, took part in the assassination of President Kennedy. This †lone assassin theory is based on the "fact," as established by the Commission, that there were three shots fired in †Dealey Plaza at 12:30 P.M. on November 22, 1963, and that all three were fired from the sixth floor of the †Texas School Book Depository Building. The Depository, however, was behind the president when he was shot, so any evidence of a bullet entering the front or side of the president's body would automatically disprove the Commission's findings.

Although a number of expert marksmen, which everyone acknowledges Oswald was not, could not duplicate the feat credited to Oswald of firing three shots in six seconds with the poor-quality rifle he allegedly used, the Commission stood by its opinion. Evidence indicating that more than three shots were fired would also automatically disprove the Commission's finding of a lone assassin because it is impossible that Oswald, or any other single person, could have fired four or more shots in the time available.

On examination of the reports of bullets found or seen at the time of the assassination as described in this book, we arrive at a total of nine. First, there are the bullets acknowledged by the Warren Commission: one that is said to have struck both Kennedy and Governor John †Connally (the †magic bullet), which is in the National Archives; one that hit the curb in front of James T. †Tague, a bystander, and caused slight injury to his cheek; and another that hit the president in the head and disintegrated (bullets #1, #2, and #3). Added to these is a bullet that struck either the left or center lane of Elm Street, as seen by both Sheriff J. E. (Bill) †Decker and railroad worker Royce G. †Skelton (bullet #4). Another bullet (#5) was found by Police Officer J. W. †Foster in the grassy area below the railroad overpass, where it was dug out of the ground by a man who was identified by Dallas police chief Jesse E. †Curry as an FBI agent but who the FBI claims was not one of its men. The man remains unidentified despite a photograph that shows him digging in the ground while Foster and Sheriff's Deputy Eddy †Walthers look on. Then there are the two mounds in the earth that Wayne and Edna

†Hartman saw near the center of Dealey Plaza, which a police officer told them were caused by two bullets, fired at the presidential limousine from the †Grassy Knoll, that missed and came to earth at that spot. No one knows what happened to these bullets (#6 and #7). Next is the bullet Virgie †Rachley saw hit the street directly behind the presidential limousine with such impact it caused sparks (bullet #8). Finally, we have the bullet that caused the †windshield damage as seen and reported by Dallas police officers Starvis †Ellis and H. R. †Freeman (bullet #9).

Even if we allow that some of these reports may be duplicate sightings of the same bullet—for example, perhaps the bullet that pierced the limousine's windshield was the same bullet Sheriff Decker saw hit the pavement near the center of Elm Street—we are still left with five to seven bullets that are definitely accounted for, far more than Oswald or any other person acting alone could have fired in the few seconds in which the shooting took place.

The †House Select Committee on Assassinations said it could account for the sounds of four gunshots. Although this was a step in the right direction, investigation of the bullet sightings recorded in this entry must be made before the number of shooters can be determined accurately.

BUNDY, VERNON

An admitted heroin addict, Bundy was a witness at
the trial of Clay †Shaw, whom New Orleans district
attorney Jim †Garrison charged with participating in
the assassination. Bundy claimed to have seen Shaw
meet secretly with Lee Harvey †Oswald in July 1963
and said Shaw gave Oswald what appeared to be a roll
of money.

📖 *On the Trail of the Assassins*

BURKLEY, DR. GEORGE

Admiral Dr. Burkley was the White House medical
officer, and therefore the personal physician to
President Kennedy. Burkley was riding in a car
toward the rear of the motorcade as it made its way
through downtown Dallas. Immediately following the
shooting, his car was directed first to the Dallas Trade
Mart, where the president had been scheduled to
deliver a luncheon address, and from there to
†Parkland Memorial Hospital. Burkley was aboard †*Air
Force One,* where he sat with Jacqueline †Kennedy and
the coffin on the flight to Washington, and he was an
observer at the autopsy. Although a uniquely qualified
expert witness because he was the only medically
trained person to see the president's body at both
Parkland and †Bethesda Naval Hospital, Burkley was

never asked to testify before the †Warren Commission.
See also AUTOPSY CONTROVERSY.
📖 *Best Evidence*

BUSH, GEORGE
George Bush, the forty-first president of the United
States, denies that he had any relationship with the
CIA prior to his 1976 appointment as its director,
though there have been charges that he was connected
to the activities of Lee Harvey †Oswald. In a November
29, 1963, memo, FBI director J. Edgar †Hoover
mentioned that an FBI agent and a member of the
Defense Intelligence Agency briefed "Mr. George Bush
of the †Central Intelligence Agency" about the
assassination. The Agency produced a George Bush,
allegedly a former employee, who denied ever having
been briefed about the assassination and claimed he
had worked for the CIA for only six months in a low-
level position examining photographs unrelated to
President Kennedy's murder. Discovered after the
death of George †DeMohrenschildt, the man many
believe was Lee Harvey Oswald's CIA control officer,
was the following entry in DeMohrenschildt's personal
telephone book: "Bush, George H. W. (Poppy) 1412 W.
Ohio, also Zapata Petroleum Midland."
📖 *Plausible Denial*

BUTLER, GEORGE
A Dallas police lieutenant, Butler was reportedly assigned responsibility for Lee Harvey †Oswald's safe transfer from Dallas Police Headquarters downtown to the Dallas County jail. Several witnesses remembered that Butler had appeared to be apprehensive and "jittery" in the moments before Oswald was killed.
□ *High Treason*

CABANA MOTEL

About midnight, the night before the Kennedy murder, Jack †Ruby visited Lawrence Meyers, a guest at the Cabana Motel. Meyers was accompanied by a female companion named Jean West, who is believed to have had ties with Oswald associate David †Ferrie, a New Orleans figure investigated by District Attorney Jim †Garrison. Staying at the Cabana Motel at the same time was alleged †Mafia courier Eugene Hale Brading, who was registered under the alias Jim †Braden. The following day, Braden was detained briefly by police near †Dealey Plaza shortly after the assassination, but was released.

📖 *Crossfire; High Treason*

CABELL, CHARLES

Brother of Dallas mayor Earle †Cabell, U.S. Army General Charles Cabell had been deputy director of the †Central Intelligence Agency during the †Bay of

Dallas mayor Earle Cabell

Pigs exercise. He was among a group of high-level CIA personnel fired by Kennedy after the Cuban invasion fiasco. Charles Cabell has been implicated in CIA schemes to recruit †Mafia hitmen to kill Fidel †Castro during the 1960s. Some researchers believe Charles Cabell may have had a motive to participate in plans to assassinate Kennedy. There is no hard evidence to prove this.

📖 *High Treason*

CABELL, EARLE

Mayor of Dallas at the time of the assassination, Earle Cabell rode with his wife six cars behind Kennedy's presidential motorcade. Although there is no evidence that he had anything to do with the assassination, the fact that Cabell's brother, General Charles †Cabell, was fired by Kennedy for the poor planning of the †Bay of Pigs invasion, and that the assassination took place in Cabell's city has been listed as a "sinister connection" by researchers Robert J. †Groden and Harrison Edward †Livingstone.

📖 *High Treason*

CABELL, MRS. EARLE

The wife of the Dallas mayor was riding in the presidential motorcade six cars back from Kennedy's limousine when the shots were fired. Mrs. Cabell was among several witnesses, including Texas senator Ralph †Yarborough, who told the †Warren Commission they could smell the distinct odor of gunpowder in †Dealey Plaza. It appears unlikely that people located at street level would smell gunpowder if all the shots were fired from six floors above them, where the odor would be quickly carried away by a breeze that was blowing that day, although it would not be inconsistent with at least one shot being fired from the †Grassy Knoll.

📖 *Crossfire*

CAIRNS, DR. A. B.
See HARPER BONE FRAGMENT.

CALLAWAY, TED
Callaway, the manager of a used-car lot on the corner of Patton Avenue and Jefferson Boulevard in Dallas, heard the sound of the gunshots that killed Police Officer J. D. †Tippit. He and another employee, Sam Guinyard, ran toward the sounds, encountering a man who was leaving the scene holding a handgun. Callaway shouted, "Hey, man, what the hell is going on?" The man slowed down briefly, muttered a

response, and rounded a corner heading west on Jefferson.

Arriving on the scene and finding Tippit dead, Callaway used the patrol car's radio to call for help and was told police were on the way. He then picked up the officer's gun, and he and a cabdriver, William †Scoggins, cruised the neighborhood in an unsuccessful attempt to locate the murderer. Callaway later picked Lee Harvey †Oswald out of a police lineup whose fairness has since been questioned for including men who bore not even the slightest resemblance to Oswald. Callaway was one of several witnesses who reported they did not see Helen Louise †Markham at the Tippit murder scene.

See also TIPPIT MURDER SCENE WITNESSES.

📖 *Warren Report*

CAMPBELL, OCHUS V.

Vice president of the †Texas School Book Depository, Campbell was standing in front of the building when President Kennedy was killed. He testified to the †Warren Commission that he heard shots "fired from a point which I thought was near the railroad tracks located over the viaduct on Elm Street," indicating the area near the †Grassy Knoll. He claimed he had no reason to notice anything unusual about the Depository Building because the shots were coming from somewhere else.

See also TEXAS SCHOOL BOOK DEPOSITORY BUILDING EMPLOYEES.

📖 *Rush to Judgment*

CAMPISI, JOSEPH

Owner of the Egyptian Restaurant in Dallas in 1963, Campisi is alleged to have had ties with †Mafia boss Santos †Trafficante and Joseph †Civello, reputed chief of Mafia don Carlos †Marcello's operations in Dallas. The night before the assassination, Jack †Ruby had dinner at the Egyptian Restaurant. Although he disclaimed intimacy with Ruby, Campisi visited him in jail after Ruby's arrest for killing Lee Harvey †Oswald.

📖 *Conspiracy*

CAMP SMITH

Despite Defense Department denials, Hawaii's Camp Smith—a U.S. Marine Corps base—was the site of a secret investigation of President Kennedy's assassination conducted by two Marine Corps teams, according to the testimony of former Marine navigator Larry Huff before the †House Select Committee on

Assassinations. Huff disclosed that on December 14, 1963, he was the navigator of a C-54 aircraft that flew ten to twelve military investigators on the way to Japan to Wake Island, where they changed planes for the second leg of the trip. During the flight Huff was told the Japan trip was part of an investigation of Lee Harvey †Oswald's involvement in the assassination. Huff said that on the return flight, he read a confidential report prepared by the Marine Corps containing a psychological evaluation of Oswald, which concluded that he was psychologically incapable of carrying out the assassination alone. This alleged report has disappeared.

📖 *High Treason*

CANADA, CAPTAIN ROBERT

Commanding officer of †Bethesda Naval Hospital in 1963, Captain Canada was present during the autopsy of President Kennedy. He played only a peripheral role in the postmortem exam and recalled nothing unusual about the body or the wounds.

See also AUTOPSY CONTROVERSY.

📖 *Best Evidence*

CANCLER, JOHN

Cancler, a convicted burglar and pimp, appeared on

television in June 1967 in an NBC "White Paper" program called "The †Case of Jim Garrison." On the show Cancler charged that the New Orleans district attorney's office had attempted to get him to put false evidence in the home of Clay †Shaw. When called before a grand jury and asked to repeat his claim, Cancler reportedly refused, pleading the Fifth Amendment protection against self-incrimination. When asked to reiterate before a criminal court judge what he had said on television, Cancler once again refused and was found guilty of contempt of court.

📖 *On the Trail of the Assassins*

CANFIELD, MICHAEL L.

Canfield is an assassination researcher and coauthor of †*Coup d'Etat in America.*

CARLIN, KAREN

Carlin was a stripper working at Jack †Ruby's nightclub during November 1963 under the name "Little Lynn." She allegedly borrowed five dollars from Ruby for carfare home to Fort Worth the night before he shot Lee Harvey †Oswald. The following morning, she called Ruby and asked for an additional $25.00, which he agreed to wire her. At 11:17 on Sunday morning, Ruby sent the money from the Western Union office in downtown Dallas, then walked to Police Headquarters nearby, making his way to the basement garage, where he shot Oswald four minutes later.

This incident would appear to support Ruby's original contention that the shooting was not planned, but was an impulsive and therefore not a conspiratorial act. Many researchers, however, believe it may have been staged, suggesting conspiracy.
See also WARNER, ROGER C.
📖 *Contract on America*; *Ruby Cover-up*

CARNES, DR. WILLIAM H.
See CLARK PANEL.

CAROUSEL CLUB
This nightclub near downtown Dallas was owned by Jack †Ruby and featured striptease acts. Ruby also had an interest in a similar operation called the Vegas Club, also in Dallas.

CARR, RICHARD R.
Richard Carr was working on the construction of the new county courthouse overlooking †Dealey Plaza the day of the assassination. He reports seeing a heavyset

man wearing a tan jacket, hat, and horn-rimmed glasses at a window on the sixth floor of the †Texas School Book Depository Building just before the shots were fired. After the shooting, Carr says he saw two men running either from behind the building or from inside it. The two jumped into a Rambler station wagon and sped north on Houston Street. A few minutes later, the heavyset man who had been on the sixth floor hurried away from the building.

Researcher J. Gary †Shaw contends that FBI agents warned Carr against testifying before the †Warren Commission and that, allegedly harassed by Dallas Police officers, Carr then moved to Montana. Trouble followed him when one day he discovered dynamite wired to his car's ignition. Another attempt on his life was foiled with the help of a neighbor who was a local police officer. After testifying at the Clay †Shaw trial, Carr was attacked by knife-wielding assassins, but despite receiving several wounds he managed to shoot one of them to death.

See also DEALEY PLAZA WITNESSES.

📖 *Crossfire; High Treason; Mortal Error*

CARR, WAGGONER

Attorney general for the state of Texas, Waggoner Carr reportedly called J. Lee †Rankin, general counsel for the †Warren Commission, on January 22, 1964, telling him he had learned that Lee Harvey †Oswald had been an "undercover agent" employed by the †Federal Bureau of Investigation. Rankin called an emergency session of the full Commission at 5:30 that evening, a session that Commission member Congressman Gerald †Ford said was the most "tense and hushed" meeting he could recall attending. As a result, Carr and other Texas officials who claimed they had also learned that since September 1962 Oswald had been FBI undercover agent #179 were summoned to Washington to give their testimony in a top-secret session on January 24. On the basis of denials by J. Edgar †Hoover and other FBI officials, the Warren Commission concluded that Oswald had not been in the FBI's employ.

See also JAWORSKI, LEON; PENA, OREST.

📖 *Rush to Judgment; Texas Connection*

CARRICO, DR. CHARLES

Dr. Carrico was the first doctor to examine the fatally wounded president at †Parkland Memorial Hospital. On the afternoon of November 22, 1963, he wrote and signed a report describing the wound in the president's throat as an entrance wound. He described it as both "small" and "round." This is not the description a doctor would use to identify a bullet exit wound, although the †Warren Report concludes this was the exit point of the †magic bullet that injured both Kennedy and Governor John †Connally. Carrico also reported that the wound in the rear of the president's head was nearly circular and measured 2 to 2¾ inches across.

See also HEAD WOUND CONTROVERSY; THROAT WOUND CONTROVERSY; TRACHEOTOMY.

📖 *Best Evidence*; *Rush to Judgment*

CARTER, ARTHUR E.

Arthur Carter was an FBI agent who took testimony from †Texas School Book Depository Building employee Bonnie Ray †Williams. The testimony has come under fire because the FBI report of this interview appears to have misquoted Williams concerning the time he was on the sixth floor of the building. The time is crucial because it puts Williams on the same floor as the alleged assassin just minutes before the shooting, yet Williams claims there was no one else on the floor with him.

📖 *Rush to Judgment*

CARTER, WILLIAM N.

On December 4, 1963, †Secret Service special agent Carter received testimony from Harold D. †Norman, a

†Texas School Book Depository Building employee who was on the fifth floor of the building when the assassination took place. Carter's report quotes Norman as saying the shots came from directly above him and that he saw "dust falling from the ceiling" below the window where Oswald allegedly stood when he fired at the president. When questioned about this by the †Warren Commission, Norman denied making either of these statements.
See also JARMAN, JAMES; WILLIAMS, BONNIE RAY.
📖 *Rush to Judgment*

CARTO, WILLIS
Carto was the president of †Liberty Lobby, which published †*Spotlight* magazine.

"THE CASE OF JIM GARRISON"
This NBC "White Paper" television program attacked the New Orleans district attorney's investigation of the Kennedy assassination. This one-sided look at Jim †Garrison's investigation caused Garrison to believe that the show was an attempt to smear him.
See also CANCLER, JOHN; LEEMANS, FRED; RUSSO, PERRY; SHERIDAN, WALTER; TORRES, MIGUEL; TOWNLEY, RICHARD.
📖 *On the Trail of the Assassins*

CASKET TEAM
The Joint Casket Bearer Team of the Military District of Washington, D.C., is responsible for handling the caskets for funerals held at Arlington National Cemetery. The Casket Team members responsible for President Kennedy's coffin were Army Lieutenant Samuel R. †Bird, Coast Guard Yeoman George A. †Barnum, Navy Seaman Hubert †Clark, Marine Corporal Timothy †Cheek, Army Specialist Douglas †Mayfield, Army Sergeant James L. †Felder, and Air Force Sergeant Richard E. †Gaudreau. Several members of the team remembered a "decoy" ambulance at the front entrance of †Bethesda Naval Hospital when they arrived there on the evening of November 22, 1963.
See also AMBULANCE CONTROVERSY; COFFIN CONTROVERSY.
📖 *Best Evidence*

CASTELLANOS, NESTOR
A Cuban exile, Castellanos was alleged to have vehemently attacked the president when he addressed a right-wing group in a Dallas suburb during October 1963. Castellanos supposedly voiced the threat "We are waiting for Kennedy the 22nd. . . . We're going to give him the works when he gets in Dallas." In light of

these ominous predictions, it is largely contradictory
that no demonstrations by Cuban exiles occurred
when Kennedy visited Dallas.
See also ANTI-CASTRO CUBANS.
◫ *Conspiracy*

CASTRO, FIDEL
The Cuban dictator has long been suspected of
ordering Kennedy's death, with the obvious motive
being retaliation for the numerous CIA plots against
his life. Proponents who support the premise are
convinced Castro sought revenge against the
American president, whom he believed was personally
responsible for the threats on his life. No hard
evidence has ever been produced linking Castro with
the assassination.

CELLAR, THE
Owned by Pat †Kirkwood, an acquaintance of Jack
†Ruby's, The Cellar was an all-night club where nine
†Secret Service agents, four of whom had motorcade
responsibilities the following day, allegedly partied until
the early hours of the night of November 21–22, while
the president slept. Secret Service agents with the
White House detail or those traveling with the president
are forbidden to drink any alcoholic beverages while "in

travel status." This rule also applies to field agents who are augmenting the White House detail, such as those in Dallas during the president's visit. Yet according to a statement attributed to the club's manager, Jimmy Hill, "those guys [the Secret Service agents] were bombed. They were drinking pure Everclear [alcohol]." Reporter Jim †Marrs accused the agents responsible for guarding the sleeping president at the Hotel Texas of leaving several Fort Worth firemen to man their posts while they went to The Cellar. Secret Service chief James J. †Rowley denied that late-night drinking affected the performance of his men; however, several officials in the motorcade offered different opinions. One of these, Senator Ralph †Yarborough, told Marrs, "All of the Secret Service men seemed to me to respond very slowly, with no more than a puzzled look" when the shots rang out in †Dealey Plaza.
📖 *Crossfire*

CENTRAL INTELLIGENCE AGENCY (CIA)
Many informed observers believe the CIA played a critical role in the president's death. The CIA has a long history of involvement in odious activities, ranging from plans to kill foreign rulers, alleged drug dealing in Southeast Asia, and even abetting the infamous Watergate burglars whose arrest ultimately

brought about the downfall of President Richard
†Nixon. It is interesting to note that in the only two
court trials in which the assassination of President
Kennedy figured, the prosecution of Clay †Shaw by
Jim †Garrison and the libel suit brought by the CIA's
E. Howard †Hunt against the publication †*Spotlight*,
people on both juries arrived at the same conclusion:
that the CIA was behind the assassination. Two books
that deal primarily with this subject are †*Plausible
Denial*, by Mark †Lane, and *Coup d'Etat in America*,
by Michael †Canfield and Alan J. †Weberman.
See also OFFICE OF STRATEGIC SERVICES; OPERATION
40; PERMINDEX.

CENTRO MONDIALE COMMERCIALE
See PERMINDEX.

CHANEY, JAMES
Dallas police motorcycle officer Chaney had the
president clearly in view when the shots were fired.
Shortly afterward, he told local television reporters
that Kennedy had been "struck in the face,"
supporting similar reports that at least one shot came
from in front of the president.
See also DEALEY PLAZA WITNESSES.
📖 *Crossfire; High Treason*

"CHARLES, PEDRO"

A letter mailed to Lee Harvey †Oswald from Havana,
Cuba, on November 28, 1963, four days after the
entire world knew Oswald was dead, and signed
"Pedro Charles," was intercepted by the †Secret
Service and turned over to the FBI labs. The letter
alluded to the "fact" that Oswald had been hired to
shoot someone. Soon after, a letter was sent to Robert
F. †Kennedy identifying "Charles" as a Castro agent.
FBI examination found that both letters were typed
on the same typewriter. Although the †Warren
Commission recognized that the "Pedro Charles"
letters were a hoax, evidently no further effort was
made to discover who was behind it or what the
motivation was.

📖 *Conspiracy*

CHASE, DR. NORMAN

Dr. Chase was among a group of medical experts
whom the †House Select Committee on Assassinations
asked to examine the medical evidence produced by
the president's autopsy. After reviewing the X rays of
the head, Chase said the wound was much too massive
to be caused by a direct-on hit by a single-jacketed
bullet such as those allegedly used by Lee Harvey
†Oswald to kill Kennedy. Such a wound would be

caused by a bullet tumbling inside the skull, or if it hit
at an angle, and would leave a large number of
fragments; yet according to Dr. James J. †Humes, who
performed the autopsy, all that was found were "tiny
dustlike particle fragments" more consistent with a
bullet driving straight through the skull and bone.
See also HEAD WOUND CONTROVERSY.
📖 *High Treason*

CHEEK, TIMOTHY
A member of the †Casket Team that moved the
president's coffin, Marine Lance Corporal Cheek spoke
to researcher David S. †Lifton, who says Cheek
substantiated the confusion surrounding the use of
two Navy ambulances and the difficulty the team
encountered locating Kennedy's coffin on arrival at
†Bethesda Naval Hospital.
See also AMBULANCE CONTROVERSY; BIRD, SAMUEL R.
📖 *Best Evidence*

CHERAMIE, ROSE
See ARCACHA SMITH, SERGIO.

CHESHER, BILL
Little is known about Chesher other than that he
allegedly had information linking Lee Harvey †Oswald

with his murderer, Jack †Ruby. Chesher never shared that information with anyone, and he died of a heart attack in March 1964.

📖 *High Treason*

CHETTA, DR. NICHOLAS

Dr. Chetta was the New Orleans coroner who performed autopsies on several individuals—including David †Ferrie—who died mysteriously, preventing them from testifying in the court case District Attorney Jim †Garrison brought against Clay †Shaw for his alleged part in the assassination. Assassination researchers term the deaths of these and some other individuals as "strange" or "related." Dr. Chetta, who was a friend and supporter of Garrison's, himself died of a heart attack on May 25, 1968. His sometime assistant, Dr. Henry Delaune, was killed on January 26, 1969.

📖 *High Treason*

CHISM, MR. AND MRS. JOHN

The Chisms and their three-year-old son were standing along the curb with their backs to the †Grassy Knoll near the now-famous Stemmons Freeway sign that partially blocked the view of the assassination in the †Zapruder film. John Chism and his wife both said the

first shots were fired just as the president's car was abreast of them. They both looked behind them to see exactly where the shots were coming from, believing the shooter was somewhere on the knoll. Mrs. Chism said, "It [the second shot] came from what I thought was behind us."
See also DEALEY PLAZA WITNESSES; GRASSY KNOLL WITNESSES.

📖 *Best Evidence*

CIVELLO, JOSEPH

Civello ran the Dallas operations of New Orleans †Mafia head Carlos †Marcello. He was also a close friend and sometime business associate of Jack †Ruby's, whose extensive ties to the underworld also ran through restaurant owner Joseph †Campisi. Author John H. †Davis charges that the FBI, under J. Edgar †Hoover, attempted to cover up Ruby's relationships with Civello, who was considered the number-one Mafia man in Dallas, and with Campisi, who was number two.

📖 *Conspiracy; Mafia Kingfish*

CLARK, HUBERT

A member of the Military District of Washington, D.C., †Casket Team, Navy Seaman Apprentice Clark

was questioned by assassination researcher David S.
†Lifton on December 19, 1967. According to Lifton,
Clark's version of the events that occurred when the
motorcade with the ambulance allegedly carrying
Kennedy's body arrived at †Bethesda Naval Hospital
supports the statements of other members of the team.
Like the others, Clark recalled that there was
confusion regarding the whereabouts of the ambulance
carrying Kennedy's coffin when the team arrived at
the hospital.

See also AMBULANCE CONTROVERSY; BIRD, SAMUEL R.
📖 *Best Evidence*

CLARK, DR. KEMP

Chairman of the Neurosurgery Division of †Parkland
Memorial Hospital, Dr. Clark was the first one to
closely examine the president's head wound. He also
pronounced the president dead and signed the death
certificate. Among the statements that Dr. Clark made
in the hours following the assassination and that
contradicted the autopsy results released later was
that the president was shot in the throat—meaning he
was shot from the front. At a press conference shortly
after the president's body was removed from Parkland
for the trip to Washington, Clark located the head
wound at the "back of his head . . . toward the right

side"—also conflicting with the autopsy report, which
placed the wound farther toward the top and front,
not just in the back.
See also EBERSOLE, DR. JOHN; HEAD WOUND
CONTROVERSY; PARKLAND PRESS CONFERENCE;
PERRY, DR. MALCOLM; TRACHEOTOMY.
📖 *Best Evidence*; *Conspiracy of Silence*

CLARK PANEL

In 1968, U.S. Attorney General Ramsey Clark
convened a panel of four doctors to review the autopsy
photographs and X rays produced at †Bethesda Naval
Hospital. Published accounts of their report said it
confirmed the finding of the †Warren Commission that
the president had been hit by two shots fired from
behind and above him. However, on closer examination, several researchers found that the Clark Panel's
report differed from the autopsy report in its
description of the location of two wounds. The doctors
on the panel were William H. Carnes, Russell Fischer,
Russell H. Morgan, and Alan R. Moritz.
See also HEAD WOUND CONTROVERSY.
📖 *Best Evidence*; *High Treason*

CLEMONS, ACQUILLA

A witness to the killing of Police Officer J. D. †Tippit,

Clemons reportedly said she saw two men take part in the shooting, neither of whom resembled Lee Harvey †Oswald. Never questioned by federal agents, Mrs. Clemons claimed she was later visited at her home by a man with a gun who she thought was a police officer. The man warned her that if she testified about the shooting, she might be killed.

See also TIPPIT MURDER SCENE WITNESSES.

📖 *Crossfire; Rush to Judgment*

COFFIN CONTROVERSY

Two basic controversies surround the coffin that allegedly contained the president's body on the trip from †Parkland Memorial Hospital to †Bethesda Naval Hospital. The first is the description of the coffin. According to the account given by William †Manchester, the coffin provided by the Dallas funeral home owned by Vernon †Oneal weighed four hundred pounds and was a top-of-the-line bronze unit that sealed hermetically, a "Britannia" model manufactured by the Elgin Casket Company. Several witnesses at Bethesda, including hospital corpsman Dennis †David and lab technologist Paul K. †O'Connor, described the coffin containing the president's body as a low-priced gray metal unit similar to a shipping coffin. A second subject of controversy involves the

time the coffin arrived at Bethesda (see †ambulance controversy). The differing descriptions of the coffin in which Kennedy's body arrived at Bethesda have led some to surmise that the president's body was removed from the expensive coffin sometime after that coffin was put aboard †*Air Force One* in Dallas.
See also BODY BAG CONTROVERSY.
📕 *Best Evidence*; *Death of a President*; *High Treason*

COMMITTEE ON BALLISTICS ACOUSTICS

Organized by the National Science Foundation, under the direction of Dr. Norman Ramsey, this group examined the acoustical evidence produced by the †Dallas police dispatch tape. The committee concluded that its analysis did not demonstrate that any shots were fired from the †Grassy Knoll. Most assassination researchers have criticized the report.
See also ACOUSTICAL EVIDENCE.
📕 *High Treason*

CONNALLY, JOHN

Connally, the governor of Texas (and, in 1963, still a Democrat), was seated in the jump seat directly in front of President Kennedy when the shots were fired. One bullet passed through the governor's body, smashing through his wrist and embedding itself in

Texas Governor John Connally and his wife, Nellie

his thigh. According to the †Warren Commission, this was the same bullet that entered Kennedy's back and exited his throat, the so-called †magic bullet on which the †single bullet theory is based. Connally has steadfastly refused to accept this theory and continues to insist that he heard a shot before he was hit, which would not be possible if the shot that struck Kennedy also hit him, since a bullet travels faster than the sound of the gun firing it. Nellie Connally, who was seated next to her husband, testified that she saw the president react physically to a shot before her husband was hit.

📖 *Best Evidence*

CONSPIRACY

This book by Anthony Summers, an investigative reporter for the BBC, was published by McGraw-Hill in 1980 (an expanded, updated edition was issued by Paragon House in 1989). It focuses on the theory that Lee Harvey †Oswald was a tool of U.S. intelligence agents who are responsible for the assassination.

CONSPIRACY THEORIES

Within hours of the assassination, many individuals began developing theories about the possible existence of conspiracies against the president's life, resulting in dozens of books about the subject. The most popular theories revolve around these groups and individuals: †anti-Castro Cubans, who blamed Kennedy for the †Bay of Pigs fiasco; Fidel †Castro, who held the Kennedy brothers responsible for a series of attempts on his life; the †Central Intelligence Agency, because the president fired several of its top men and vowed to clean house in the Agency; members of the military-industrial complex, who believed Kennedy was about to end U.S. involvement in the †Vietnam War; †right-wing extremists, who opposed Kennedy's policy of "appeasement" toward the Soviet Union; members of the †Mafia, because the president's brother, Attorney General Robert F. †Kennedy, had turned the powers of the federal government against the underworld; and backers of Vice President Lyndon B. †Johnson, unhappy with the news that Kennedy intended to drop him from the ticket before the 1964 election.

These theories, and perhaps as many as half a dozen others, all have adherents who are able to muster from the misinformation and inconsistencies enough circumstantial evidence and supposition to give them the ring of credibility.

CONTRACT ON AMERICA

Published in 1988 by Zebra Books and written by David E. †Scheim, *Contract on America: The Mafia Murder of President John F. Kennedy* focuses on underworld characters who had both motive and means to kill the president.

COOPER, JOHN SHERMAN

A three-time Republican senator from Kentucky, Cooper was selected by President Lyndon B. †Johnson to serve as a member of the †Warren Commission. Cooper is said to have objected to the †single bullet theory from the very outset. He also is credited, along with Commission member Senator Richard B. †Russell, with influencing the Commission staff to investigate the CIA link with Lee Harvey †Oswald more thoroughly.

📖 *Conspiracy; Plausible Denial*

COUCH, MALCOLM

A cameraman for a local Dallas television station, Couch was riding in a press car eight or nine cars back from the lead car in the Kennedy motorcade. He testified that when the shots were fired, another passenger in the car, photographer Robert H.

†Jackson, yelled that a rifle was protruding from a window of the †Texas School Book Depository Building. Couch said he looked up in time to see a rifle barrel being withdrawn into the window on what appeared to be the sixth or seventh floor.

He also claimed that an individual named Wes †Wise, "who works for [television station] KRLD," told him he saw Jack †Ruby coming around the side of the Depository Building five to ten minutes after the shooting. Wise never testified before the †Warren Commission.

See also DILLARD, THOMAS.

📖 *Rush to Judgment; Warren Report*

COUP D'ETAT IN AMERICA
Written by Michael L. †Canfield and Alan J. †Weberman and published in 1975 by The Third Press, the book *Coup d'Etat in America: The CIA and the Assassination of John F. Kennedy* focuses on what the authors claim was the CIA's involvement in the assassination, including deploying "assassination squad" teams at the scene in Dallas.

CRAFARD, CURTIS LAVERNE
A drifter who worked at odd jobs in Jack †Ruby's †Carousel Club, "Larry" Crafard told FBI

investigators that he frequently saw Bernard
†Weissman in the club. Weissman had placed an
inflammatory anti-Kennedy ad in the *Dallas Morning
News* the day of the assassination, and was revealed
by Crafard to be on personal terms with Ruby.
Crafard further said he heard Ruby refer to
Weissman by name.
See also AMERICAN FACT-FINDING COMMITTEE.
📖 *Rush to Judgment*

CRAIG, ROGER D.

A deputy sheriff of Dallas County in November
1963, Craig appears to be another victim of post-
assassination duress because his testimony conflicted
with the official findings of the †Warren Commission.
Named Officer of the Year in 1960, Craig had a
neatly ordered life that seemingly crumpled after the
assassination, and he ultimately committed suicide.
Craig figured prominently in three controversial
incidents immediately following the assassination.
The first was his eyewitness account that shortly
after the shooting, he saw a man running down the
hill on the north side of Elm Street from the
direction of the †Texas School Book Depository
Building and jump into a Rambler station wagon that
had slowed to pick him up. Later at Police

Headquarters, he identified Lee Harvey †Oswald as the man he saw get into the car. The Warren Commission version was that Oswald boarded a public bus and then switched to a taxicab to flee the area of the shooting. Police Captain Will †Fritz, who conducted Oswald's interrogation, denied that Craig was ever in the same room with the suspect, yet a photograph published in 1969 clearly showed Craig standing inside the office during Oswald's questioning.

About ten minutes after the shooting Craig was approached by the family of Arnold †Rowland. Mr. Rowland told him he saw two men at the sixth-floor window of the Depository Building. (Mrs. Rowland disagreed with her husband, but neither of their accounts lend credence to the Warren Commission's †lone assassin theory.) Shortly after this exchange, Craig and another officer found the rifle that Oswald allegedly used, except that he identified it by its markings as a 7.65-caliber Mauser, not a †Mannlicher-Carcano.

Craig's life was thrown into turmoil when he refused to recant his testimony. Several attempts were made on his life, and following the breakup of his marriage, he shot himself.

See also BOONE, EUGENE L.; MOONEY, LUKE; WADE, HENRY W.; WEITZMAN, SEYMOUR.
📖 *Crossfire; High Treason; Rush to Judgment*

CRAIG, WALTER

Under pressure from its critics that the interests of the man accused of killing President Kennedy, Lee Harvey †Oswald, were not being protected, the †Warren Commission appointed Walter Craig, then president of the American Bar Association, to participate in the hearings in a role vaguely similar to that of a defense attorney. Critics charge that Craig's participation was virtually nil and that his awareness of the facts of the case was practically nonexistent. There is no record of Craig's having called even a single witness to testify in Oswald's defense or of his ever having recalled a witness for cross-examination.
📖 *Rush to Judgment*

CRENSHAW, DR. CHARLES A.

A surgeon at †Parkland Memorial Hospital, Crenshaw was there when the president was brought in. Never called to testify by any official body, Crenshaw wrote, with Jens Hansen and J. Gary †Shaw, an account of his experiences in a book titled *JFK: Conspiracy of*

Silence, published by Signet in 1992. In the book Crenshaw claims that he was fully aware at the time that the wounds to the president's head and throat were caused by bullets fired from in front of Kennedy. He also claims that while he was working to save Lee Harvey †Oswald's life after Jack †Ruby shot him, he received a telephone call from President Lyndon B. †Johnson telling him that a man standing by in the operating room would take Oswald's deathbed confession of the assassination.

See also TRACHEOTOMY.

📖 *Conspiracy of Silence*

CRESCENT CITY GARAGE

This automobile parking garage in New Orleans, owned by Adrian †Alba, had contracts to garage vehicles owned by the †Federal Bureau of Investigation, the †Secret Service, and the †Office of Naval Intelligence. It was also a hangout for Lee Harvey †Oswald, who worked next door at the †William Reily Coffee Company.

📖 *On the Trail of the Assassins*

"CROSS, RON"

"Ron Cross" was the pseudonym used by an undercover CIA case officer when he testified before

the †House Select Committee on Investigations that "Maurice †Bishop" was actually David Atlee †Phillips.
📖 *Conspiracy*

CROSSFIRE

Published by Carroll & Graf in 1989, *Crossfire: The Plot That Killed Kennedy* is the work of Dallas journalist Jim †Marrs. This book reviews in depth much of what was known about the assassination through 1989, and provides some additional witness information. The book focuses on those groups with the motive and means to carry out the assassination of an American president. It was one of the sources for the Oliver †Stone film †*JFK*.

CUBAN REVOLUTIONARY COUNCIL (CRC)

The CRC was an †anti-Castro group allegedly organized by CIA agent E. Howard †Hunt whose purpose was to discredit the pro-Castro †Fair Play for Cuba Committee. The CRC headquarters was located at †544 Camp Street in New Orleans.
See also BANISTER, GUY.
📖 *Crossfire; High Treason*

CUBELA, ROLANDO

In 1961, Cuban official Rolando Cubela, a former

assassin for Fidel †Castro during the revolution to overthrow the Batista government, allegedly attempted to defect but was persuaded by the †Central Intelligence Agency to remain in place. Cubela became a CIA informer under the code name AM/LASH. On the same day Kennedy was assassinated, Cubela was in Paris, France, meeting with a CIA contact to discuss plans to kill Castro. Nothing came of the plans.

In February 1966, Cubela was arrested and was later convicted by the Cuban government of conspiracy against Castro and of treason. He was sentenced to twenty-five years in prison. Some researchers have cited the AM/LASH plots against Castro as motivation for Castro's involvement in Kennedy's death, alleging that Cubela was actually a double agent. Cubela passionately denied this, and no hard evidence exists to support such an assumption.

📖 *Conspiracy; Reasonable Doubt*

CUNNINGHAM, CORTLANDT

An FBI firearms expert, Cortlandt was asked by the †Warren Commission to examine the bullets allegedly recovered from the shooting scene of police officer J. D. †Tippit. Because the bullets were too badly mangled, he was unable to positively identify them as having been fired from a revolver reportedly owned by Lee Harvey †Oswald.

📖 *Rush to Judgment*

CURRY, JESSE E.

Dallas police chief Curry rode in the lead car of the presidential motorcade. Immediately after the shots were fired, he shouted orders over the police radio, commanding officers to rush to the overpass just ahead of his car to "see what happened up there." The following day, he told reporters the shots came from behind him. Six years after the assassination, Curry was quoted as saying that there was still no hard evidence that Lee Harvey †Oswald fired the rifle that was allegedly used to kill President Kennedy. He wrote a book, *The JFK Assassination File*, published in 1969 by the American Poster and Printing Company.

📖 *Crossfire; Rush to Judgment*

CUSTER, JERROL F.

One of two X-ray technicians at the †Bethesda Naval Hospital morgue when the president's body was brought in for the autopsy, Custer reportedly said that the president's wounds clearly indicated to him that Kennedy had been shot from the front. Custer also claims that while he was taking the X-ray plates of the president's wounds to be developed, he saw Jacqueline †Kennedy enter the hospital. According to official records, the coffin containing the president's body was inside a Navy ambulance parked directly outside the main entrance to the hospital when Mrs. Kennedy entered the building. Custer's statement, if true, means the president's body had already been X-rayed before the coffin allegedly containing his body was unloaded.

On May 28, 1992, Custer attended a press conference along with the autopsy photographer, Floyd A. †Riebe, to discuss recent publicity concerning the autopsy. According to a Reuter wire service story of May 29, 1992, Custer said the X rays that had been released to the public showing Kennedy's head wounds were "wrong." Custer then went into detail to demonstrate that the published X rays had been tampered with and did not reflect the president's actual wounds. He was quoted as saying that his job was to locate bullet fragments. He then confirmed a report by one of the Navy doctors present that a complete bullet was recovered under Kennedy's back when his body was moved. This bullet has never been accounted for in the evidence inventory of the case. Custer described the scene at the autopsy as "total chaos."

See also AMBULANCE CONTROVERSY; AUTOPSY CONTROVERSY; JENKINS, JAMES C.; O'CONNOR, PAUL K.; OSBORNE, DR. DAVID; REED, EDWARD F.; X-RAY CONTROVERSY.

📖 *Best Evidence*

D

DALLAS CONFERENCE
In 1991, assassination researcher Harrison Edward
†Livingstone gathered together for the first time a
number of the people who were present in the
†Parkland Memorial Hospital emergency room when
the wounded president was brought in, and several
who were present when the autopsy was performed at
†Bethesda Naval Hospital. These doctors, nurses, the
ambulance driver, technicians, and other specialists
discussed as a group such topics as the president's
head and back wounds, the condition of his body, the
items used to wrap the body, and the autopsy
photographs. The tremendous differences among the
descriptions of various key medical details underscore
the possibility that Kennedy's wounds were altered
between the time the body left Parkland and the time
the autopsy was performed.
📖 *High Treason 2*

DALLAS COUNTY JAIL INMATES
See MITCHELL, WILLIE; POWELL, JOHN.

DALLAS POLICE

The Dallas Police Department, under the direction of its appointed chief, Jesse E. †Curry, and the man responsible for day-to-day operations, Captain Will †Fritz, has come under fire from numerous sources because of what many charge was extremely poor performance during the president's visit to the city. Critics point out that among other lapses, the security Dallas police afforded the motorcade ended one block short of the shooting scene; the investigation of the shooting scene was concentrated on the †Texas School Book Depository Building, despite the fact that many police officers on the scene thought the shots were fired from the area of the †Grassy Knoll; and the interrogation and protection of the suspect Lee Harvey †Oswald was inconsistent with professional police procedures.
📖 *Texas Connection*

DALLAS POLICE DISPATCH TAPE

It is standard operating procedure for the Dallas Police Department to record all conversations broadcast over police frequencies. Just before the assassination, the microphone on a motorcycle in the motorcade escort believed to be Officer H. B. †McLain's jammed in the open position. This meant the sounds of activity near the scene, including the gunshots, were recorded on the dispatch tape. Much controversy has raged around the vital subject of the number of shots recorded—with some experts contending there were three, while others claim there were four—and over the direction of the shots seemingly recorded on the tape. The original copy of the recording is missing from the †National Archives in Washington, D.C.

See also ACOUSTICAL EVIDENCE; FERRELL, MARY.

📖 *High Treason*

DANIELS, HAWK

Hawk Daniels, a federal investigator, took part in an investigation concerning alleged plans by former Teamsters boss Jimmy †Hoffa to kill Attorney General Robert F. †Kennedy, and possibly also the president. Daniels, who later became a judge, claims he listened in on two 1962 telephone conversations in which Hoffa asked Louisiana Teamsters official Edward Partin to obtain plastic explosives for him so he could arrange to blow up Robert Kennedy's home.

📖 *Conspiracy*

DANIELS, NAPOLEON J.

A former member of the Dallas police force, Daniels stated repeatedly that he saw a man somewhat resembling Jack †Ruby enter the Main Street auto entrance ramp leading to the lower level of Dallas Police Headquarters moments before Lee Harvey †Oswald was shot. He claims the man went unchallenged by Officer Roy †Vaughn, who was guarding the entrance at the time. Vaughn denied this.
📖 *High Treason; Rush to Judgment*

DARK-COMPLEXIONED MAN (OR MEN)

Several people in †Dealey Plaza at the time of the assassination reported seeing at least two men with rifles at the sixth-floor window of the †Texas School Book Depository Building. It is possible that one of them might have been Lee Harvey †Oswald, but the second man was said to have had a very dark complexion. He was variously described as either Hispanic or Negro by these witnesses. In addition, Deputy Sheriff Roger D. †Craig reported that he saw a dark-skinned man driving a Rambler station wagon away from the scene after another man, who had light skin, ran down a slope from the Book Depository Building and jumped into the car before it sped away. Another dark-complexioned man appears somehow to have been associated with the so-called †Umbrella Man, whose mysterious behavior in Dealey Plaza before, during, and after the assassination has been a focus of researchers' scrutiny.

See also EUINS, AMOS L.; HENDERSON, RUBY; POWELL, JOHN; ROWLAND, ARNOLD

📖 *Crossfire*

DAVID, DENNIS

A petty officer in the Medical Service Corps stationed at the Naval Medical School at †Bethesda Naval Hospital when the president's body arrived, David has been quoted as claiming he helped unload the coffin allegedly containing Kennedy's body, a direct contradiction of the official report filed by the †Casket Team, which unloaded the coffin. David's tale also conflicts with the †O'Neill and Sibert report on the autopsy. David has also reportedly provided other information about the events at Bethesda that dispute certain findings of the †Warren Commission.

See also AMBULANCE CONTROVERSY; BODY BAG CONTROVERSY; COFFIN CONTROVERSY.

📖 *Best Evidence*

DAVIS, AVERY

An employee in the †Texas School Book Depository

Building, Mrs. Avery Davis was standing in front of
the building entrance when the assassination took
place. She reportedly told FBI agents that she thought
the shots had come from the overpass in front of the
motorcade.

See also ADAMS, VICTORIA; TEXAS SCHOOL BOOK
DEPOSITORY BUILDING EMPLOYEES.

📖 *Rush to Judgment*

DAVIS, BARBARA AND VIRGINIA

Barbara Davis and her sister-in-law Virginia R. Davis
claim they witnessed a man running from the
direction of the area where Officer J. D. †Tippit was
shot. The man stopped in front of Barbara Davis's
house, where he opened his revolver and allowed
several spent shells to fall to the ground. The women
retrieved the shells and gave them to a police officer
investigating Tippit's murder. Barbara Davis said the
man was wearing a dark sport coat. When she was
shown the light tan jacket Lee Harvey †Oswald was
wearing when he was arrested shortly after the
shooting, she said it was not the one worn by the man
she saw empty the gun.

See also TIPPIT MURDER SCENE WITNESSES.

📖 *Rush to Judgment*

DAVIS, JOHN H.

John Davis is the author of *Mafia Kingfish: Carlos Marcello and the Assassination of John F. Kennedy,* published by McGraw-Hill in 1989. This book is a major source of information linking the assassination to organized crime.

DAVIS, RED

Researchers Robert J. †Groden and Harrison Edward †Livingstone claim that Red Davis, a member of the Dallas Police Department, told Officer Roy †Vaughn that Assistant Police Chief Charles †Batchelor escorted Jack †Ruby to the basement of Police Headquarters, where Ruby killed Lee Harvey †Oswald. *See also* DANIELS, NAPOLEON J.
📖 *High Treason*

DAVIS, THOMAS

A convicted bank robber, Thomas Eli Davis III was a part-time undersea salvage operator who also took part, along with Jack †Ruby, in running guns to Cuba. Davis was allegedly arrested by Moroccan security forces because he had in his possession a letter that discussed Lee Harvey †Oswald and the assassination. Intervention by a CIA agent is credited with winning

Davis's release. Davis died of accidental electrocution in 1973.

📖 *Conspiracy; Ruby Cover-up*

DAVIS, VIRGINIA R.

See DAVIS, BARBARA AND VIRGINIA.

DAY, J. CARL

Dallas police lieutenant Day claimed to have lifted Lee Harvey †Oswald's †palmprint from the †Mannlicher-Carcano rifle allegedly used to kill Kennedy. Inexplicably, Day ignored normal police procedure and failed to photograph the print and protect it with cellophane, even though he followed procedure with other, less valuable prints found on the rifle. No residue of the purported palmprint was found when the rifle was examined by the FBI.

See also DRAIN, VINCENT; LATONA, SEBASTIAN FRANCIS.

📖 *Rush to Judgment*

DEALEY PLAZA

The scene of the Kennedy assassination is located at the western edge of downtown Dallas. Situated on slightly over three acres, it is crossed by Main Street, Elm Street, and Commerce Street, all three leading to entrances to the freeway system, including Stemmons Freeway, which the motorcade took to †Parkland Memorial Hospital after the shooting. Named for George B. Dealey, founder of the *Dallas Morning News* and an early civic leader, the plaza was the site of the first home, store, and courthouse in Dallas.

DEALEY PLAZA WITNESSES

At least four hundred people were in and around †Dealey Plaza when President Kennedy was killed. Not all of them witnessed the assassination, and of those who did, not all have spoken up about what they saw. Entries have been included in this book for the following people who were on the scene and who have testified or in some other way given witness to the events of November 22, 1963: Associated Press photographer James W. Altgens; Danny Garcia Arce; Police Officer Marrion L. Baker; Secret Service agent Glen Bennett; Hugh Betzner, Jr.; Charles Brehm; Howard L. Brennan; Police Officer E. D. Brewer; Charles Bronson (*see* BRONSON FILM); Mrs. Earle Cabell, wife of the Dallas mayor; Richard R. Carr; Police Officer James Chaney; Governor John Connally; TV cameraman Malcolm Couch; Deputy Sheriff Roger D. Craig; Sheriff J. E. (Bill) Decker; *Dallas Morning News* photographer Thomas Dillard;

Robert E. Edwards; Amos L. Euins; Ronald B.
Fischer; Police Officer Bobby W. Hargis; Police
Sergeant D. V. Harkness; Wayne and Edna Hartman;
Police Officer Clyde A. Haygood; Ruby Henderson;
Secret Service agent Clinton Hill; Jean Hill; Ed
Hoffman; Robert Hughes; Texas State Highway
Patrolman Hurchel Jacks; Assistant Press Secretary
Malcolm Kilduff; W. W. Mabra; Police Officer B. J.
Martin; Bill and Gayle Newman (*see* NEWMAN
FAMILY); Jean Newman; Arnold Rowland; NBC
cameraman Dave Weigman; Deputy Constable
Seymour Weitzman; Robert H. West; Linda Willis;
Philip L. Willis.

DEAN, PATRICK T.

Dallas police sergeant Dean claims that shortly
after Jack †Ruby's arrest, Ruby told him that he had
premeditated the murder of Lee Harvey †Oswald and
had entered the police garage by simply walking
down the Main Street entrance ramp. Although
several other officers belatedly corroborated Dean's
statement about how Ruby entered the building, it
remains questionable. Dean, who had known Ruby
for several years, took a lie-detector test answering
questions he allegedly wrote himself, but failed to
achieve a result that would clearly indicate whether

he was telling the truth.

See also DANIELS, NAPOLEON J.; GRIFFIN, BURT W.; VAUGHN, ROY.

📖 *Conspiracy; Rush to Judgment*

THE DEATH OF A PRESIDENT

Written by noted author William †Manchester and published in 1967 by Harper & Row, this book is a fairly straightforward account of the assassination and the events preceding and following it, through the president's burial. Commissioned to write the book by the Kennedy family, Manchester later had a falling out with Robert F. †Kennedy and the late president's widow, Jacqueline, that resulted in a well-publicized legal battle. The outcome was that certain passages were deleted from Manchester's manuscript and the Kennedy family divorced itself from the work, meaning it was no longer a Kennedy-authorized version of the assassination but Manchester's own history of the events. In a 1988 foreword to a reissue of the book, Manchester discounted all conspiracy theories concerning President Kennedy's assassination.

DEBRUEYS, WARREN

An FBI agent, deBrueys was stationed in New

Orleans and has been identified as Lee Harvey
†Oswald's contact with the Bureau.
See also PENA, OREST.
📖 *Plausible Denial*

DECKER, J. E. (BILL)
Dallas County sheriff Decker was riding in the lead
car of the presidential motorcade when the fatal shots
were fired. He immediately dispatched all available
deputies to the railroad yard behind the †Grassy Knoll
to "see what happened there," and secure the area
pending the arrival of detectives. His deputies
established a command post behind the stockade fence
on the knoll, which they maintained for at least two
more hours. Newspaper reports the afternoon of the
shooting quoted Decker as saying that after he heard
the first shot, he thought he saw a bullet bounce off
the pavement.
See also DEALEY PLAZA WITNESSES; ELLIS, STARVIS;
GRASSY KNOLL WITNESSES.
📖 *High Treason; Rush to Judgment*

DELGADO, NELSON
A Marine who served for a while with Lee Harvey
†Oswald, Delgado testified that Oswald was a
supporter of Fidel †Castro, and had spoken of joining

the Cuban army. In testimony conflicting with statements made by others about the subject, Delgado described Oswald's marksmanship abilities as a "big joke," saying he often missed the target sheet entirely. Delgado also claimed that FBI agents attempted to get him to change several portions of his testimony so it would more closely align with the findings of the †Warren Commission.

See also ANDERSON, EUGENE D.

📖 *Rush to Judgment*

DEMOHRENSCHILDT, GEORGE

An oil geologist who formed a close friendship with Lee Harvey †Oswald, DeMohrenschildt claimed to be the son of a marshal of nobility in czarist Russia, and was therefore entitled to call himself a baron. DeMohrenschildt is believed to have been an espionage agent for Nazi Germany in the United States and Mexico during World War II and later to have been associated with American intelligence agencies, especially the CIA, for whom he was an informant. Reports indicate that DeMohrenschildt may have been instrumental in getting Oswald a job in 1962 with a graphic arts company that processed photos taken by the †U-2 spy planes that flew regular surveillance missions over Soviet territory—a strange

George DeMohrenschildt

employer for a man who had once defected to the Soviet Union.

In March 1977, just hours after arranging an interview with an investigator from the †House Select Committee on Assassinations, DeMohrenschildt was found dead of a shotgun blast in the mouth. The death was ruled a suicide.

See also JAGGERS-CHILES-STOVALL; MENDOZA, DR. CHARLES.

📖 *Conspiracy; Crossfire*

DILLARD, THOMAS

Dillard was a photographer for the *Dallas Morning News*. He was riding in the press car toward the rear of the presidential motorcade when Kennedy was shot. A few seconds after the final shot, he took two photographs of the †Texas School Book Depository Building. The †Warren Report said one of Dillard's photos showed a partially opened window on the sixth floor of the building. Dillard's photo was among those examined by experts hired by the †House Select Committee on Assassinations who determined that boxes visible in photos taken before and after the shooting had been "rearranged." This led assassination researcher Jim †Marrs to question how it was possible that Lee Harvey †Oswald had time to rearrange boxes on the sixth floor and be discovered on the second floor by a police officer at almost the same time.

See also BAKER, MARRION L.; COUCH, MALCOLM.

📖 *Crossfire; Warren Report*

DODD, RICHARD C.

A railroad worker who had taken time to watch the presidential motorcade pass through †Dealey Plaza, Dodd told assassination researcher Mark †Lane that he had seen puffs of smoke rising from the corner of the stockade fence atop the †Grassy Knoll. This observation was supported by statements from other railroad workers who were standing nearby.

See also OVERPASS WITNESSES.

📖 *Rush to Judgment*

DONAHUE, HOWARD

A ballistics expert, Donahue conducted a study of the shots that killed President Kennedy. His work is chronicled in the book *Mortal Error, The Shot That Killed JFK,* written by Bonar Menninger and published by St. Martin's Press in 1992. Donahue and Menninger hypothesize that the fatal head wound inflicted on the president was caused by the accidental discharge of a rifle carried by †Secret Service Agent George †Hickey, who was riding in the car directly

behind the president's limousine. Agent Samuel
†Kinney, who rode in the same car, has denied that
Hickey fired a shot.

DORMAN, ELSIE
An employee of a publisher with offices in the †Texas
School Book Depository Building, Dorman was filming
the motorcade from the window of her fourth-floor
office when the shooting took place. There is no record
that she was ever questioned by any official
investigators.
See also TEXAS SCHOOL BOOK DEPOSITORY BUILDING
EMPLOYEES.
📖 *Crossfire*

DOUGHERTY, JACK E.
An employee of the †Texas School Book Depository
Building, Dougherty was questioned by †Warren
Commission staff members. Although the Commission
concluded that Lee Harvey †Oswald entered the
building the morning of the assassination carrying a
long paper package, which he reportedly claimed
contained curtain rods and which the Commission
believed concealed the †Mannlicher-Carcano rifle he
used to kill President Kennedy, Dougherty testified
that he saw Oswald enter the building and that he

was positive that Oswald carried nothing in his hands. *See also* FRAZIER, BUELL WESLEY.

📖 *Rush to Judgment*

DOWNTOWN LINCOLN-MERCURY

Several salesmen at the Dallas Downtown Lincoln-Mercury automobile dealership testified to the [†]Warren Commission that on November 9, 1963, a man calling himself Lee Oswald came into the showroom, inquired about buying a Mercury Comet, and took the car on a reckless test drive. The man also told the salesmen that he expected to be coming into a large sum of money in a few weeks' time. The Warren Commission concluded that this man could not have been Lee Harvey [†]Oswald, who, it said, was elsewhere that day. Some researchers speculate that the man calling himself Oswald may have been an impersonator leaving a false trail of evidence.

See also BOGARD, ALBERT G; BROWN, ORAN; PIZZO, FRANK; WILSON, EUGENE M.

📖 *Rush to Judgment*

DOX, IDA

Dox prepared a series of drawings that accurately reproduced the Kennedy autopsy photographs for the [†]House Select Committee on Assassinations. Photographs of the

drawings were then taken, and these photos were used in the Committee's investigation. The decision to use drawings rather than photos was ostensibly made to spare the Kennedy family the pain of having the public view actual photos of the president's corpse.
📖 *Best Evidence*

DOYLE, HAROLD
Doyle is one of three †hoboes found near the scene and taken in for questioning by the Dallas police shortly after the shooting. Initially charged for vagrancy, all three were later released. There has been confusion about their identities, what they were doing in the railroad yard behind the †Grassy Knoll, and why they were released so quickly.
See also ABRAMS, GUS W.; GEDNEY, JOHN FORRESTER.
📖 *High Treason 2*

DRAIN, VINCENT
Drain was the FBI agent who took the †Mannlicher-Carcano rifle allegedly found in the †Texas School Book Depository Building to the FBI labs in Washington, D.C., for examination in the early hours of November 23, 1963. The FBI found no usable fingerprints on the weapon, and on Sunday afternoon,

November 24, Drain returned it to the †Dallas police.
See also LATONA, SEBASTIAN FRANCIS; PALMPRINT
ON RIFLE.
📖 *Best Evidence*

DUDMAN, RICHARD

A correspondent for the *St. Louis Post-Dispatch,*
Dudman wrote several articles about the assassination
investigation during December 1963 that fueled
controversies that persist today. These included
interviews conducted during the first week of December
with some of the doctors at †Parkland Memorial
Hospital who had worked to save the president's life,
who insisted the wound in Kennedy's throat was a
bullet entry wound, not an exit wound. On December
18, Dudman reported that two †Secret Service agents
visited the Parkland surgeons with a copy of the
autopsy report from †Bethesda Naval Hospital.
Following this visit, the Dallas doctors changed their
opinion of the wound to "conform" to the Bethesda
autopsy report. The Parkland doctors told Dudman that
they had not been coerced into changing their minds.
See also AUTOPSY CONTROVERSY; MCCLELLAND, DR.
ROBERT N.; PERRY, DR. MALCOLM; TRACHEOTOMY.
📖 *Best Evidence*

DUFFY, JAMES R.

An attorney, Duffy (no relation to the present author) wrote *Who Killed JFK? The Web: The Kennedy Assassination Cover-up,* published by Shapolsky in 1989. Based on official documents, this book examines the life and connections of Lee Harvey †Oswald and looks at various conspiracy theories.

DULANEY, DR. RICHARD

A resident at †Parkland Memorial Hospital, Dulaney was shown copies of photographs of the president's head wound allegedly taken at the time of the autopsy. He is reported as saying that these photos showed a wound different from the one he remembers seeing in an unobstructed view afforded when another doctor lifted Kennedy's head.

See also HEAD WOUND CONTROVERSY.

📖 *High Treason*

DULLES, ALLEN W.

A member of the †Warren Commission, Dulles was director of the †Central Intelligence Agency from 1953 through 1961. Many critics find it hard to justify Dulles's selection for the Commission. He had spent most of his life in the same intelligence organization

Allen W. Dulles, with the then-presidential candidate John F. Kennedy

that President Kennedy had sworn to break up and had himself been forced out by Kennedy after the †Bay of Pigs fiasco.

DURAN, SILVIA

A young Mexican woman who was employed in the Cuban Embassy in †Mexico City in 1963, Duran was approached several times in late September and early October of that year by an American calling himself Lee Harvey †Oswald. The man wanted to arrange for a visa to Cuba, from where, he said, he intended to travel to the Soviet Union. Later, after reportedly making statements that the man she met in Mexico City might not be the same man she saw Jack †Ruby kill on television, Duran was arrested twice by Mexican authorities, allegedly at the instigation of the †Central Intelligence Agency.

□ *Conspiracy; Plausible Denial*

EBERSOLE, DR. JOHN

Ebersole was the radiologist who took autopsy X rays of the president's wounds at †Bethesda Naval Hospital. He allegedly told a reporter from his hometown newspaper that he took numerous X rays of the body in an effort to locate a bullet that the autopsy doctors believed entered through the president's back but did not exit. No bullet was ever found. He is also reported as saying that the †tracheotomy opening in the president's throat, which was originally a bullet wound, had been sutured closed. The doctors at †Parkland Memorial Hospital denied that the wound had been closed. In fact, Dr. Kemp †Clark recalled that the tracheotomy tube was left in the body when the body was prepared for shipment to Washington.
See also X-RAY CONTROVERSY.
📖 *Best Evidence*

EDDOWES, MICHAEL

Eddowes wrote a book originally titled *Khrushchev*

Killed Kennedy and later republished by Clarkson N.
Potter as *The Oswald File* (1977). Its main premise is
that while Lee Harvey †Oswald was living in the
Soviet Union, he was taken prisoner and replaced by
the KGB with a Soviet agent who assumed Oswald's
identity. According to Eddowes, it was this KGB agent
who later murdered the president. The issue was put
to rest when Eddowes sued the state of Texas to have
the body in Oswald's grave exhumed; it was, and was,
in fact, found to be the real Oswald.
📖 *High Treason*

"EDUARDO"
"Eduardo" was an alias used by E. Howard †Hunt,
according to Marita †Lorenz.

EDWARDS, ROBERT E.
Dallas County employee Edwards was standing with
Ronald B. †Fischer across from the †Texas School Book
Depository Building at the intersection of Elm and
Houston streets when something at a sixth-floor
window of the building caught his attention. He could
see the head and shoulders of a man who was wearing
either a white T-shirt or light-colored sport shirt.
Edwards reported that it seemed odd to him that the
man was not watching for the motorcade, but was

staring "transfixed" toward the end of Elm Street near the overpass.

📖 *Crossfire*

EDWARDS, SHEFFIELD
A CIA operative believed to be involved in plots to kill Fidel †Castro, Edwards was also a reported liaison between the CIA and mob hitmen.
See also BISSELL, RICHARD.

📖 *High Treason*

ELLIS, STARVIS
Dallas Police Officer Ellis told the †House Select Committee on Assassinations that he rode his motorcycle alongside the first car in the presidential motorcade. He reported seeing a bullet strike the pavement, but no such bullet was ever accounted for, and Ellis was never questioned by the †Warren Commission.
See also DECKER, J. E. (BILL); WINDSHIELD DAMAGE.

📖 *Crossfire*

EPSTEIN, EDWARD JAY
Epstein is the author of three books dealing with the assassination: *Inquest: The Warren Commission and the Establishment of Truth,* published by Viking in

1966; *Counterplot,* published by Viking in 1969; and *Legend: The Secret Life of Lee Harvey Oswald,* published by Ballantine in 1978. The first established Epstein as a critic of the †Warren Report. Epstein's thesis is that Lee Harvey †Oswald was an undercover operative of the American intelligence community. *Counterplot* is an attack on the assassination investigation conducted by New Orleans district attorney Jim †Garrison.

EUINS, AMOS L.

According to testimony by James †Underwood, who was assistant news director for KRLD-TV in Dallas at the time of the assassination, Euins, who was fifteen years old at the time, told a Dallas motorcycle police officer that he saw a "colored man" with a rifle lean out the sixth-floor window of the †Texas School Book Depository Building. Following allegedly threatening telephone calls to his family, Euins, who is black himself, recanted his statement and told the †Warren Commission that he didn't know whether the man he saw was white or "colored."

See also DARK-COMPLEXIONED MAN (OR MEN); POWELL, JOHN; ROWLAND, ARNOLD.

📖 *Rush to Judgment*

EWING, MICHAEL

Ewing was a staff member of the †House Select Committee on Assassinations. He is the coauthor, with Bernard Fensterwald, of *Assassination of JFK by Coincidence or Conspiracy?* produced by the Committee to Investigate Assassinations and published by Kensington Publishing Corporation in 1977.

EXECUTIVE ACTION

This was a code name reserved for covert CIA activities involving Agency plans to assassinate unfriendly foreign leaders.
See also ZR/RIFLE.
□ *Conspiracy*

EXNER, JUDITH

A stunning beauty and an intimate of Chicago mob leader Sam †Giancana, Exner also engaged in an affair with President Kennedy beginning in March 1960. The liaison ended after March 1962, when it is thought that FBI director J. Edgar †Hoover confronted Kennedy with his knowledge of the affair and the fact that Exner was linked to Giancana. Exner later wrote about the affair in a book titled *My Story,* published by Grove in 1977.
□ *Crossfire*

FAIR PLAY FOR CUBA COMMITTEE (FPCC)

A pro-Castro organization active during the 1960s, the FPCC did not have a chapter in New Orleans, which was home to so many Cubans exiled from their homeland. During the summer of 1963, Lee Harvey †Oswald created an FPCC chapter—with an address at †544 Camp Street—that was nothing more than a paper organization naming him the president and only member. Some assassination researchers believe Oswald fabricated this group to help him establish a facade as a pro-Castro sympathizer.

📖 *Conspiracy*

FBI TELEX MESSAGE

On November 17, 1963, the following telex message was sent to all FBI offices in the United States:
URGENT: 1:45 AM EST 11-17-63 HLF 1 PAGE
TO: ALL SACS
FROM: DIRECTOR
THREAT TO ASSASSINATE PRESIDENT KENNEDY IN

DALLAS TEXAS NOVEMBER 22 DASH TWENTY THREE
NINETEEN SIXTY THREE. MISC INFORMATION
CONCERNING. INFORMATION HAS BEEN RECEIVED BY
THE BUREAS [*sic*] BUREAU HAS DETERMINED THAT A
MILITANT REVOLUTIONARY GROUP MAY ATTEMPT TO
ASSASSINATE PRESIDENT KENNEDY ON HIS PROPOSED
TRIP TO DALLAS TEXAS NOVEMBER TWENTY TWO DASH
TWENTY THREE NINETEEN SIXTY THREE. ALL
RECEIVING OFFICES SHOULD IMMEDIATELY CONTACT
ALL CIS, PCIS LOGICAL RACE AND HATE GROUP
INFORMANTS AND DETERMINE IF ANY BASIS FOR
THREAT. BUREAU SHOULD BE KEPT ADVISED OF ALL
DEVELOPMENTS BY TELETYPE. OTHER OFFICES HAVE
BEEN ADVISED. END AND ACK PLS.

According to New Orleans district attorney Jim
†Garrison, William S. †Walter, an FBI employee of the
New Orleans office, claimed that following the assas-
sination, the file copies of this message and a duplicate
sent shortly afterward disappeared from the office.
📖 *On the Trail of the Assassins*

FEDERAL BUREAU OF INVESTIGATION (FBI)

According to Mark North, author of *Act of Treason: The
Role of J. Edgar Hoover in the Assassination of
President Kennedy* (Carroll & Graf, 1992), FBI director
J. Edgar †Hoover knew of a †Mafia plot to kill Kennedy

but did nothing to stop it. On Kennedy's election in 1960, Hoover began actively to collect potentially damaging information on the Kennedy family. Being an old acquaintance of Kennedy's father, Joseph P. Kennedy, Sr., Hoover was well aware of Kennedy Sr.'s shadier business dealings and felt that John Kennedy would be vulnerable to political blackmail.

By 1962, FBI surveillance of Mafia hideouts had revealed the depth of the mob's resentment of the Kennedys' anti-Mafia crusade. Hoover's own relationship with the Kennedys was not much better. President Kennedy had ousted many former FBI agents from the †Secret Service, the State Department, the †Central Intelligence Agency, the Immigration and Naturalization Service, and other agencies. In return, Hoover publicly criticized Kennedy's policies while secretly gathering information on Kennedy's affairs with Marilyn Monroe, Judith †Exner, and other women. Hoover also quarreled with Attorney General Robert F. †Kennedy, whom he felt was overstepping his authority.

There has been some speculation that Lee Harvey †Oswald may have secretly been an FBI agent, a charge that Hoover himself denied in a written statement to the †Warren Commission.

FBI agents assisted in many aspects of the official investigation into the president's death. Among the

more important documents produced by FBI agents was the †O'Neill and Sibert report on the autopsy performed at †Bethesda Naval Hospital.
📖 *See also* QUIGLEY, JOHN.

FELDER, JAMES L.

Army Sergeant James Felder was a member of the †Casket Team charged with transporting the president's coffin. Felder was interviewed by researcher David S. †Lifton. According to Lifton, Felder substantiated reports of confusion at †Bethesda Naval Hospital involving the use of two Navy ambulances and the team's difficulty locating Kennedy's coffin during a thirty-minute interval following its arrival at the hospital.
See also AMBULANCE CONTROVERSY; BIRD, SAMUEL R.
📖 *Best Evidence*

FENSTERWALD, BERNARD

Fensterwald was the coauthor, with Michael †Ewing, of *Assassination of JFK by Coincidence or Conspiracy?,* published by Kensington Publishing Corporation in 1977.

FERRELL, MARY

A Dallas-based assassination researcher who has

devoted countless hours probing into the president's murder, Ferrell has contributed to numerous books on the subject. It was Ferrell who alerted the †House Select Committee on Assassinations to the existence of a Dictabelt recording of sounds at the assassination scene; this recording became known as the †Dallas police dispatch tape. An analysis of this tape led the Committee to admit that four shots were fired in †Dealey Plaza, rather than the three originally acknowledged by the †Warren Commission. Ferrell also reportedly claimed that Captain Will †Fritz, the man who interrogated Lee Harvey †Oswald, told a friend that Lyndon B. †Johnson called while Oswald was in custody and said, "You've got your man, the investigation is over."

See also ACOUSTICAL EVIDENCE.

📖 *Conspiracy; High Treason*

FERRIE, DAVID

Photographs of David Ferrie show a man of outlandish appearance. This is partially because he suffered from a disease that caused him to lose all the hair on his body, including his head and eyebrows. He usually compensated for this by wearing a cheap red wig and obviously phony eyebrows. Ferrie had a reputation as an excellent pilot who flew dangerous missions into

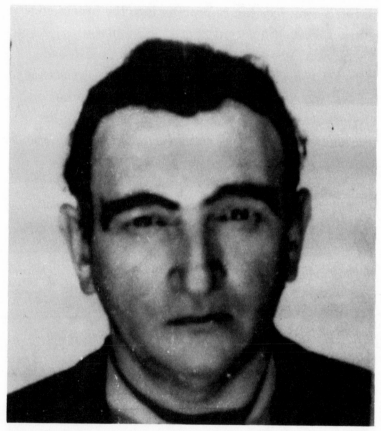

David Ferrie

Cuba before the †Bay of Pigs invasion. He was active in right-wing organizations in New Orleans, especially with †anti-Castro Cubans. He was also an associate of Guy †Banister's and did work for mafioso Carlos †Marcello and members of his organization. Ferrie also had connections with Lee Harvey †Oswald that dated back at least a dozen years before the assassination. Ferrie died of what officials termed natural causes on February 22, 1967, shortly after New Orleans district attorney Jim †Garrison implicated him in Kennedy's assassination.

📖 *Conspiracy; Heritage of Stone; On the Trail of the Assassins.*

FILMS OF THE ASSASSINATION
See ARNOLD, GORDON; BRONSON FILM; DORMAN, ELSIE; HUGHES, ROBERT; MUCHMORE, MARIE; NIX, ORVILLE; OLIVER, BETTY; WEIGMAN, DAVE; ZAPRUDER FILM.

FINCK, DR. PIERRE
A forensic pathologist, Dr. Finck attended at the autopsy on the president's body conducted at †Bethesda Naval Hospital. Finck testified that the depth of the wound in the president's back was "the first fraction of an inch." This was the wound allegedly

caused by the †magic bullet, which supposedly passed through Kennedy's body and also caused the wounds to Governor John †Connally. When asked by the †Warren Commission whether the magic bullet could have inflicted the wound in Connally's wrist, Dr. Finck replied, "No; for the reason that there are too many fragments described in that wrist." By contrast, the magic bullet is almost entirely intact.

See also SHAW, DR. ROBERT.

📖 *Best Evidence; High Treason*

FIRING SEQUENCE CONTROVERSY

The †Warren Commission concluded that Lee Harvey †Oswald fired three times at President Kennedy from the sixth floor of the †Texas School Book Depository Building. Despite reports from people at the scene of as few as two shots to as many as six, the Commission settled on three because three spent cartridges were allegedly found in the †sniper's nest on the sixth floor of the building. At first the Warren Commission established that two bullets hit Kennedy and one wounded Texas governor John †Connally. This view of events was later changed to correspond with evidence proving that a bystander, James T. †Tague, was injured when a bullet hit the pavement at his feet. Thus was created what has become known as the

†magic bullet theory, according to which one bullet wounded both Kennedy and Connally, and another killed Kennedy, leaving a third to cause the injury to Tague. The Commission relied on the †Zapruder film to establish the timing of the shots, and concluded that Oswald had fired all three in 4.8 to 5.6 seconds. Three men rated master marksmen by the National Rifle Association were asked by the Commission to simulate Oswald's firing sequence. The men, positioned about thirty feet off the ground (rather than sixty feet, the level of the Depository Building's sixth floor), each fired six shots at a stationary target. One of these three "masters" was able to match Oswald's alleged timing; the other two failed. Not one of the eighteen shots hit the targeted head and neck. All parties in the assassination debate agree that Oswald could not be called a "master" shot, and he was further handicapped because the sight on his alleged rifle was not aligned accurately.

See also MANNLICHER-CARCANO RIFLE; SIMMONS, RONALD.

📖 *Rush to Judgment*

FISCHER, RONALD B.

A Dallas County employee, Fischer was standing on the corner of Elm and Houston streets with Robert E.

†Edwards just before the presidential motorcade entered †Dealey Plaza when he observed a man at the sixth-floor window of the †Texas School Book Depository Building. The man wore either a white T-shirt or a light-colored sport shirt. Fischer noticed that the man stared "transfixed" at Elm Street, looking in the direction of the railroad overpass. He said later he thought the shots that were fired at the president came from the west side of the building, which is the direction of the †Grassy Knoll.
📖 *Crossfire*

FISCHER, DR. RUSSELL
Maryland state medical examiner Fischer headed the panel of four doctors established by Attorney General Ramsey Clark in 1968 to review the autopsy photographs and X rays of the president's wounds. *See also* CLARK PANEL.
📖 *Best Evidence*; *High Treason*

FITZGERALD, DESMOND
A CIA officer involved in plots to kill Fidel †Castro, FitzGerald once identified himself to Cuban official Rolando †Cubela as a senator who represented Attorney General Robert F. †Kennedy. He told Cubela

that a coup against Castro would have U.S. government backing, and that Kennedy favored assassinating Castro.

📖 *Conspiracy; High Treason*

544 CAMP STREET

This was the address of a seedy three-story building in New Orleans that figured prominently in Lee Harvey †Oswald's activities in that city. When Oswald was arrested in August 1963 following a fight with †anti-Castro Cubans who objected to his distributing pro-Castro literature, he was in possession of pamphlets rubber-stamped with the address FPCC, 544 Camp Street, New Orleans. The letters FPCC stood for the †Fair Play for Cuba Committee. The Camp Street address was an odd location for a pro-Castro group, since it was the address of the anti-Castro †Cuban Revolutionary Council. Also at 544 Camp Street were the offices of Guy †Banister, a supporter of anti-Castro groups with reported links to the U.S. intelligence community and the underworld. Other offices in this shabby corner building were used by various Cuban exile groups planning the overthrow of Castro.

See also BRINGUIER, CARLOS.

📖 *Conspiracy; Crossfire*

FOLSOM, ALLISON

When Marine Corps Lieutenant Colonel Folsom
testified before the †Warren Commission, he read aloud
the score Lee Harvey †Oswald received on a Russian-
language test. Did Oswald receive instruction in
Russian while he was in the Marines? Why? Despite
Folsom's evidence, supporters of the Commission
contend that Oswald taught himself Russian because
he planned to defect to the Soviet Union.
📖 *Heritage of Stone*

FONZI, GAETON

A Philadelphia journalist who was hired by the †House
Select Committee on Assassinations, Fonzi traveled
widely collecting information to be used in the
Committee's investigation of the president's
assassination. Fonzi later wrote that the Committee's
investigation had been inadequate and recommended
that another investigation of the Kennedy
assassination be opened.

FORD, GERALD

Congressman (later President) Ford was selected by
Lyndon B. †Johnson to serve on the †Warren
Commission. Assassination researcher Mark †Lane
has charged that Ford secretly leaked to the FBI

information gathered by the Commission's staff during its investigation. Ford coauthored, with John R. Stiles, a book titled *Portrait of the Assassin,* published in 1965 by Simon & Schuster.
See also WARREN COMMISSION MEMBERS.
📖 *Plausible Denial*

FOSTER, J. W.

Dallas police officer Foster was one of two officers assigned to stand on the railroad overpass that spanned Elm Street, and under which the presidential motorcade would pass. After the shooting, Foster reportedly searched the area below and found a tear in the grass where a bullet had hit the ground. Ordered to guard the spot, Foster remained there until an unidentified man, described as an FBI agent, removed the slug and took it with him. A photo showed a sandy-haired man in a suit removing the slug while Foster, in uniform, looked on. Nothing was ever heard about this slug again.
See also HARTMAN, WAYNE AND EDNA; OVERPASS WITNESSES.
📖 *Crossfire*

FOX, SYLVAN

In 1965, Pulitzer Prize–winning journalist Sylvan Fox wrote the first book challenging the †Warren Report.

Fox's work, *The Unanswered Questions About the Kennedy Assassination,* published by Award Books in 1965, was based solely on the Warren Commission's hearings and is credited by many private researchers with sparking their interest in investigating the assassination.

FRAZIER, BUELL WESLEY

Frazier was the †Texas School Book Depository Building employee who drove Lee Harvey †Oswald to work the day of the assassination. The †Warren Commission made much of Frazier's testimony that Oswald carried a long, paper-wrapped parcel with him into the building that day, which he told Frazier contained curtain rods. When the Commission showed Frazier a paper package with the dismantled †Mannlicher-Carcano rifle wrapped inside, he told them Oswald's package was much shorter. Frazier described the package Oswald had with him as about twenty-seven inches long. The rifle allegedly found inside the building could not be dismantled to that short a length; a package containing the purported murder weapon had to be no less than 34.8 inches long. Frazier said Oswald carried the package against his body from under his armpit down to the palm of his hand, in such a manner that it wasn't readily visible to

others. Like many other building employees, such as
Joe R. †Molina, Frazier was standing in front of the
Depository Building when the president's motorcade
passed. When the Commission asked him what he
heard, he replied that he thought the shots "come [*sic*]
from down there, you know, where that underpass is."
See also DOUGHERTY, JACK E.; RANDLE, LINNIE MAE.
📖 *Rush to Judgment*

FRAZIER, ROBERT
A ballistics and firearms expert employed by the FBI,
Frazier testified before the †Warren Commission that he
examined Commission Exhibit #399, more commonly
known as the †magic bullet, at the FBI labs. He said the
bullet was "clean" of any traces of blood or tissue and
that its weight loss, which he placed at three grains,
could be attributed to the manufacturing process. If
this is true, it means the bullet would have had to pass
through both Kennedy and John †Connally, doing
extensive damage to the bone in Connally's wrist,
without being damaged itself. When pressed about the
possibility that the bullet did wound both men, Frazier
said it was "possible but I don't say that it probably
occurred." Frazier also testified that the bullet holes in
Kennedy's suit jacket and shirt were five and three-
eighths and five and three-quarters inches below the

collar. This contradicts the †Warren Report, which places the wound at the base of the president's neck.
See also THROAT WOUND CONTROVERSY.

📖 *Best Evidence*; *Warren Commission Report*

FREEMAN, H. R.

H. R. Freeman was a Dallas motorcycle police officer. *See* WINDSHIELD DAMAGE.

FRIENDS OF DEMOCRATIC CUBA

An †anti-Castro Cuban organization. *See* SEWALL, FRED.

FRITZ, WILL

Dallas police captain Fritz interrogated Lee Harvey †Oswald after his arrest. Fritz was allegedly one of the police officers who first identified the rifle found in the †Texas School Book Depository Building as a Mauser, not the †Mannlicher-Carcano the †Warren Commission concluded was the weapon that killed Kennedy. He reportedly made contradictory claims regarding whether prints were found on the rifle.
See also BOONE, EUGENE L.; CRAIG, ROGER D.; MOONEY, LUKE; WADE, HENRY W.; WEITZMAN, SEYMOUR.

📖 *High Treason*; *Rush to Judgment*

GALLOWAY, DR. CALVIN

Admiral Galloway was commanding officer of the
National Naval Medical Center at Bethesda when the
president's body arrived, and he attended the autopsy.
News reports suggested that he drove the ambulance
supposedly containing the president's remains from the
front entrance of †Bethesda Naval Hospital around to
the rear, where the coffin was unloaded, an activity he
later denied, although he admitted being in the
ambulance. According to confidential reports, Galloway
later called each military person present during the
autopsy into his office individually and requested a
signed statement acknowledging that they would not
discuss what they had seen during the autopsy under
penalty of a court-martial. Galloway was never
subpoenaed to testify before the †Warren Commission.
See also AMBULANCE CONTROVERSY; BODY BAG
CONTROVERSY; CASKET TEAM.
□ *Best Evidence*

GANNAWAY, W. P.

Captain Gannaway was commanding officer of the
Dallas Police Department's Special Service Bureau.
When questions arose about the swiftness with which
the police broadcast a description of Lee Harvey
†Oswald as a suspect in the president's shooting,
Gannaway reportedly said matters were facilitated by
a roll call of †Texas School Book Depository Building
employees that determined that only Oswald was
missing. Author Mark †Lane challenged this
explanation, pointing out that the police broadcast
was made at 12:45 P.M., while many building
employees who had been outside the building when
the shots were fired at 12:30 still remained outside,
unable to reenter because police officers had sealed off
all the entrances.
See also REVILL, JACK.
📖 *Rush to Judgment*

GARNER, DARRELL WAYNE

Garner was the boyfriend of Betty Mooney
†MacDonald and the suspect—later released—in the
attempted murder of Warren †Reynolds, who was a
witness to the murder of Dallas police officer J. D.
†Tippit.

GARNER, DOROTHY ANN
An employee in the †Texas School Book Depository
Building, Garner told police that she was on the
fourth floor of the building when the shooting took
place, and that she thought the shots came from "a
point to the west of the building," which would place
the shooter in the area of the †Grassy Knoll.
📖 *Crossfire; Rush to Judgment*

GARRISON, JIM
Garrison, the New Orleans district attorney,
conducted his own investigation of the assassination
based on evidence that Lee Harvey †Oswald had lived
in New Orleans and had had contacts with numerous
individuals whom Garrison considered highly
motivated to kill President Kennedy. In 1967,
Garrison indicted businessman Clay †Shaw on charges
that he participated in a conspiracy to murder the
president. Although unable to produce convincing
evidence for the court, Garrison alleged that Shaw
was a †Central Intelligence Agency operative and that
the assassination had been a CIA plot. On March 1,
1969, Shaw was acquitted. Several jurors later stated
that Garrison did persuade them that the
assassination was the result of a conspiracy, although

New Orleans district attorney Jim Garrison

he failed to prove that Shaw was a party to it.

Garrison has written two books, *A Heritage of Stone* (Putnam, 1970) and *On the Trail of the Assassins* (Warner, 1991). He was the leading character in Oliver †Stone's film †*JFK*.

📖 *Plausible Denial*

GAUDET, WILLIAM GEORGE

An employee of the CIA for twenty years, Gaudet allegedly obtained a tourist card to visit Mexico at the same time as Lee Harvey †Oswald. These cards were issued by the Mexican consulate in New Orleans in September 1963. According to records, Oswald was issued card number 824085, and Gaudet card number 824084. Gaudet reportedly first admitted, then denied knowing Oswald, and denied that he had ever traveled to Mexico with Oswald, although he doesn't recall why he obtained the tourist card.

See also MEXICO CITY.

📖 *Conspiracy*

GAUDREAU, RICHARD E.

An Air Force sergeant, Gaudreau was a member of the Military District of Washington, D.C., †Casket Team that handled President Kennedy's coffin at †Bethesda Naval Hospital. Researcher David S.

†Lifton reports that Gaudreau and his wife, Barbara, substantiate the story of the confusion over which of two Navy ambulances at the scene actually contained the coffin with the president's body in it.

See also AMBULANCE CONTROVERSY; BIRD, SAMUEL R.; CHEEK, TIMOTHY.

📖 *Best Evidence*

GEDNEY, JOHN FORRESTER

Gedney is said to be one of three †hoboes Dallas police picked up for questioning near the scene shortly after the shooting. Initially charged with vagrancy, all three were later released. There has been confusion about their identities, what they were doing in the railroad yard behind the †Grassy Knoll, and why they were released so quickly.

📖 *High Treason 2*

GIANCANA, SAM

Giancana (real name, Momo Salvatore Guingano) was a Chicago †Mafia boss involved in CIA plots to kill Fidel †Castro. He was also the target of attacks by Attorney General Robert F. †Kennedy, despite the fact that the president had been having an affair with Giancana's paramour, Judith †Exner. Robert Kennedy ordered the FBI to make life difficult for Giancana,

Mafia boss Sam Giancana

which it did by shadowing his every move so closely that other mob figures kept their distance from him, effectively isolating him from business and social associates. In desperation, Giancana went to court and obtained an injunction against the FBI.

In 1975, Giancana was murdered just as the Senate Intelligence Committee was preparing to question him about his role in the CIA-Mafia plots to kill Castro. He was shot once in the back of the head and six times around the mouth in an obviously clear statement as to why he was killed. The fact that Giancana was killed with a .22-caliber pistol rather than the larger-caliber guns preferred by professional hitmen led some observers to suspect he was murdered by a killer within the intelligence community.

See also MARCELLO, CARLOS; ROSELLI, JOHNNY; TRAFFICANTE, SANTOS; ZR/RIFLE.

📖 *Conspiracy; Crossfire*

GIESECKE, DR. ADOLPH

Dr. Giesecke was an anesthesiology professor at Southwestern Medical School in Dallas and part of the team that worked on the mortally wounded president at †Parkland Memorial Hospital. When assassination researcher Harrison Edward †Livingstone described the head wound as a large blowout in the back of the head, Giesecke agreed that that was the wound he saw. This differs from the description of the wound in the report of the autopsy conducted at †Bethesda Naval Hospital. When asked by the †Warren Commission if he had seen another wound or a bullet hole below the large wound in the back of the head, Giesecke replied he had not. Dr. Giesecke did say that he thought he saw a wound in the president's left temple, as did Dr. Marion †Jenkins of Parkland Memorial Hospital, and Norman †Similas, a witness at the scene of the shooting.

See also HEAD WOUND CONTROVERSY; TEMPLE WOUND CONTROVERSY.

📖 *High Treason; Rush to Judgment*

GOLDBERG, ALFRED

A staff member of the †Warren Commission and, with Norman †Redlich, one of the main authors of the †Warren Report, Goldberg attempted to get the FBI to investigate the forty-minute time lag between the shooting and the discovery of the so-called †sniper's nest and the rifle on the sixth floor of the †Texas School Book Depository Building. According to David S. †Lifton, Goldberg wrote two letters to J. Edgar †Hoover urging him to look into the matter, but Hoover declined.

📖 *Best Evidence*

GOLZ, EARL

A *Dallas Morning News* reporter, Golz has been a
tenacious searcher of the truth about the
assassination and instrumental in discovering
important evidence. In 1978, he located a man who at
the time of the shooting had been serving a three-day
sentence at the Dallas County Jail on †Dealey Plaza.
The man claimed that he and several other prisoners
saw two †dark-complexioned men at the sixth-floor
window of the †Texas School Book Depository Building
adjusting the sight of a rifle. That same year, Golz
was one of two researchers who uncovered the
existence of the †Bronson film, which many believe
shows movement in two windows of the building's
sixth floor.
📖 *Reasonable Doubt*

GONZALEZ, HENRY

A Democratic congressman from San Antonio, Texas,
Gonzalez rode in the presidential motorcade when
Kennedy was killed and later served as chairman of
the †House Select Committee on Assassinations.
Gonzalez resigned from the Committee in a dispute
with Chief Counsel Richard A. †Sprague over control
of the Committee's investigative machinery. Gonzalez
later charged that the Committee was a "put-up job,"

Congressman Henry Gonzalez, chairman of the House Select Committee on Assassinations

and that it was "never intended to work."
📖 *High Treason*

GRANT, EVA
Eva Grant was Jack †Ruby's sister. Grant had an on-and-off relationship with Ruby that would occasionally result in long periods during which they did not speak to each other. She testified to the †Warren Commission about Ruby's family life, his reaction to the Kennedy assassination, and the ad placed in the *Dallas Morning News* by the †American Fact-Finding Committee.
📖 *Ruby Cover-up*

GRASSY KNOLL
After the †Texas School Book Depository Building, the Grassy Knoll is the most widely known location identified with the assassination. Dozens of witnesses, including civilians, police officers, and people riding in the presidential motorcade, testified that at least some of the shots fired at the president came from the knoll. Situated to the south and west of the Book Depository, the knoll rises up from Elm Street toward the railroad yards behind it. Near the crest is a wooden stockade fence that many witnesses believe served as a cover for the person or persons who shot the president.

According to author John H. †Davis, two days
before the assassination, two Dallas police officers on
routine patrol saw a group of men standing behind the
fence engaged in what appeared to be mock target
practice. The men sped off in a nearby car before the
officers could question them.
See also SMOKE FROM THE GRASSY KNOLL.
📖 *Mafia Kingfish*

GRASSY KNOLL WITNESSES
At the time of the shooting, dozens of people were
scattered across the face of the †Grassy Knoll. Of those
who witnessed the assassination from the knoll and
were called to testify, virtually all claim the shots fired
at President Kennedy came from somewhere behind
them. Grassy Knoll witnesses include Gordon †Arnold;
Lee †Bowers; Mr. and Mrs. John †Chism; Emmett J.
†Hudson; Mary E. †Woodward; and Abraham Zapruder
(*see* ZAPRUDER FILM).

GRAVES, L. C.
Dallas police detective Graves walked on Lee Harvey
†Oswald's left while escorting the prisoner through
the basement garage at Dallas Police Headquarters,
where Jack †Ruby shot and killed him. Graves told
the †Warren Commission he was surprised that the

reporters and television cameras were allowed so close to the prisoner, since he was under the impression that tight security arrangements had been made. He claimed that Police Chief Jesse E. †Curry had said "the newsmen were well back in the garage." Graves also admitted that he was unaware that both the Dallas police and the FBI had received telephoned threats to Oswald's life prior to escorting him to the garage.

See also LEAVELLE, JAMES R.; MONTGOMERY, L. D.

📖 *Rush to Judgment*

GREENER, CHARLES W.

Greener was the owner of the †Irving Sports Shop.

GREER, WILLIAM

Secret Service agent Greer was driving the presidential limousine when Kennedy was shot. Some critics charge that when the first shot was fired, instead of immediately speeding off, he slowed the car almost to a stop, turned to look at the president, and pulled away only after the fatal shot had struck Kennedy in the head. Greer also drove the ambulance carrying the president's official coffin from †Andrews Air Force Base to †Bethesda Naval Hospital. Greer was one of two Secret Service agents present at the autopsy who described the alleged neck wound as a shoulder wound.

See also KELLERMAN, ROY; SHANEYFELT, LYNDAL.

📖 *Best Evidence*; *High Treason*

GREGORY, DR. CHARLES

An orthopedic surgeon, Dr. Gregory operated on Governor John †Connally's wrist. The †Warren Report concludes that the wrist wound was caused by the †magic bullet, which supposedly first passed through the president's body, then Connally's body, then his wrist. Dr. Gregory said the bullet "behaved as though it never struck anything except him." Dr. Gregory also testified that he removed two metal fragments from Connally's wrist and that another remained lodged in the governor's chest. The magic bullet had virtually no weight loss, which raises the question of where these fragments came from, and further suggests the possibility that another bullet, unaccounted for by the Commission, could have been fired by a second gunman.

📖 *High Treason; Reasonable Doubt*

GRIFFIN, BURT W.

Griffin served as assistant counsel to the †Warren Commission. When he questioned Dallas police

sergeant Patrick T. †Dean about his testimony that
Jack †Ruby claimed he had entered the Police
Headquarters garage by simply walking down the
Main Street entrance ramp, Griffin lost his temper
and called Dean "a damned liar."
See also VAUGHN, ROY.
□ *Best Evidence*; *Rush to Judgment*

GRINNAN, JOSEPH P.

Known locally as an independent oil operator and an
area coordinator for the John Birch Society, Grinnan
took part in preparing an anti-Kennedy newspaper
advertisement that appeared in the *Dallas Morning
News* the day the president arrived in Dallas and was
assassinated.
See also AMERICAN FACT-FINDING COMMITTEE;
WEISSMAN, BERNARD.
□ *Warren Report*

GRODEN, ROBERT J.

A photographic expert, Groden created an enhanced
version of the †Zapruder film, which was broadcast on
a late-night television program on March 6, 1976, and
became instrumental in reopening the assassination
investigation in 1976 by the newly formed †House
Select Committee on Assassinations. After examining

the autopsy photos, Groden told the Committee that
four of the photographs showed evidence of forgery.
The Committee rejected this claim. Groden is the
coauthor of *JFK: The Case for Conspiracy,* published
by Manor Books in 1967, and, with Harrison Edward
†Livingstone, of *High Treason,* published by Berkley in
1990.
📖 *Best Evidence*; *High Treason*

GROODY, PAUL
Groody was the director of the Miller Funeral Home
in Dallas, where Lee Harvey †Oswald's body was
embalmed. According to David S. †Lifton, Groody told
him that during the predawn hours of November 25,
1963, several FBI agents demanded time alone with
Oswald's body and took prints of the dead man's
fingers and palms. Groody said they left "black gook"
on Oswald's hands, which he subsequently removed.
See also MOSELEY, JACK; PALMPRINT ON RIFLE.
📖 *Best Evidence*

GROSSMAN, DR. ROBERT
A neurosurgeon at †Parkland Memorial Hospital,
Grossman was never called to testify by either the
†Warren Commission or the †House Select Committee
on Assassinations. He reportedly told a reporter from

the *Boston Globe* that he saw a large hole in the back of the president's head that was too large for a bullet entry wound.

See also HEAD WOUND CONTROVERSY.

📖 *High Treason*

GUINN, DR. VINCENT

A nuclear chemist consulted by the †Warren Commission, Dr. Guinn examined fragments collected from the wounds that allegedly came from the †magic bullet. His findings indicated that they were, in fact, part of that bullet. The †House Select Committee on Assassinations later asked him to reexamine this material, but Guinn discovered that the fragments sent to him from the National Archives were not the same weight of those listed in the National Archives records. In addition, other fragments originally considered as evidence in this case vanished completely.

See also NATIONAL ARCHIVES, DOCUMENTS MISSING FROM.

📖 *Best Evidence*; *High Treason*

GUSTAFSON, PATRICIA

Gustafson is the married name of Patricia †Hutton.

HALL, LORAN
Loran Hall was an activist in anti-Castro circles.
See ODIO INCIDENT.

HARBISON, CHARLES
Charles Harbison, a Texas highway patrolman, was
assigned to guard Governor John †Connally's hospital
room. Harbison reportedly claimed that someone,
possibly a doctor, gave him more than three bullet
fragments that had been removed from Connally's
body. He allegedly turned them over to an FBI agent.
See also BELL, AUDREY; BORING, FLOYD; GREGORY,
DR. CHARLES; MAGIC BULLET.
📖 *Conspiracy*

HARDIE, JULIUS
Julius Hardie, a Dallas resident, gave an interview
that was published in the August 27, 1978, issue of
the *Dallas Morning News* in which he claimed that on
the morning of the assassination, he saw three men on
the overpass bordering †Dealey Plaza. Two of the men

carried long guns, either rifles or shotguns, he couldn't be sure which. No record can be found of the report Hardie said he filed with the FBI directly following the assassination.

📖 *Reasonable Doubt*

HARGIS, BOBBY W.

This Dallas motorcycle patrolman was riding on the left side of the presidential limousine, just a few feet from Mrs. Kennedy, when the shots were fired. The shot that hit the president's head blew portions of his skull and brain matter against Hargis, who testified to the †Warren Commission that the material hit him in the face so hard that at first he thought he had been shot. When he realized what had happened, Hargis stopped his motorcycle and, leaving it running, dismounted and ran in the direction of the wooden fence atop the †Grassy Knoll, where he thought the shots had come from. When he reached the fence, he looked around and was surprised to find nothing. Evidently thinking the gunman had escaped across the railroad tracks, he remounted his motorcycle and sped under the overpass, where once again he found nothing suspicious. Later, Hargis said he thought the shooting had come from behind the president's limousine, a perception that explains neither his immediate response to the shooting

nor the direction from which the material from the
president's head flew when it hit him in the face.
See also BREHM, CHARLES; MARTIN, B. J.
📖 *Crossfire; Rush to Judgment*

HARKNESS, D. V.

Dallas police sergeant Harkness testified to the †Warren
Commission that after the shooting, he ran to the rear
of the †Texas School Book Depository Building toward
the railroad yard. Behind the building, he encountered
a group of men who identified themselves as †Secret
Service agents. The Secret Service denies that any of its
agents were posted in the area of †Dealey Plaza when
the motorcade passed through; they were all said to be
in vehicles in the motorcade. Harkness's report of
encountering Secret Service agents where none were
supposed to be is just one among many such reports.
Harkness was also the officer who searched the boxcars
that were about to depart the railyard behind the
†Grassy Knoll and discovered and arrested the three
†hoboes whose identities, presence near the
assassination scene, and premature release by the
Dallas police have aroused such controversy.
See also HILL, JEAN; SMITH, L. C.; SECRET SERVICE
AGENTS, UNKNOWN.
📖 *On the Trail of the Assassins*

HARPER BONE FRAGMENT
On the evening of Saturday, November 23, 1963, the
day after the assassination, a college student named
William Allen Harper found a piece of bone in the
grassy area to the left of Elm Street, opposite the
†Grassy Knoll. He took it to his uncle, Jack Harper, a
doctor at Methodist Hospital in Dallas, who gave it to
the hospital's chief pathologist, Dr. A. B. Cairns.
Cairns—and, reportedly, other doctors—identified it
as a piece of bone from the rear of a human skull. (Yet
others who have seen the fragment have been less
certain.) The bone was turned over to FBI agent
James †Anderton, who, at the instruction of assistant
FBI director Alan Belmont, forwarded it to the FBI lab
in Washington despite a †Secret Service request that it
be sent to the White House. According to some
investigators, the difficulty of matching the fragment
to a precise location in President Kennedy's skull
indicates that the head wound was altered.
See also ANGEL, DR. LAWRENCE; HEAD WOUND
CONTROVERSY.
📖 *Best Evidence*

HARRELSON, CHARLES V.
On September 1, 1980, reputed Mafia hitman Charles

Harrelson was arrested for the ambush killing of U.S. district court judge John H. Wood, Jr., of San Antonio, Texas. During the six hours he held off Texas law officers, Harrelson reportedly admitted not only killing Wood but also participating in the assassination of President Kennedy. Indicted along with Harrelson in Judge Wood's murder was Joe Marcello, brother of New Orleans Mafia boss Carlos †Marcello. During interviews with several reporters and assassination researchers, Harrelson, who is in federal prison in Texarkana, has played coy about his involvement in the Kennedy assassination. Several researchers, including Fort Worth graphics expert Jack †White, are convinced that Harrelson was one of the three †hoboes arrested near the scene of the shooting and then quickly released following the assassination.
📖 *Crossfire; Mafia Kingfish*

HARTMAN, WAYNE AND EDNA
Interviewed in 1986 by author Jim †Marrs, the Hartmans claim that immediately after the shooting, they ran to the grassy area on the south side of Elm Street, opposite the †Grassy Knoll. A police officer told them shots had been fired at the president from the area across the street, pointing to the Grassy Knoll. Then

Edna saw two parallel mounds on the ground and asked if they were from moles. The officer is said to have responded, "Oh no, ma'am, that's where the bullets struck the ground." The Hartmans contacted the FBI and told their story, emphasizing that the two mounds pointed toward the Grassy Knoll. Marrs claims that the FBI reports the Hartmans as saying the mounds pointed toward the †Texas School Book Depository Building.
See also FOSTER, J. W.
📖 *Crossfire*

HATHAWAY, PHILIP B.
A few minutes before noon on November 22, 1963, Hathaway and a coworker, John Lawrence, were walking toward Main Street, hoping to find a good spot from which to watch the presidential motorcade, when Hathaway spotted a man carrying a cloth-and-leather rifle case that seemed to be packed with a long gun. He described the man, whom he took to be a †Secret Service agent, as approximately six feet five inches tall, thick in the chest, and weighing more than 250 pounds. Hathaway said the mysterious rifleman appeared to be in his early thirties, had dirty-blond crew-cut hair, and was wearing a gray business suit. Lawrence also saw the man, but, because of the press

of the crowd, he failed to see the rifle case.
See also OWENS, ERNEST JAY.
📖 *Crossfire*

HAYGOOD, CLYDE A.

Haygood, a Dallas police motorcycle officer, was still on Main Street at the tail end of the motorcade when he heard the shooting. He immediately raced his motorcycle to the corner of Houston Street, turned right and then left on Elm. Upon seeing numerous police officers and civilians running up the †Grassy Knoll, he parked his motorcycle and followed, but found nothing suspicious. After speaking to a man he believed was a railroad detective, Haygood returned to his motorcycle. He was then approached by James T. †Tague, a witness whose testimony contributed to the formulation of the †single bullet theory. Tague told Haygood he was standing on the curb separating Main and Commerce streets, directly opposite the Grassy Knoll, when a piece of concrete flew up from the curb and hit his face, causing a small cut that was still bleeding. Deputy Sheriff Eddy †Walthers then accompanied Tague to the spot where he had been standing to look for bullet marks. Haygood was also approached by an unidentified man who told him the first shot had been fired from the †Texas School Book Depository Building. Haygood

immediately radioed this information to the police
dispatcher. Other police officers were also directed to the
Depository Building by an unknown witness.
See also BREWER, E. D.; HARGIS, BOBBY W.
📖 *Best Evidence; Crossfire*

HEAD WOUND CONTROVERSY

When the president was examined at †Parkland
Memorial Hospital in Dallas, his head wound was
described as located at the rear of the skull. Dr.
Charles †Carrico estimated the size of the wound at
2 to 2 ¾ inches across. During the autopsy at
†Bethesda Naval Hospital Dr. Thornton †Boswell
prepared a drawing of the skull showing the wound
reaching much higher across the top, with
measurements noted at 3.9 by 6.7 inches. In addition,
three individuals at Parkland reported seeing a bullet
wound in the president's left temple: Father Oscar
†Huber, Dr. Marion †Jenkins, and Dr. Robert N.
†McClelland. McClelland mentioned this left temple
wound as the cause of death in his hospital report.
The conflicting descriptions of the head wound have
led some researchers to believe that the wound was
altered between Parkland and Bethesda in order to
cover up the real direction from which the fatal shot
came. They believe that conspirators may have

changed the wound's placement and enlarged it to
make it plausible that both the bullet's entry and exit
occurred toward the rear of the head, rather than that
the bullet entered the front of the head or the right
side (i.e., the side toward the †Grassy Knoll).
See also AUTOPSY CONTROVERSY; TEMPLE WOUND
CONTROVERSY; THROAT WOUND CONTROVERSY.
📖 *Best Evidence*

HEINDEL, JOHN R.

Heindel said he had known Lee Harvey †Oswald while
both were in the Marines, and that many of his Marine
buddies called him by the nickname "Hidell." This may
be the source of one of Oswald's known aliases.
See also ALIASES USED BY OSWALD.
📖 *Conspiracy; Rush to Judgment*

HELMS, RICHARD

Helms served in the †Central Intelligence Agency as
deputy director in charge of covert operations,
including assassinations (1962–1965), and as director
(1966–1973). He was convicted of lying to a Senate
committee. Helms was the CIA liaison with the
†Warren Commission and has come under heavy fire
from many assassination researchers who charge that
he did everything within his power to hinder the

CIA director Richard Helms

investigation. When asked by the †House Select Committee on Assassinations why the CIA did not interview Lee Harvey †Oswald when he returned to the United States after having defected to the Soviet Union, Helms replied that "military officers" were under the jurisdiction of Defense Department intelligence agencies. Oswald, however, was never an officer in the Marines. The widespread belief that Oswald was employed by the CIA is supported in part by an FBI memorandum turned up by the Assassinations Committee. The memo states, "We did not know definitely whether or not he had any intelligence assignments at that time."
📖 *High Treason; Plausible Denial; Reasonable Doubt*

HEMMING, GERRY PATRICK

A former CIA agent who had once worked with supporters of Fidel †Castro before the success of Castro's revolution in Cuba, Hemming later joined in support of anti-Castro forces. According to defense testimony provided by Marita †Lorenz during the libel suit brought by E. Howard †Hunt against †*Spotlight* magazine, Hemming was one of a group of men assigned to kill President Kennedy. Lorenz's testimony also fingered Hunt and Frank †Sturgis as being other members of this assassination squad. Hemming is also alleged to have

Gerry Patrick Hemming

been Lee Harvey †Oswald's sergeant during the time Oswald was stationed in Japan at †Atsugi Air Base.

Hemming is alleged to have told Anthony Summers, author of †*Conspiracy*, that he met Oswald outside the Cuban consulate in Los Angeles in January 1959. Summers reports that Hemming claimed that Oswald was attempting to gain access to representatives of Castro's government and that he suspected Oswald was working for either an American intelligence or law enforcement agency.

📖 *Conspiracy*

HENCHCLIFFE, MARGARET

Henchcliffe, a nurse with extensive experience in dealing with bullet wounds, was in the emergency room at †Parkland Memorial Hospital when the president was brought in following the shooting. She described the hole in Kennedy's throat as the size of the tip of her little finger and identified it as "an entrance bullet hole." When asked by †Warren Commission assistant counsel Arlen †Specter if it could have been a bullet exit wound, she said she had never seen an exit wound "that looked like that."

See also PARKLAND MEMORIAL HOSPITAL STAFF; TRACHEOTOMY.

📖 *Best Evidence*; *High Treason*

HENDERSON, RUBY

Ruby Henderson reports that a few minutes before the president's motorcade arrived in †Dealey Plaza, she saw two men at an upper-floor window of the †Texas School Book Depository Building. She thought one man might have been a Mexican because his skin was dark in color.

See also DARK-COMPLEXIONED MAN (OR MEN); EUINS, AMOS L.; POWELL, JOHN; ROWLAND, ARNOLD; WALTHER, CAROLYN.

📖 *Conspiracy*

HESS, JACQUELINE

Jacqueline Hess was in charge of the "mysterious deaths project" of the †House Select Committee on Assassinations. She developed a list of twenty-one people connected in some way to the assassination and its aftermath who died under mysterious circumstances.

📖 *High Treason*

HICKEY, GEORGE

†Secret Service agent Hickey was riding in the car directly behind the president's limousine when the shots were fired. In some photos taken at the time, Hickey can be seen standing on the car's running

board or sitting atop the rear deck. Bonar Menninger, the author of a book titled *Mortal Error: The Shot That Killed JFK* (St. Martin's, 1992), which is based on the work of ballistics expert Howard †Donahue, charges that Hickey accidentally fired the fatal shot that struck Kennedy's head. Although Hickey never answered the book's publisher's requests to respond to *Mortal Error*'s allegations, Secret Service agent Samuel †Kinney denied that Hickey had fired a shot.
📖 *Mortal Error*

HICKS, JIM
Hicks is suspected by some assassination researchers of holding open a radio-transmitting microphone during the assassination in an attempt to disrupt police communications so as to give the assassins time to escape. Hicks's fate is difficult to establish. A CIA photo taken of a man in †Mexico City that is supposed to be Lee Harvey †Oswald is said by researchers Robert J. †Groden and Harrison Edward †Livingstone to strongly resemble Hicks.
📖 *High Treason*

HIDELL, ALEK JAMES
Alek James Hidell (also "A. Hidell") was one of the †aliases used by Oswald.

HILL, CLINTON

A †Secret Service agent, Hill is familiar from films as well as photographs taken during the assassination that show him rushing toward the presidential limousine after the first shot, mounting the rear step plate on the bumper, and pushing Mrs. Kennedy off the rear deck, where she had crawled in pursuit of a skull fragment, and back into the relatively safer passenger seat. Hill later testified that he saw that a portion of Kennedy's head had been blown away and lay on the rear seat. Many experts say that this fatal injury is more consistent with a gunshot to the front of the head, not to the rear as the †Warren Commission concluded. Hill testified to the Commission that the wound in the president's back was six inches below the neckline, and that "a portion of [his] head on the right rear side was missing."

See also HEAD WOUND CONTROVERSY; THROAT WOUND CONTROVERSY.

📖 *Best Evidence*

HILL, GERALD L.

Dallas police sergeant Hill was one of the officers who arrested Lee Harvey †Oswald for shooting Police Officer J. D. †Tippit. He told an NBC television interviewer that Oswald refused to identify himself.

Hill said he was identified by items inside his billfold. The arresting officers radioed to the dispatcher that they had arrested "one Lee Harvey Oswald." This immediate identification of the suspect as Oswald has led many to question the allegation that at the time of his arrest, Oswald carried identification naming himself as A. Hidell, the name that links him with the rifle allegedly found in the †Texas School Book Depository Building. No mention of an identification card with the name Hidell on it was made by Hill or other officers involved in the arrest of Oswald.
See also BENTLEY, PAUL.
📖 *Rush to Judgment*

HILL, JEAN
Jean Hill is famous as the "lady in red" because she wore a red coat the day of the assassination and is clearly visible in many photographs of the event. Hill and her friend Mary †Moorman were in †Dealey Plaza to see a motorcycle police officer whom Hill wanted to date. They were standing across the street from the †Grassy Knoll when the motorcade turned onto Elm Street. Hill stepped forward and called to the president, hoping he would look her way so Moorman could take his picture with her Polaroid camera. As Hill called out the president's name, she heard

gunshots, then saw Kennedy fall back as the fatal bullet struck his head. Hill claims that at least some of the shots she heard came from the Grassy Knoll area, and even recalls seeing a man up there with what appeared to be a gun. After the president's limousine pulled away, Hill raced to the Grassy Knoll and looked around. She was then grabbed by several men, who walked her to the sheriff's office and questioned her about shots hitting the ground where she had been standing. She said that she knew nothing about any such shots but that she had seen a gunman on the Grassy Knoll. Hill also claims to have seen a man whom she was later able to identify as Jack †Ruby in the Dealey Plaza area both before and after the shooting. She coauthored, with Bill Sloan, a book titled *JFK: The Last Dissenting Witness,* published by Pelican in 1992.

See also DEALEY PLAZA WITNESSES.

📖 *Best Evidence*; *Crossfire*

HOBOES, THREE

Minutes after the fatal shots were fired at President Kennedy, Dallas police officers discovered three tramps inside a railroad freight car attached to a train waiting to leave the railyard behind the †Grassy Knoll and the †Texas School Book Depository Building.

Photos taken by press photographers on the scene show the three being taken in for questioning.

Over the years, various researchers have attempted to identify these men and link them to the assassination. Among those who have been alleged to have been disguised as these hoboes are E. Howard †Hunt, Frank †Sturgis, and Charles †Harrelson, but there has been no proof of these allegations. In early 1992, the television program "A Current Affair" claimed to have found the original arrest records for the three men, identifying them as Gus W. †Abrams, Harold †Doyle, and John Forrester †Gedney and saying that they were unconnected to the assassination.
📖 *High Treason 2*

HOBSON, MRS. ALVIN

An employee in the †Texas School Book Depository Building, Mrs. Hobson was on the fourth floor when the shooting took place. She told the FBI she did not think the shots came from her building.
See also TEXAS SCHOOL BOOK DEPOSITORY BUILDING EMPLOYEES.
📖 *Best Evidence*

HOFFA, JIMMY

James R. Hoffa was the national Teamsters Union

president. He reportedly had close ties to Richard M. †Nixon and contributed large amounts of Teamsters money to Nixon's presidential race against John Kennedy. Hoffa hated the Kennedys, especially Robert, who targeted many of Hoffa's †Mafia friends and reportedly voiced threats against them more than once. Hoffa vanished in July 1972 and has never been found. On January 14, 1992, the *New York Post* published an interview with Frank †Ragano, who claimed to be Hoffa's attorney, in which Ragano said that in early 1963 he delivered a message from Hoffa to Mafia bosses Carlos †Marcello and Santos †Trafficante that they had to kill President Kennedy. "This has to be done," Ragano quoted Hoffa as saying. *See also* KENNEDY, ROBERT F.; MCCLELLAN COMMITTEE.

📖 *High Treason*

HOFFMAN, ED

A deaf-mute since birth, Hoffman was among the crowd standing along the Stemmons Freeway waiting for the presidential motorcade to exit †Dealey Plaza. Deciding he wanted a better view of the president, Hoffman was making his way toward the plaza when he saw a man running behind the wooden fence at the top of the †Grassy Knoll. The man, dressed in a dark

business suit, was clutching a rifle, which he threw to
another man, who dismantled it and put it inside a
tool bag. The men went off in different directions.
Hoffman, not having heard the shots because of his
deafness, wondered what was going on until the
presidential limousine sped past him and he glimpsed
the president's bloody body in the back seat. Perhaps
because of his inability to speak, he was unable to get
any police officers on the scene to communicate with
him. Several attempts over the years to tell his story
to the FBI met with no interest, and his own family
advised him to stay out of it. Finally, in 1985,
assassination researcher Jim †Marrs discovered
Hoffman's story.
📖 *Crossfire*

HOLLAND, SAM

A railroad supervisor, Holland was working on the
overpass when he stopped to watch the presidential
motorcade. He stated that the shots came from his
left, and when he looked that way, he saw a puff of
smoke rise behind the wooden fence atop the †Grassy
Knoll. Along with other railroad workers, including
James †Simmons, he ran to the spot and found it
empty. On the ground, impressed in the damp earth,
were hundreds of footprints that looked as if they had

been made by someone (or perhaps more than one person) who was there a long time, pacing back and forth.

See also JOHNSON, CLEMMON; MILLER, AUSTIN; REILLY, FRANK; SMOKE FROM THE GRASSY KNOLL.
📖 *Reasonable Doubt*

HOLMES, HARRY D.

Holmes was the postal inspector for the Dallas Post Office in 1963. He testified that Oswald had rented a postal box but that it had been closed on May 14, 1963. He said postal regulations require that when a box is closed, the portion of the box application that lists names of persons other than the applicant who are authorized to receive mail at the box be destroyed. This meant he could not tell the †Warren Commission whether A. Hidell, the name used to order the alleged assassination weapon, was authorized to receive mail at the box to which the rifle was sent. Holmes was wrong. Postal regulations require that the entire application remain on file for two years after a box is closed. The *New York Times* of November 30, 1963, quotes Holmes as saying that no one other than Oswald was authorized to receive mail at the box he had rented. If this was true, why was mail addressed to A. Hidell put in Oswald's postal box?

See also ALIASES USED BY OSWALD; POST OFFICE
BOX 2915.
📖 *Rush to Judgment*

HOOVER, J. EDGAR

Hoover has come under fire from assassination
researchers because he consistently supported the
idea that Lee Harvey †Oswald was the sole assassin
and that he was not part of a larger conspiracy. Few
assassination researchers have implicated Hoover or
the †Federal Bureau of Investigation in President
Kennedy's assassination. One exception is Texas
attorney Mark North, who wrote a book on the
subject, *Act of Treason: The Role of J. Edgar Hoover in
the Assassination of President Kennedy,* published in
1992 by Carroll & Graf.
📖 *High Treason*

HOSTY, JAMES

Hosty was an FBI agent in the Bureau's Dallas office.
During the weeks prior to the assassination, he made
several routine visits to the home of Ruth †Paine,
where Marina †Oswald was living with her children.
He said he wanted to speak with Lee Harvey †Oswald,
and asked how he could get in touch with him. He was
given the address of the †Texas School Book

President John F. Kennedy, with his brother, Attorney General Robert F. Kennedy, and FBI director J. Edgar Hoover

Depository Building, where Lee worked. When Oswald learned of the visits, he slipped into a dark mood and sought out Hosty at the FBI office. Upon learning that Hosty was not in, Oswald left a note for him in which he told the agent to stop bothering his wife or he would report the visits to "the proper authorities." Hosty thought little of the note and left it in his work tray. Soon after Oswald was murdered, Hosty claims his superior, Special Agent-in-Charge L. Gordon †Shanklin of the Dallas office, ordered him to destroy the note, which he did. Although Shanklin denies this, few believe him. Hosty was later disciplined, perhaps for talking too much about Oswald.
□ *Conspiracy; Plausible Denial*

HOUSE SELECT COMMITTEE ON ASSASSINATIONS
The Committee was established in 1976 to look into the assassinations of President Kennedy and civil rights leader Martin Luther King, Jr. From the beginning, the Committee was hampered by the fact that most of its appointed members were young congressmen who had little power on Capitol Hill. An effort to include investigations of the murder of Robert F. †Kennedy and the attempted murder of Alabama governor George Wallace was rejected.

The Committee went through a series of changes

and turmoil among its members and staff, but in the end actually accomplished more than the †Warren Commission had done in seeking the truth. The Committee concluded that there was a conspiracy to kill the president. It placed the blame on organized crime, a favorite target of its second chief counsel, G. Robert †Blakey (who replaced Richard †Sprague). Many believe Blakey had ties too close to the CIA to permit an objective investigation of that agency's potential involvement in the assassination. The Committee concluded that four shots were fired at the president, not the three the Warren Commission claimed. At least one Committee member, Congressman Christopher Dodd, said he believed the evidence indicated that three gunmen fired at the president.

Many assassination researchers criticize the Committee's work. Its report, issued in January 1979, differed from the Warren Commission's findings. Without a doubt it left much undone, but it did take a small step toward finding the truth. Critics of both the Warren Commission and the House Select Committee wonder whether it is possible for a body representing the federal government to conduct an impartial investigation of an assassination in which agencies of that government appear to have played a role.

See also ACOUSTICAL EVIDENCE; GONZALEZ, HENRY.
□ *High Treason*

HOWARD, LAWRENCE
See ODIO INCIDENT.

HUBER, OSCAR
A Catholic priest from nearby Holy Trinity Church in
Dallas, Father Huber administered the last rites to
President Kennedy in the †Parkland Memorial
Hospital emergency room. He has been quoted as
saying that he saw a "terrible wound" over Kennedy's
left eye.
See also JENKINS, DR. MARION; MCCLELLAND, DR.
ROBERT N.; SHAW, DR. ROBERT; TEMPLE WOUND
CONTROVERSY.
□ *Best Evidence*

HUDKINS, LONNIE
As early as January 1964, rumors surfaced that Lee
Harvey †Oswald had been connected in some way to a
U.S. government intelligence agency. Lonnie Hudkins
was the author of an article published in the *Houston
Post* on New Year's Day containing information that
Oswald had been an informant for the FBI. When
confronted with this, the †Warren Commission

discussed the question of what to do about the allegations, but ultimately made no genuine effort to uncover the truth.

📖 *Rush to Judgment*

HUDSON, EMMETT J.

A member of the crew that maintained the grounds at †Dealey Plaza, Hudson was seated on the steps leading to the top of the †Grassy Knoll when the president was shot. He told a †Warren Commission attorney that the shots came "from above and behind" him, which clearly indicates the wooden picket fence at the top of the knoll. Jim †Marrs's reading of his testimony led Marrs to the conclusion that the Commission attorney who questioned Hudson swayed him from identifying the knoll as the source of the shots and led him to respond in the affirmative when asked if he thought they came from the †Texas School Book Depository Building.

📖 *Crossfire*

HUFF, LARRY

See CAMP SMITH.

HUGHES, ROBERT

Hughes was standing at the southwest corner of

Houston and Elm streets filming the motorcade as it turned from Houston onto Elm. His filming included scanning the front of the ⁺Texas School Book Depository Building. Several photographic experts who viewed the film believe it shows two people at the sixth-floor windows of the building as the motorcade passed. The ⁺Warren Commission asked the FBI to examine the film. The FBI report stated that the image some believed were two men was "probably a stack of boxes." The Warren Commission, evidently seeking to bolster its ⁺lone assassin theory, changed the word "probably" to a much more definitive "determined . . . to be the shadow from the cartons near the window." The Hughes film remains one of the more controversial pieces of evidence in the assassination investigation.

See also BRONSON FILM; SELZER, ROBERT.

📖 *Rush to Judgment*

HUMES, DR. JAMES J.

U.S. Navy pathologist Commander Humes conducted the autopsy on the president's body at ⁺Bethesda Naval Hospital. Humes has come under fire from every critic of the ⁺Warren Report. He admits burning the first draft of his autopsy report, which many consider highly unethical and indicative of serious differences between the original findings and certain vital points in the final report. Humes is the only doctor present at the autopsy who claims to have seen a bullet entry wound in the rear of the president's head.

See also AUTOPSY CONTROVERSY; HEAD WOUND CONTROVERSY; LUNDBERG, DR. GEORGE.

📖 *Best Evidence*

HUNT, E. HOWARD

A CIA agent, E. Howard Hunt gained national notoriety in 1973 for his role in the infamous Watergate scandal that ultimately brought down Richard M †Nixon's presidency. In a 1985 libel trial that was virtually ignored by the media, Hunt sued the publication †*Spotlight* over an article it published implicating him in the Kennedy assassination. The jury found for *Spotlight,* and the jury foreperson, Leslie †Armstrong, offered the opinion that the evidence had convinced her that the CIA had killed Kennedy and that Hunt had played a role in the conspiracy. The trial was the centerpiece of defense attorney Mark †Lane's 1991 best-seller, †*Plausible Denial,* published by Thunder's Mouth Press.

Hunt was the agent in charge of the CIA station in †Mexico City in September 1963, when Lee Harvey †Oswald allegedly visited the Soviet and Cuban

E. Howard Hunt

embassies there, ostensibly to arrange for his return
to the Soviet Union.
📖 Plausible Denial

HUNT, H. L.
At the time of the assassination, H. L. Hunt was
reputed to be the richest man in America, perhaps the
world. He appeared to have close ties to both the FBI
and the CIA, and was a strong supporter of right-wing
causes. His son Nelson Bunker †Hunt is said to have
partially underwritten the cost of an anti-Kennedy
newspaper advertisement that appeared in the *Dallas
Morning News* the day of the assassination. Hunt's oil
profits were said to be threatened by Kennedy's
announced plans to end the oil depletion allowance. A
note written by Lee Harvey †Oswald addressed to "Mr.
Hunt" has raised speculation as to whether it was
intended for the oil tycoon, one of his sons, or the CIA
agent E. Howard †Hunt.
See also AMERICAN FACT-FINDING COMMITTEE.
📖 *High Treason; Texas Connection*

HUNT, DR. JACKIE
Dr. Hunt was in the emergency room at †Parkland
Memorial Hospital when the president was brought in
after the shooting. She never saw the back of Kennedy's

head because he was lying on his back while she looked at him. She stood directly over him. She rejected the veracity of the photograph from the autopsy showing a wound reaching across the top of the president's head because she said she would have seen that from where she stood. The wound described to her by doctors who had seen it was in the rear of the head only.

📖 *High Treason*

HUNT, NELSON BUNKER

Son of H. L. †Hunt, Nelson was one of a small group of people who paid to place a full-page anti-Kennedy advertisement in the *Dallas Morning News* the day of the assassination.

See also AMERICAN FACT-FINDING COMMITTEE.

📖 *Texas Connection*

HUTTON, PATRICIA

Nurse Patricia Hutton (married name, Gustafson) was one of the first †Parkland Memorial Hospital staff members to reach President Kennedy when his limousine arrived there. She attempted unsuccessfully to place a compress on the head wound. She described the wound as the size of a fist and at the back of the head, an account that does not agree with the autopsy report.

📖 *High Treason*

INGRAM, HIRAM

A deputy sheriff in Dallas, Ingram was a close friend
of Deputy Sheriff Roger D. †Craig's. Researchers
Robert J. †Groden and Harrison Edward †Livingstone
allege that Ingram died under mysterious
circumstances following a fall that broke his hip and
report that Ingram claimed he knew there had been a
conspiracy to kill the president.
📖 *High Treason*

IRVING SPORTS SHOP

Located on Irving Boulevard in Irving, Texas, a Dallas
suburb, the Irving Sports Shop was brought into the
investigation when, at 6:30 P.M. on Sunday, November
24, 1963, an anonymous male caller told an FBI agent
in the Bureau's Dallas office that Lee Harvey †Oswald
had had a rifle sighted, or prepared for the mounting
of a sight, at the shop. Similar calls were received by
the Dallas police and a local television station.

Acting on this information, FBI agents visited the shop the next day and found a repair tag indicating that a rifle had been sighted for a customer named "Oswald." The man who did the work, Dial D. Ryder, claimed he never worked on an Italian-manufactured rifle similar to the one allegedly found in the †Texas School Book Depository Building. Further, the ticket indicated that three holes were drilled in the rifle to mount the sight, while the rifle alleged to be Oswald's required only two holes for the mount. Speculation has escalated that an impersonator using Oswald's name had a rifle sighted at the shop, then later tipped off the FBI and police to lead them to this "evidence" against Oswald.

📖 *Conspiracy; Rush to Judgment*

ITEK CORPORATION

Itek is a company that processes and analyzes photographs and films. In 1966, United Press International was asked to examine a film of the assassination made by Orville †Nix, who recorded the events from a section of †Dealey Plaza facing the †Grassy Knoll. Some investigators claim that the film, which shows the Grassy Knoll in the background at the moment Kennedy was shot, reveals light flashes and the image of a gunman. Scientists at Itek, who were consulted by UPI, concluded that the image was actually the shadow of a tree. Itek, through contractual agreements, has links to the CIA and other government agencies.

📖 *Crossfire*

JACKS, HURCHEL

Texas state highway patrolman Jacks drove Vice
President Lyndon B. †Johnson's car in the motorcade
and raced to the hospital behind Kennedy's limousine.
Jacks claimed to have gotten a good look at the
president's head wound before a †Secret Service agent
covered Kennedy's head with a jacket. In a state police
report dated November 28, 1963, Jacks claimed it
appeared to him that a bullet had hit Kennedy "above
the right ear or near the temple." He also said the
Secret Service assigned him to prevent anyone from
taking pictures of the presidential limousine while it
was parked outside †Parkland Memorial Hospital.
See also NEWMAN FAMILY; SITZMAN, MARILYN.
📖 *Best Evidence; High Treason*

JACKSON, ROBERT H.

A photographer for the *Dallas Times-Herald,* Jackson
is reported to have claimed that immediately after the
shots were fired, he saw a rifle barrel disappear into a

window on an upper floor of the †Texas School Book
Depository Building. In an unusual departure from
scientific method, the surgeon in charge of Kennedy's
autopsy at †Bethesda Naval Hospital, Dr. James J.
†Humes, referred to Jackson's report in his autopsy
report (autopsy reports generally do not include such
nonmedical information).
📖 *Best Evidence*

JAGGERS-CHILES-STOVALL

This Dallas graphic arts company did top-secret work
for the military, including processing photographs
taken by the †U-2 spy planes that regularly flew
surveillance missions over Soviet territory. Lee Harvey
†Oswald worked at this company for six months
following his return from the Soviet Union. It has been
alleged that the job was arranged by Oswald's friend
George †DeMohrenschildt, a CIA informant. When
Oswald was arrested following the shooting of J. D.
†Tippit, he was said to be carrying a Dallas Public
Library card that included his employer's name,
Jaggers-Chiles-Stovall, and the name Jack L. Bowen.
See also BOWEN, JOHN "JACK."
📖 *Conspiracy*

JARMAN, JAMES, JR.

An employee in the †Texas School Book Depository
Building, James Jarman, Jr., was one of three black
men whom several people on the street below said
they saw at the fifth-floor windows (directly below the
so-called †sniper's nest) either immediately before or
during the shooting. When asked by †Warren
Commission member Gerald †Ford where he thought
the shots came from, Jarman answered, "from below,"
not from above.
See also CARTER, WILLIAM N.; NORMAN, HAROLD D.;
WILLIAMS, BONNIE RAY.
📖 *Rush to Judgment*

JAWORSKI, LEON

Jaworski, who later gained national celebrity as the
special prosecutor appointed by Richard M. †Nixon in
the Watergate scandal, was asked by the †Warren
Commission to investigate rumors that Lee Harvey
†Oswald had ties to either the †Federal Bureau of
investigation or the †Central Intelligence Agency.
Jaworski reported that his investigation had
uncovered no such relationships.
📖 *High Treason*

JENKINS, JAMES CURTIS
James Curtis Jenkins was one of two technicians (the other was Paul K. †O'Connor) who removed Kennedy's body from its coffin before the autopsy at †Bethesda Naval Hospital. Jenkins has said that the official autopsy report does not describe what he saw. He reports that he was in the room during the entire procedure and recalls seeing damage to the president's head near his right ear, leading him to believe there might be a bullet entry wound in that location. According to some reports, he also claimed that the president's head was wrapped in towels when the body was removed from the coffin in which it had arrived. The nurses at †Parkland Memorial Hospital claim no towels were placed inside the coffin before it was closed and taken away. The discrepancies between descriptions of the body, its wrapping, and the coffin when they left Parkland and when they arrived at Bethesda have led some investigators to conclude that the president's body was tampered with during the trip from Dallas to Washington or while the body lay in wait at Bethesda for the autopsy to be performed. *See also* AMBULANCE CONTROVERSY; AUTOPSY CONTROVERSY; BODY BAG CONTROVERSY; X-RAY CONTROVERSY.
📖 *Best Evidence*; *High Treason 2*

JENKINS, DR. MARION

Like the reactions and observations of many of the other doctors who worked on President Kennedy at †Parkland Memorial Hospital, those of Dr. Jenkins immediately following the experience are of vital importance to anyone desiring the truth about Kennedy's wounds. Jenkins, an anesthesiologist, is reported as saying that while he was checking for the president's pulse, he felt the wound on Kennedy's left temple. This is probably the same wound that Father Oscar †Huber alluded to.

See also HEAD WOUND CONTROVERSY; MCCLELLAND, DR. ROBERT N.; TEMPLE WOUND CONTROVERSY.

📖 *High Treason*

JFK

Directed by Oliver †Stone, and starring Kevin Costner as New Orleans district attorney Jim †Garrison, this film was released in 1991. Even before it was completed, the film and its director came under heavy and intense attack by the establishment press. In a manner that mixes fact and fiction, the film follows the investigation of Garrison through the end of the trial of Clay †Shaw. It is based on Garrison's book *On the Trail of the Assassins* (Warner, 1991), and on Jim †Marrs's book, *Crossfire:*

The Plot That Killed Kennedy (Carroll & Graf, 1989),
as well as on other, uncredited sources.

JOHNSEN, RICHARD

Secret Service agent Johnsen was given a bullet
allegedly found on a stretcher at †Parkland Memorial
Hospital by Darrel C. †Tomlinson. This was at
approximately 2:00 P.M. on the day of the assassination. Johnsen returned to Washington aboard †*Air
Force One* with the president's body and entourage. At
7:30 P.M., he turned the bullet over to Secret Service
chief James J. †Rowley, who sent it to the FBI
laboratory. This became the famous †magic bullet that
allegedly wounded both Kennedy and Governor John
†Connally. Its origin is still a clouded issue.
📖 *Best Evidence*

JOHNSON, CLEMMON

A railroad worker, Johnson watched the presidential
limousine make its way through †Dealey Plaza from the
railroad overpass directly in front of and above the
motorcade. He reported seeing white †smoke from the
area of the †Grassy Knoll just after the shots were fired.
See also HOLLAND, SAM; MILLER, AUSTIN; REILLY,
FRANK; SIMMONS, JAMES.
📖 *Best Evidence*

JOHNSON, LADY BIRD

Wife of Vice President Lyndon B. †Johnson, Lady Bird (Claudia Alta Taylor Johnson) rode with her husband in the motorcade. At †Parkland Memorial Hospital, she attempted to console Mrs. Kennedy while doctors worked to save the president's life. Mrs. Johnson witnessed her husband's swearing in as president aboard †*Air Force One,* and returned with him to Washington.

📖 *Death of a President*

JOHNSON, LYNDON B.

Some assassination researchers identify Vice President Johnson as the man with the most to gain by Kennedy's death. He knew he was in jeopardy of being dumped from the Democratic party ticket by the president and reportedly had a strong personal hatred for Kennedy because he had beaten Johnson badly in the contest for the 1960 Democratic presidential nomination. According to Madeline †Brown, a woman alleged to be Johnson's mistress at the time of the assassination, Johnson knew about the plot to kill Kennedy before it happened. Craig I. Zirbel's best-selling 1991 book, *The Texas Connection: The Assassination of President John F. Kennedy,* is devoted exclusively to the supposition "that Vice President

Lyndon B. Johnson was involved" in the conspiracy to kill President Kennedy. During his years in the White House, Johnson is variously reported to have voiced the opinion that responsibility for the assassination belonged to †Castro, the †Central Intelligence Agency, or supporters of South Vietnam president †Ngo Dinh Diem, who had been murdered three weeks earlier at what many believed were the orders of President Kennedy.

See also VIETNAM WAR.

📖 *Best Evidence*; *Conspiracy*; *High Treason*

JOHNSON, PRISCILLA

A journalist who interviewed Lee Harvey †Oswald when he was in the Soviet Union in 1959, Johnson became Marina †Oswald's biographer after the assassination. Johnson's relationship with Marina Oswald came to wide attention because she was with Marina when the latter discovered the bus ticket stubs that contributed to the belief, now in disrepute, that Oswald had traveled to †Mexico City for meetings at the Soviet and/or Cuban embassies there. Johnson's husband, George McMillan, later wrote a book about the assassination of Martin Luther King, Jr. (*The Making of an Assassin: The Life of James Earl Ray*, Little, Brown, 1976), that Mark †Lane asserts contains

fabricated information fed to McMillan by the FBI.
📖 *Plausible Denial*

JONES, MILTON R.
Sixteen-year-old Milton Jones was a passenger on a
Dallas bus just after the time of the assassination on
November 22, 1963. The †Warren Commission reported
that when Lee Harvey †Oswald left the †Texas School
Book Depository Building, he boarded a westbound
bus on Elm Street, asked the driver, Cecil J.
†McWatters, for a transfer, and got off a few blocks
later. Investigators identified the driver based on a
bus transfer allegedly found in Oswald's pocket when
he was arrested. McWatters was asked about the
passenger. He said a man did board his bus at Elm
and Murphy streets, and when McWatters told him
the president had been shot, the man smiled. This
remark led to headlines about "The Smiling Assassin."
McWatters later identified Oswald in a lineup as
resembling a passenger on his bus, but not the man
who asked for the transfer. The following day, when
Milton Jones boarded McWatters's bus, the driver
recognized him as the passenger who had asked for
the transfer and had smiled at the news that Kennedy
had been shot.
📖 *Rush to Judgment*

JONES, ROBERT

In 1963, Army Lieutenant Colonel Jones was the operations officer for the 112th Military Intelligence Group headquartered near San Antonio, Texas. It was not widely known at the time that military intelligence agents were on duty in Dallas the day of the assassination. Jones testified that when he heard news of the assassination, he contacted his agents in Dallas for information and was told that an A. J. Hidell had been arrested. Cross-checking military intelligence files, he identified the name Hidell as an alias used by Lee Harvey †Oswald. He called the Dallas FBI office with this information and spoke to Agent-in-Charge L. Gordon †Shanklin, who has been accused of giving the order to destroy a note written to one of his agents by Oswald. When investigators for the †House Select Committee on Assassinations asked to see the files Jones referred to, they were told the files had been destroyed five years earlier as a matter of "routine."

See also ALIASES USED BY OSWALD; HOSTY, JAMES.
📖 *Conspiracy*

JONES, DR. RONALD

A senior surgical resident at †Parkland Memorial Hospital, Dr. Jones was among the first doctors to see

Kennedy when he was brought into the emergency room. He testified that the wound in the president's throat was an entry wound, not an exit wound. If correct, this means Kennedy was shot from the front. Dr. Jones described the wound as "very small and relatively clean-cut as you would see in a bullet that is entering rather than exiting from a patient." Jones has been described as having worked on more than one hundred victims of gunshot wounds in the five years preceding President Kennedy's assassination. *See also* THROAT WOUND CONTROVERSY; TRACHEOTOMY.

📖 *Best Evidence*; *High Treason 2*

KANTOR, SETH

The author of *The Ruby Cover-up* (Zebra Books, 2nd printing, 1992; originally titled *Who Was Jack Ruby?*), Kantor is a rarity among assassination writers because he was in the motorcade that day and was present later at †Parkland Memorial Hospital while the president's body was still there. Formerly a reporter for the *Dallas Times-Herald,* Kantor had known Jack †Ruby well as a source of information. He told the †Warren Commission that he saw Ruby in Parkland Memorial Hospital just minutes before the announcement of the president's death. Kantor claims he not only saw Ruby but spoke briefly with him about what had happened. Ruby denied this, and the Commission chose to discount Kantor's testimony. Kantor was also on the scene when Ruby shot Lee Harvey †Oswald.

See also RUBY AT PARKLAND; TICE, WILMA.

📖 *Rush to Judgment*

KARAMESSINES, TOM

An assistant to CIA director Richard †Helms, Karamessines allegedly wrote a memorandum in 1966 expressing concern that the presence of CIA man E. Howard †Hunt in Dallas the day of the assassination would become known. Hunt denied rumors about this. He even filed suit against Michael L. †Canfield and Alan J. †Weberman, the authors of the book †*Coup d'Etat in America,* who claimed Hunt was one of the †hoboes who were detained by the Dallas police after the shooting.
📖 *High Treason*

KELLERMAN, ROY

†Secret Service agent Kellerman rode in the front passenger seat of the presidential limousine as it crawled through †Dealey Plaza at a pace much slower than the forty-four miles per hour Secret Service regulations required. Kellerman remained with the president at †Parkland Memorial Hospital and was present during the autopsy at †Bethesda Naval Hospital. He reportedly described the wound caused by the †magic bullet, which supposedly entered the lower portion of Kennedy's neck, as "the hole that was in his shoulder."
📖 *Best Evidence*

KENNEDY, JACQUELINE BOUVIER

President John F. Kennedy's attractive wife, "Jackie," as she is affectionately called by the press and the public, rode in the limousine seated next to her husband when he was shot. An extremely popular First Lady, she enjoyed a personal popularity that some say even eclipsed that of her husband. A sorrowing nation shared her bereavement, and the world admired her stately dignity during the president's funeral. Mother of John Kennedy, Jr., and Caroline Kennedy, she later married Greek shipping tycoon Aristotle Onassis and became an editor for the Doubleday Company.

KENNEDY, JOHN F.

Thirty-fifth president of the United States, Kennedy was the first Roman Catholic and the youngest man to hold that office. He was also the fourth president to be murdered in office. The second son of a wealthy Boston family, John distinguished himself in the U.S. Navy in World War II aboard PT boats operating in the Pacific theater. Elected to the Senate as a conservative Democrat in 1952, he married Jacqueline Bouvier the following year. In 1957 he won a Pulitzer Prize for biography for his book *Profiles in Courage*. Defeated by the more liberal Adlai Stevenson forces in his bid for his party's vice-presidential nomination in 1956, he captured the presidential nomination in 1960 and went on to beat Vice President Richard M. †Nixon in the general election by the closest margin in history.

Kennedy's administration was rocked by the failed invasion of Cuba by U.S.-supported Cuban exiles in 1961, known to history as the †Bay of Pigs fiasco. A high point was the confrontation with the Soviet Union over the shipment of missiles to Cuba in 1962, in which Kennedy faced down Soviet dictator Nikita Khrushchev. When he was assassinated, Kennedy was on a tour of major Texas cities to win votes for his reelection campaign the following year among Texas Democrats, who had lost enthusiasm for his administration. Kennedy died at 1:00 P.M. central standard time on November 22, 1963, of a gunshot wound that caused massive damage to his head. He was pronounced dead at †Parkland Memorial Hospital in Dallas, Texas, by Dr. Kemp †Clark. His death was announced by Malcolm †Kilduff.

KENNEDY, REGIS
An FBI agent, Regis Kennedy allegedly confiscated a film of the assassination that later disappeared without, as far as is known, ever being viewed.
See also OLIVER, BETTY.
📖 *High Treason*

KENNEDY, ROBERT F.

Younger brother of John, Robert Kennedy served as
his attorney general and stayed on as Lyndon B.
†Johnson's attorney general until 1964. Robert made
powerful enemies among the leaders of gangster
organizations with his crusade to drive them out of
business. Robert Kennedy was in Washington, D.C.,
on the day of the assassination; he met †*Air Force
One* as it arrived at †Andrews Air Force Base that
evening and accompanied Mrs. Kennedy in the
ambulance to †Bethesda Naval Hospital. Elected to
the Senate from New York in 1965, he was assassinated on June 5, 1968, just after his victory in the
California primary in his race for the Democratic
presidential nomination.

KILDUFF, MALCOLM

Assistant press secretary to President Kennedy,
Kilduff was filling in for Press Secretary Pierre
Salinger during Kennedy's trip to Texas. Kilduff had
the task of announcing to the press and the nation that
the president was dead. Kilduff said that when the
shots were fired, he looked directly up at the †Texas
School Book Depository Building because that was the
location from which he believed they had come.
📖 *High Treason 2*

KILGALLEN, DOROTHY

A nationally known syndicated newspaper columnist and panelist on the celebrated television program "What's My Line?," Kilgallen covered Jack †Ruby's trial, interviewed Ruby, and traveled to both Dallas and New Orleans in quest of the truth about the Kennedy assassination. It was reliably reported that in November 1965 the columnist claimed she was going to blow the Kennedy assassination story "wide open." Within a week, she was found dead under what the New York City medical examiner called "circumstances undetermined." Her death was ultimately termed a suicide, although no real evidence supported this finding.

☵ *High Treason*

KINNEY, SAMUEL

Secret Service agent Kinney was driving the "Queen Mary," the Secret Service follow-up car that was directly behind the presidential limousine. Kinney reportedly said he saw one shot hit the "right side of the head." In late 1991, Kinney wrote to St. Martin's Press, publisher of Bonar Menninger's 1992 book *Mortal Error: The Shot That Killed JFK,* in defense of Secret Service agent George †Hickey, who the book claims accidentally fired the shot that hit Kennedy's head, the fatal shot. Hickey himself did not answer the publisher's request for a response to the book's allegations.

◻ *Best Evidence*; *Mortal Error*

KIRKWOOD, PAT
Kirkwood was the owner of a Fort Worth nightclub, The †Cellar, reportedly visited by †Secret Service agents the night before the assassination. Their drinking lasted until the early morning hours of the day the president was murdered. The consumption of alcohol while on assignment was in direct violation of Secret Service rules, yet no action was taken against these men.

◻ *High Treason*

KLEIN'S SPORTING GOODS COMPANY
A Chicago-based mail-order company, Klein's was asked by the FBI to check its files for an order from a person named Hidell after a coupon from one of the firm's ads in †*American Rifleman* was discovered among Lee Harvey †Oswald's possessions. Klein's reported that it had shipped a †Mannlicher-Carcano rifle with the serial number C2766 to a customer named A. Hidell, at †post office box 2915 in Dallas, Texas. The post office box was one rented by Oswald. The fact that Oswald chose to

order the weapon through the mail, which required giving the seller a name and address for shipping purposes, instead of purchasing one from any of over a dozen stores in Dallas that carried the same rifle and required no identification, has prompted †Warren Commission critics to question why such a paper trail leading directly to the alleged assassin was created.
📖 *High Treason; Reasonable Doubt*

KOSTIKOV, VALERIY VLADIMIRICH

Kostikov was allegedly a KGB agent stationed in †Mexico City in the early 1960s. Reportedly, one of his responsibilities was to initiate or approve assassination plans in the Western Hemisphere. The CIA provided the †Warren Commission with evidence in the form of photos and tape-recorded phone conversations that Lee Harvey †Oswald was one of Kostikov's agents. The implication was that Oswald killed Kennedy on the orders of the Soviet intelligence organization. Critics see the CIA's role in supplying this evidence as a way of covering its own part in the assassination.
📖 *Plausible Denial*

KOUNAS, DOLORES A.

Dolores Kounas was employed by the McGraw-Hill book publishing company, which maintained offices on

the third floor of the †Texas School Book Depository
Building. She testified that she was standing on Elm
Street across from the building when the presidential
motorcade passed. She said she did not look up at the
building when the shots were fired at Kennedy
because it was her impression that they had come
from a location to the west of her position, somewhere
near the overpass, which is in the general direction of
the †Grassy Knoll.
See also DEALEY PLAZA WITNESSES; GRASSY KNOLL
WITNESSES.
□ *Crossfire; Rush to Judgment*

KRAMER, MONICA
Monica Kramer was an American tourist who visited
the Soviet Union during 1961 and met Lee Harvey
†Oswald there twice.
See also NAMAN, RITA.

KUZMUK, WALTER
An officer of the †Central Intelligence Agency, Kuzmuk
testified on behalf of E. Howard †Hunt in the latter's
suit against the publication †*Spotlight,* which
published an article accusing Hunt of being in Dallas
on November 22, 1963, and having a connection to the
assassination. Kuzmuk claimed he lived near Hunt in

the Washington suburbs and drove to work with him almost every day, and that his office was two doors away from Hunt's office. He said that on November 22, he saw Hunt drive past him as he left a Washington restaurant at the time the president was being shot in Dallas. Kuzmuk was unable to testify about Hunt's whereabouts during the last two weeks of November, but he did recall this chance sighting in Washington on that particular day.

📖 *Plausible Denial*

LANDIS, PAUL

[†]Secret Service agent Landis was riding in the car directly behind Kennedy's limousine when the shots were fired. He reported that his reaction to the shot that hit the president's head was that it was fired "from somewhere toward the front, right-hand side of the road." ⊓ *Conspiracy; Crossfire*

LANE, MARK

Attorney Lane was a critic of the [†]Warren Report even before it was published. He has spent almost thirty years pursuing the truth behind the assassination. His works on the subject include books, screenplays, and documentary films. His two most important books are [†]*Rush to Judgment* (1966; reissued, 1992), a detailed critique of the [†]Warren Commission's methods and findings, and [†]*Plausible Denial* (1991), in which he asserts that the CIA was responsible for the assassination of John F. Kennedy. Both books are now published by Thunder's Mouth Press.

Lane represented Lee Harvey [†]Oswald's mother, Marguerite [†]Oswald, before the Warren Commission and attempted, unsuccessfully, to represent the interests of the dead Oswald. He complained that although the Commission had set up panels to investigate *why* Oswald had killed Kennedy, it did not assign anyone to investigate whether it was Oswald who actually shot him.

📖 *Rush to Judgment*

LANZ, PEDRO DIAZ

Lanz was a Cuban pilot who, according to Marita [†]Lorenz, was among a group of men who transported arms to Dallas shortly before the assassination. She also claims she saw Lanz and several others looking over a street map of Dallas before the trip.

See also STURGIS, FRANK.

📖 *High Treason; Plausible Denial*

LATONA, SEBASTIAN FRANCIS

Latona was a fingerprint expert who in 1963 had been employed by the FBI for thirty-two years. On November 23, 1963, he examined the [†]Mannlicher-Carcano rifle that was sent to Washington, allegedly the assassination weapon. He reported that he was unable to find any prints on the rifle that were of any value in identifying the person who had used it. After the rifle was returned to Dallas, a †palmprint belonging to Lee Harvey †Oswald was discovered on it by the Dallas police, a story that was accepted as true by the †Warren Commission.

See also DAY, J. CARL; DRAIN, VINCENT.

📖 *Rush to Judgment*

LATTIMER, DR. JOHN

Dr. Lattimer was the first physician permitted to examine what were alleged to be the autopsy photographs and X rays of President Kennedy's skull. This was done at the National Archives in January 1972. Lattimer told a *New York Times* reporter that what he saw validated the findings of the †Warren Commission. Lattimer was not a pathologist but a urologist (a specialist in the urinary system) and therefore a rather odd choice for the honor he was given. Lattimer's statements concerning the head wounds bothered many doctors, including Dr. Cyril H. †Wecht, who at the time was the president of the American Academy of Forensic Sciences. Wecht called Lattimer "unbelievably unqualified" in the area of forensic pathology, and described him as "a guy who never moves above the belly button."

See also HEAD WOUND CONTROVERSY.

📖 *Best Evidence*; *High Treason 2*

LAWRENCE, JACK

Lawrence was employed by the †Downtown Lincoln-Mercury dealership in Dallas, where Lee Harvey †Oswald allegedly shopped for a car and went for a test drive. Lawrence's job began one month before the assassination, and ended the day following Kennedy's murder. The night before the president was killed, he borrowed a dealership car to drive home and did not report to work on time the next day. He stumbled into work thirty minutes after the shooting, pale, sweating, and with mud on his clothes. He ran into the men's room, where he vomited. When other dealership employees found the car in the parking lot behind the †Grassy Knoll next to the †Texas School Book Depository Building, they called the police. Lawrence was arrested and held for twenty-four hours, then released. It is alleged that Lawrence gave his employer fictitious references when he was hired.
📖 *High Treason*

LAWRENCE, JOHN
See HATHAWAY, PHILIP B.

LAWRENCE, PERDUE
Dallas police captain Perdue Lawrence told the †House Select Committee on Assassinations that the †Secret

Service altered his motorcycle escort pattern for the president's limousine. Lawrence claimed he wanted four motorcycles on each side and slightly to the rear of the car, but Secret Service agent Winston †Lawson declared that that was too many and reduced the number to two on each side.

📖 *High Treason*

LAWSON, WINSTON

Lawson was the †Secret Service agent in charge of planning security for the president's trip to Dallas. In addition to Dallas police captain Perdue †Lawrence's charge that Lawson changed the motorcycle escort, it was also alleged that Lawson prevented the Dallas police from putting a police car in the motorcade. Lawson denied that he had removed the car, claiming he "could not recall" who took the car out of the motorcade. The †House Select Committee on Assassinations found the security precautions for the Dallas visit "uniquely insecure."

📖 *High Treason*

LEAVELLE, JAMES R.

Dallas police detective Leavelle was one of the two men handcuffed to Lee Harvey †Oswald when he was shot by Jack †Ruby. It is reported that Leavelle

objected to taking Oswald through the basement
garage, which was the announced route to the police
car he would ride in to the county jail. Leavelle
suggested that a safer route was straight out the first
floor of the building, which would have permitted
Oswald and his guards to avoid the press and others
who had gathered in the building's basement. His
suggestion was ignored.
See also GRAVES, L. C.; MONTGOMERY, L. D.
📖 *Rush to Judgment*

LEEMANS, FRED

Fred Leemans was interviewed in June 1967 on the
NBC television network broadcast of a "White Paper"
program called "The †Case of Jim Garrison." The show
appeared to many to be an attempt to discredit New
Orleans district attorney Jim †Garrison, who had
brought charges against Clay †Shaw for his alleged
participation in a conspiracy to kill President Kennedy.
Leemans, whom Garrison later identified as the
proprietor of a "Turkish bath" in New Orleans, told a
nationwide audience that the district attorney's office
had offered him $2,500 to testify that Shaw had visited
his Turkish bath in the company of Lee Harvey
†Oswald. Leemans said he decided not to testify because
it would have been immoral. According to Garrison, the

grand jury hearing evidence about the charges against
Shaw decided Leemans's statements were so outlandish
that they did not bother calling him to testify.
□ *On the Trail of the Assassins*

"LEOPOLDO"
See ODIO INCIDENT.

LESTER, DICK
According to news reports, Dallas night watchman
Dick Lester discovered a bullet near the railroad
tracks that pass over †Dealey Plaza. A struggle
reportedly ensued between the FBI and the †House
Select Committee on Assassinations over the Bureau's
request to remove the assassination bullets from the
National Archives to compare them with the bullet
Lester found. The Committee forbade National
Archives personnel to release the bullets.
See also NATIONAL ARCHIVES, DOCUMENTS MISSING
FROM.
□ *High Treason*

LEWIS, L. J.
Lewis was an employee of the Reynolds Motor
Company in the Oak Cliff section of Dallas. Along with
several fellow employees, he witnessed a man running

from the scene of Officer J. D. †Tippit's murder. Lewis said the man was carrying either a pistol or a revolver, which he was attempting to hide behind his belt. The FBI interviewed Lewis on January 21, 1964. When Lewis read the report of that interview, he discovered factual errors, which he corrected and submitted in an affidavit to the †Warren Commission. Lewis could not identify Lee Harvey †Oswald as the man he saw running with a gun in his hand, despite the fact that he had obviously gotten a good look at the gun. *See also* PATTERSON, B. M.; REYNOLDS, WARREN. 📖 *Rush to Judgment*

LIBERTY LOBBY
Liberty Lobby is the right-wing organization that publishes †*Spotlight* magazine.

LIEBELER, WESLEY J.
An assistant counsel for the †Warren Commission and a professor at UCLA Law School, Liebeler is a primary character in David S. †Lifton's investigation of the assassination, †*Best Evidence.* His association with Lifton evidently helped Liebler change his mind about various aspects of the medical evidence contained in the †Warren Report.
📖 *Best Evidence*

LIFTON, DAVID S.

David S. Lifton is an assassination researcher and the author of the 1980 best-selling book †*Best Evidence: Disguise and Deception in the Assassination of John F. Kennedy.* Originally published by Macmillan, the book was reissued in 1988 by Carroll & Graf.

LIPSEY, RICHARD A.

Lipsey was the aide to General Philip C. †Wehle. When questioned by researcher David S. †Lifton, Lipsey said he was "absolutely" sure that a second, or "decoy," ambulance was used when the president's body was taken from †Andrews Air Force Base to †Bethesda Naval Hospital for the autopsy. According to Lifton, Lipsey claimed that the ambulance in which Jacqueline †Kennedy and Attorney General Robert F. †Kennedy rode contained an empty coffin. The president's body, he said, was in another ambulance that rode farther back in the motorcade.
See also AMBULANCE CONTROVERSY.
📖 *Best Evidence*

LIVINGSTONE, HARRISON EDWARD

The author of four novels, Livingstone is the coauthor, with Robert J. †Groden, of *High Treason: The Assassination of President John F. Kennedy and the*

New Evidence of Conspiracy (1989; reissued by
Berkley Books, 1990). He is also the author of *High
Treason 2: the Great Cover-up: The Assassination of
President John F. Kennedy* (Carroll & Graf, 1992).
Both books have been best sellers.

LONE ASSASSIN THEORY

The †Warren Commission, appointed by President
Lyndon B. †Johnson, concluded that one man killed
President Kennedy. That man was Lee Harvey †Oswald.
The Commission "found no evidence that either Oswald
or Jack †Ruby was part of any conspiracy, domestic or
foreign, to assassinate President Kennedy." In the years
since the Commission's report was published, numerous
independent researchers have uncovered connections or
alleged connections that link both Oswald and Ruby to
the †Federal Bureau of Investigation, the †Central
Intelligence Agency, anti- and pro-Castro Cuban
groups, and the †Mafia.
See also MAGIC BULLET; SINGLE BULLET THEORY.

LOPEZ, EDWIN J.

Lopez was an attorney employed by the †House Select
Committee on Assassinations. He was assigned
responsibility for investigating the charges that Lee
Harvey †Oswald had visited the Cuban and Soviet

embassies in †Mexico City. The †Central Intelligence Agency supplied the Committee with a photograph that it claimed showed Oswald at the Soviet embassy, but Lopez concluded that the man in the photograph was not Oswald. Because all the so-called evidence came from the CIA, that agency has been accused of attempting to manufacture a link between Oswald and a communist country.

📖 *High Treason*

LORENZ, MARITA

A former mistress of Cuban dictator Fidel †Castro, Lorenz was a key witness at the trial that resulted from E. Howard †Hunt's suit against the publication †*Spotlight.* The case is the basis for Mark †Lane's best-seller, †*Plausible Denial* (Thunder's Mouth Press, 1991). Recruited by the CIA, Lorenz turned on Castro and eventually was employed by a number of American intelligence and police agencies. Lorenz claims she drove to Dallas a few days before the Kennedy assassination with a group of heavily armed men, including several exiled Cuban leaders and Frank †Sturgis, a CIA operative. She said that in Dallas, the group met with CIA official E. Howard Hunt, and later, the night before the assassination, with Jack †Ruby in a Dallas motel room. Hunt denied

Marita Lorenz

he was in Dallas at the time, but the jury ultimately dismissed Hunt's lawsuit against *Spotlight*.

See also LANZ, PEDRO DIAZ; OPERATION 40.

📖 *Plausible Denial*

LOVELADY, BILLY NOLAN

A now-famous photograph taken by James W. †Altgens seconds after the first shot was fired shows a man standing in the front entrance of the †Texas School Book Depository Building whom many believe looked like Lee Harvey †Oswald. Obviously, if it was Oswald, he could not have been on the sixth floor of the building at the same time, shooting at the president. For reasons that appear vague, the †Warren Commission identified the man as Billy Nolan Lovelady, a building employee. No one on the Commission had ever seen Lovelady, yet they reached this conclusion. The man in the photo is wearing a white undershirt under a dark, heavy-textured shirt open halfway to the waist. Lovelady told the FBI he was wearing a red-and-white-striped sport shirt the day of the assassination. He also told the FBI he believed the shots came from "that knoll," and he "did not at any time believe the shots had come from the Texas School Book Depository Building."

See also SHELLEY, WILLIAM.

📖 *Best Evidence*; *Rush to Judgment*

LUNDBERG, DR. GEORGE
Dr. Lundberg is the editor of the *Journal of the American Medical Association*. During the third week of May 1992, the same week Oliver †Stone's film †*JFK* was released on video for home viewing, a major news event was an article published in the AMA journal. The eleven-thousand-word article was based on an interview with Dr. James J. †Humes and Dr. Thornton †Boswell, both participants in the Kennedy autopsy conducted at †Bethesda Naval Hospital. Both Humes and Boswell defended the conclusions reached in the autopsy report and denounced continuing speculation surrounding President Kennedy's assassination. Dr. Lundberg appeared on television network news programs and was a guest on the "Larry King Live" show on CNN to discuss the article. Critics of the autopsy, including noted forensic pathologist Dr. Cyril H. †Wecht, were stunned that the comments of the two doctors were treated as revelations, because the article revealed nothing new but simply restated what was in the autopsy report and what the physicians had discussed before the †Warren Commission.

On May 29, 1992, the Reuter wire service carried a report in which two men who were present in the autopsy room at Bethesda, technologist Jerrol F.

†Custer and autopsy photographer Floyd A. †Riebe, charged that the autopsy X rays and photographs are forgeries and that the wounds they depict are not the same wounds they saw during the autopsy.

MABRA, W. W.

Assassination researcher Jim †Marrs reports that
Mabra, who is identified as a Dallas County bailiff,
was standing on the corner of Main and Houston
streets when the shooting took place. Mabra is quoted
as saying that he saw people run toward the †Grassy
Knoll, where he thought at first the shots may have
originated.
See also DEALEY PLAZA WITNESSES.
📖 *Crossfire*

MCCAMY, CALVIN

McCamy was a photographic expert who was asked by
the †House Select Committee on Assassinations to
examine the autopsy photos of President Kennedy. He
told the Committee that it was "extremely unlikely"
the photos had been tampered with, or that they
showed a body other than the president's.
📖 *Best Evidence*

MCCLELLAN COMMITTEE

This Senate committee, whose official name was the
Senate Select Committee on Improper Activities in the
Labor or Management Field and which was chaired by
Senator John McClellan, was formed in the 1950s to
investigate links between unions and organized crime.
Senator John F. Kennedy was a committee member,
and his brother, Robert F. †Kennedy, was its chief
counsel. The committee marks the beginning of the
war between the Kennedy brothers and union leaders
with ties to the underworld, such as Teamsters boss
Jimmy †Hoffa.

MCCLELLAND, DR. ROBERT N.

Dr. McClelland stood at the head of the table on which
President Kennedy was placed when he was brought
into †Parkland Memorial Hospital. He is quoted as
saying that before the doctors had received any
information about the location of the person or
persons who had shot the president, it was their
impression that one bullet had "entered through the
front of the neck," coursed up the vertebrae and exited
"the rear of the skull." McClelland prepared a hospital
report at about 4:45 P.M. the day of the assassination.
That report is part of Commission Exhibit #392 in the
†Warren Report. The second-to-last line of

McClelland's report reads, "The cause of death was due to massive head and brain injury from a gunshot wound of the left temple."
See also HUBER, OSCAR; PARKLAND MEMORIAL HOSPITAL STAFF; SHAW, DR. ROBERT.
📖 *Best Evidence*; *Warren Report*

MCCLOY, JOHN J.
McCloy was chairman of the board of Chase Manhattan Bank before he became an adviser to President Kennedy in 1961. In 1963, President Lyndon B. †Johnson appointed McCloy to the †Warren Commission. Twice during the Commission's proceedings, McCloy voiced confusion about the evidence presented. On the question of the †magic bullet, he is recorded as saying, "This bullet business leaves me confused." When discussing the FBI report of the president's wounds, he said, "It left my mind muddy as to what really did happen."
📖 *Best Evidence*

MACDONALD, BETTY MOONEY
Betty MacDonald was the real name of a stripper who had worked at Jack †Ruby's nightclub using several stage names and aliases. She provided an alibi for Darrell Wayne †Garner, who was briefly accused of the

attempted murder of Warren †Reynolds, a witness to the shooting of J. D. †Tippit. In February 1964, MacDonald was found dead in a Dallas jail cell, where she was being held on a misdemeanor charge.
📖 *High Treason*

MCDONALD, NICK

M. N. McDonald was the Dallas police officer whom Johnny †Brewer, a shoe-store manager, supposedly led to Lee Harvey †Oswald inside the †Texas Theatre. McDonald claimed that when he asked Oswald, who was seated near the rear of the theater, to rise, Oswald punched him in the face and reached for a handgun that was hidden in his waistband. When Oswald was subdued, he allegedly blurted out, "Well, it's all over now."
📖 *Conspiracy*

MCGUIRE, DENNIS "PEANUTS"

An employee of Oneal's Funeral Home, McGuire helped place the president's body inside the coffin at †Parkland Memorial Hospital.
See also BODY BAG CONTROVERSY; ONEAL, VERNON; RIKE, AUBREY.
📖 *Best Evidence*; *High Treason 2*

MCHUGH, GODFREY

Brigadier General McHugh was President Kennedy's Air Force aide. He rode near the back of the motorcade in a car that was still on Main Street when the shooting took place. McHugh stayed in the back cabin of †*Air Force One,* where Kennedy's coffin was, throughout the trip from Dallas to †Andrews Air Force Base, and continued to accompany the coffin until it was delivered to †Bethesda Naval Hospital.

See also O'BRIEN, LAWRENCE F.; O'DONNELL, KENNETH; POWERS, DAVE.

📖 *Best Evidence; Death of a President*

MCLAIN, H. B.

A Dallas police motorcycle officer, McLain was riding about 150 feet behind the presidential limousine as it drove through †Dealey Plaza. McLain reportedly admitted that the police radio transmitter mounted on his motorcycle had experienced many problems, and that the microphone sometimes became stuck in the open position. An acoustical examination of the †Dallas police dispatch tape that recorded events at the assassination scene led experts to estimate that the open microphone that picked up the sound of the shots was about 154 feet behind the president when

the third shot heard on the tape was fired.
See also ACOUSTICAL EVIDENCE.
📖 *High Treason*

MCNAMARA, ROBERT
Secretary of Defense under presidents Kennedy and
Johnson, McNamara is regarded by many
assassination researchers as an integral part of the
military-industrial complex that viewed Kennedy as a
barrier to its planned all-out war in Southeast Asia.
Within a month of Kennedy's death, McNamara told
Lyndon B. †Johnson that the United States had to have
"major increases" in military personnel in Vietnam.
See also VIETNAM WAR.
📖 *High Treason*

MCNEIL, CINDY
A Houston, Texas, attorney, McNeil examined the
autopsy photographs that were allegedly taken of
President Kennedy. She reportedly concluded that the
subject of the photos is a wax model, not a human body.
High Treason 2

MCVICKAR, JOHN
McVickar was an official of the American embassy in
Moscow when Lee Harvey †Oswald arrived there on

October 31, 1959, in an unsuccessful attempt to renounce his U.S. citizenship. McVickar told the †Warren Commission he thought Oswald's behavior was that of someone who "had been tutored," that he seemed to be "using words he had learned, but did not fully understand," and that it seemed others had "guided him and encouraged him in his actions." While McVickar's observations would appear vital to understanding Oswald's motivation, they were not included in the †Warren Report, even though several pages are devoted to the incident.

📖 *Conspiracy*

MCWATTERS, CECIL J.
McWatters was a Dallas bus driver who was traced through a bus transfer ticket allegedly found in Lee Harvey †Oswald's possession when he was arrested. The †Warren Commission reported that Oswald boarded a westbound bus on Elm Street shortly after the assassination, requested a transfer, then got off a few blocks later. When questioned, McWatters said he recalled a young man who boarded his bus and smiled upon being told the president had been shot. This comment led to newspaper headlines about "The Smiling Assassin." Although McWatters identified Oswald during a lineup as one of his passengers, he

did not identify him as the smiling young man; he later identified sixteen-year-old Milton R. †Jones as the passenger who had smiled on learning of Kennedy's death.
📖 *Rush to Judgment*

MCWILLIE, LEWIS

McWillie was a Dallas gambling associate and close friend of Jack †Ruby's who ran the Tropicana nightclub in Havana before Fidel †Castro's revolution succeeded. McWillie, who had close ties to †Mafia boss Santos †Trafficante, was a familiar sight to airport employees in both Dallas and New Orleans as one of Ruby's regular traveling companions. Jack Ruby's relationship with McWillie is just one of several links he had with Mafia bosses who had reasons to kill Kennedy.
📖 *Conspiracy*

MAFIA

The "Mafia" is the name given to the organized criminal underworld whose members are primarily, but not exclusively, of Italian descent. Three leading Mafia figures have been connected to the assassination of President Kennedy: Sam †Giancana, Carlos †Marcello, and Santos †Trafficante.

The hatred of mob leaders for the Kennedy brothers went back to the 1950s, when John was a member of the †McClellan Committee, which investigated links between labor unions and racketeers, and Robert F. †Kennedy was the committee's counsel. When John was elected president he appointed his brother attorney general. The new attorney general stepped up the campaign against organized crime. His task force dealing with Mafia leaders and activities caused a serious threat to the mob's financial empire. More than once, death threats against the lives of both Kennedys were made by mob and mob-related figures, including Jimmy †Hoffa and Trafficante.

Ironically, many of the mob figures who were targets of federal investigations were also in an alliance with the †Central Intelligence Agency during the early 1960s to plot the assassination of Cuban dictator Fidel †Castro. The Mafia was smarting from the loss of its lucrative Havana gambling casinos and drug traffic and so had a vested interest in replacing Castro with someone more friendly to its business interests.

See also ALEMAN, JOSÉ; ROSELLI, JOHNNY.

📖 *Conspiracy; Mafia Kingfish*

MAGIC BULLET

The so-called magic bullet, officially known as
Commission Exhibit #399, is at the heart of the
†Warren Commission's finding that Lee Harvey
†Oswald was the assassin of President Kennedy and
that there was no conspiracy to kill the president.
This bullet, which was allegedly found on a gurney in
†Parkland Memorial Hospital after Kennedy's body
had left Dallas, supposedly entered Kennedy's back,
exited his throat, entered Governor John †Connally's
back, broke a rib bone, exited his chest, entered his
wrist, where it caused severe bone damage, and
entered the fatty part of his thigh. The bullet
allegedly discovered at Parkland is also called the
"pristine bullet" because it was in near-perfect
condition. Tests by several government agencies,
including the U.S. Army, attempting to duplicate the
tissue and bone damage the magic bullet caused to two
men have consistently failed to yield a bullet in any
condition other than badly mangled and flattened.
Critics of the Warren Commission charge that a bullet
doing the extensive damage this one allegedly did
could not survive in almost perfect condition.

The magic bullet is at the crux of the dispute over
whether one or more gunmen took part in the
assassination. The so-called †single bullet theory

appears to have been formulated, despite the reported objections of three Commission members, to satisfy the finding that only three shots were fired and still accommodate testimony that a bystander, James T. †Tague, was injured by a bullet that hit the pavement in front of him. To reject the single bullet theory can only result in recognizing that more than one person shot at the president.

See also BELL, AUDREY; BORING, FLOYD; GREGORY, DR. CHARLES; HARBISON, CHARLES; LONE ASSASSIN THEORY; OSBORNE, DR. DAVID; TOMLINSON, DARREL C. 📖 *High Treason*

MANCHESTER, WILLIAM

A noted author, William Manchester was commissioned by the Kennedy family to write an "authorized" history of the assassination. When the manuscript did not turn out as the Kennedys liked, they sued Manchester in an attempt to prevent the book's publication.

See also THE DEATH OF A PRESIDENT.

MANNLICHER-CARCANO RIFLE

A Mannlicher-Carcano 6.5-caliber Italian-made carbine is alleged to be the rifle that was used to kill the president. Of course, if more than one assassin was firing at Kennedy that day, then this would have

The Mannlicher-Carcano rifle, the alleged assassination weapon, being carried from the Texas School Book Depository Building by Dallas police lieutenant J. Carl Day

been only one of several weapons used in the ambush—if it was used at all. Questions have been raised as to why Lee Harvey †Oswald, using the †alias A. Hidell, would go through the trouble of ordering a poor-quality rifle through the mail, leaving a paper trail that any law enforcement agency could trace, instead of simply purchasing a more sophisticated model over the counter using an assumed name at any of at least a dozen stores in Dallas. Added to this is the inability of FBI sharpshooters to fire this bolt-action rifle accurately in the time frame Oswald did. Finally, there is strong evidence to indicate that the rifle originally found on the sixth floor of the †Texas School Book Depository Building was actually a German-made 7.65-caliber Mauser. Knowledgeable small-arms experts appear unanimous in their assessment of the Mannlicher-Carcano as a "poor" weapon, "crudely made," with "terrible" action. To a layman, such a rifle seems a poor selection for an assassination, where accuracy is vital.

See also ALBA, ADRIAN; *AMERICAN RIFLEMAN* ADVERTISEMENT; AMMUNITION CLIP; ANDERSON, EUGENE D.; BOONE, EUGENE L.; CRAIG, ROGER D.; FIRING SEQUENCE CONTROVERSY; MOONEY, LUKE; PALMPRINT ON RIFLE; WADE, HENRY W.; WEITZMAN, SEYMOUR.

Mafia boss Carlos Marcello

MARCELLO, CARLOS

Born in Tunisia of Sicilian parents, Marcello was for decades the reputed head of the †Mafia organization in the South. Marcello, who lived in New Orleans, has been linked to the assassination by many researchers because he had become a prime target in Attorney General Robert F. †Kennedy's crusade against organized crime. He was hastily—and temporarily—deported from the United States under orders from the attorney general in 1961; for Marcello this was an extremely humiliating episode. He allegedly commented that Robert was the tail to his brother's dog, and the only way to stop the tail was to cut off the dog's head. It has also been reported that he repeatedly voiced death threats against the president. *See also* ROSELLI, JOHNNY; TRAFFICANTE, SANTOS. ⌸ *Conspiracy; Mafia Kingfish*

MARCHETTI, VICTOR

A former CIA official, Marchetti resigned in 1969 and became famous when his book *The CIA and the Cult of Intelligence* was published by Knopf in 1974. In 1978, †*Spotlight* magazine published an article by Marchetti implying that E. Howard †Hunt and Frank †Sturgis of the †Central Intelligence Agency were involved in the Kennedy assassination, and that the Agency was planning to hand them over to the †House Select Committee on Assassinations as sacrificial lambs. This was, according to Marchetti, a way of exposing only limited information that would deter congressional and private investigators from looking too hard at the Agency. Because of the article, Hunt filed a lawsuit against *Spotlight*. The case went to a jury, which found for the publication. The foreperson of the jury, Leslie †Armstrong, later told the press that *Spotlight*'s attorney, Mark †Lane, had convinced her that the CIA was behind the assassination.

📖 *Plausible Denial*

MARKHAM, HELEN LOUISE

Helen Louise Markham was allegedly a witness to the shooting death of Dallas police officer J. D. †Tippit. The †Warren Commission relied heavily on her testimony despite the fact that she appeared habitually to give varying accounts of the incident, even providing a description of the killer that could in no way fit Lee Harvey †Oswald. A reading of her testimony before the Commission leads one to ask how the Commission used her statements to conclude that Oswald shot Tippit. The Commission lawyer asked her five times whether she had recognized any of the men in a lineup that took place less than three and a half hours after the shooting—and where she picked out Lee Harvey Oswald as Tippit's killer. Among Markham's more outlandish statements was that she talked to Tippit for a brief time before he died, even though the medical authorities said he died instantly. Other witnesses claim they did not see Markham anywhere near the dead officer in the minutes just after the shooting. *See also* TIPPIT MURDER SCENE WITNESSES.

📖 *Crossfire; Rush to Judgment*

MARRS, JIM

A Dallas journalist, Marrs has spent years investigating the assassination, including interviewing hundreds of witnesses and experts. He is the author of *Crossfire: The Plot That Killed Kennedy*, published in 1990 by Carroll & Graf. This is one of the two books on which Oliver †Stone's film †*JFK* is based.

MARTIN, B. J.

Martin was one of the two motorcycle officers who rode to the left of the president's limousine in the motorcade. He reported that his uniform, helmet, and windshield were splashed with blood, confirming that Kennedy's skull exploded to the rear and left. *See also* HARGIS, BOBBY W.

📖 *Best Evidence*

MARTIN, JACK

Martin was an associate of Guy †Banister's in New Orleans. The day of the assassination, Banister, who was known as a heavy drinker, got drunk and pistol-whipped Martin over a reference Martin made to the strange people who had been hanging around Banister's office during the previous summer. After the beating, Martin told police that he thought one of Banister's friends, David †Ferrie, had driven to Texas to act as the getaway pilot for Lee Harvey †Oswald. He later told New Orleans district attorney Jim †Garrison that he had seen Oswald in Banister's office several times.

📖 *On the Trail of the Assassins*

MARTIN, JAMES H.

While she was being held in Secret Service custody in the months following the assassination, Marina †Oswald signed a contract with Martin, who then acted as her business manager and literary agent. Because of the public's perception of her as the hapless wife of an evil assassin (who had also been a cruel husband), Marina received tens of thousands of dollars in donations from people around the country, and, according to Martin's testimony before the †Warren Commission, Marina by 1964 had received

nearly $135,000 in advances from publishers.
📖 *High Treason; Rush to Judgment*

MATTOX, JIM
On August 8, 1990, Texas attorney general Jim Mattox announced that he was going to open an investigation of the Kennedy assassination because he had received new evidence from two researchers. Mattox also said his mother had told him that she saw Jack †Ruby and Lee Harvey †Oswald eating dinner together in a restaurant where she had once worked as a waitress. Mattox was voted out of office, and nothing ever came of this investigation.
📖 *High Treason 2*

MAYFIELD, DOUGLAS
Army Specialist Mayfield was a member of the †Casket Team that handled the president's coffin in Washington. *See also* AMBULANCE CONTROVERSY; BIRD, SAMUEL R.
📖 *Best Evidence*

MEAGHER, SYLVIA
An early critic of the †Warren Commission, Meagher indexed by subject the twenty-six volumes of assembled data, testimony, and evidence published by the Commission. This *Subject Index to the Warren*

Commission Report and Hearings and Exhibits was later augmented with an index to the materials collected by the †House Select Committee on Assassinations and published by Scarecrow Press in 1980 under the title *Master Index to the JFK Assassination Investigation: The Reports and Supporting Volumes of the House Select Committee on Assassinations and the Warren Commission.* (Meagher collaborated with Gary Owens on the latter volume.)

In September 1966, Meagher participated in a televised panel discussion of the assassination at the Theater of New Ideas in New York City. Pitting a group of critics against lawyers for the Warren Commission, the discussion was the first direct confrontation between the two sides about the contradictions concerning the autopsy report. Meagher further challenged the Commission in her book †*Accessories After the Fact* (1967), a presentation of the view, which many support, that the Warren Commission deliberately concealed the truth.
📖 *Best Evidence*

MENDOZA, DR. CHARLES
Mendoza was a mysterious Dallas physician to whom George †DeMohrenschildt, a CIA informant and friend of Lee Harvey †Oswald's, was referred in June 1976,

two months after Mendoza registered with the Dallas County Medical Association. In the fall of 1976 DeMohrenschildt, who had extensive and long-standing connections to the intelligence community, completed a manuscript naming FBI and CIA officials who were ostensibly involved in the assassination of President Kennedy. Shortly after he began receiving treatment from Mendoza, a therapy his wife says included intravenous injections of undetermined drugs, DeMohrenschildt began to suffer severe mental problems. He was admitted to †Parkland Memorial Hospital and was administered electroshock therapy; he quickly deteriorated emotionally, and apparently ended his own life with a shotgun blast. Mendoza departed Dallas in December 1976, almost immediately after DeMohrenschildt was hospitalized. He left only a false forwarding address. According to researcher Jim †Marrs, DeMohrenschildt's wife, Jeanne, believed her husband was programmed to take his own life on command through mind control and behavior modification techniques administered by Mendoza.
📖 *Crossfire; High Treason*

MERCER, JULIA ANN

On November 22, 1963, Julia Ann Mercer signed an affidavit for the Dallas Sheriff's Department

describing in detail an incident she witnessed in
†Dealey Plaza early in the morning of the day
President Kennedy was assassinated. Driving west on
Elm Street, Mercer encountered an illegally parked
green Ford pickup truck with Texas tags. The truck
was half on the curb, blocking her lane. As she waited
for traffic in the lane to her left to clear so she could
drive around the truck, she observed a "white male
who appeared to be in his late 20s or early 30s,
wearing a grey jacket, brown pants, and plaid shirt,"
remove what appeared to be a rifle case from the back
of the truck. The case was about three and a half to
four feet long, and tapered from about eight inches at
its broadest to four inches at the narrowest point. The
man carried the rifle case up the grassy incline that
forms part of the overpass bordering Dealey Plaza.

Mercer claimed the entire incident took place in
plain view of three Dallas police officers who stood
talking nearby. When she was able to pull her car
around the truck, she got a good look at the driver,
whom she later recognized as Jack †Ruby, both from a
photo she claims to have been shown by police and
again when his picture was broadcast on television as
Lee Harvey †Oswald's murderer. The †Warren
Commission, while accepting her affidavit describing
the incident, never called Mercer as a witness. There

is no evidence that either the Ford truck, which had the words "Air Conditioning" emblazoned in black letters on the driver's door, or the three police officers were ever identified or located.

📖 *Crossfire; Rush to Judgment*

METZLER, JAMES E.

A Navy corpsman third class, Metzler was on duty at †Bethesda Naval Hospital when the coffin allegedly containing the president's body was brought in through the receiving dock at the rear of the hospital. He watched the †Casket Team bring in the coffin, and then helped remove the body and place it on an autopsy table.

Although he was in the room for only five or ten minutes before he was told to leave, Metzler was able to observe that the body was wrapped in a sheet. A second sheet was wrapped around the head. When Metzler left the room, he was stopped by a group of about ten men whom he took to be government agents. He showed them his Navy identification. Several days later, Metzler was summoned to the office of Admiral Calvin †Galloway and was asked to sign a statement affirming that he would not talk about the events of that night under penalty of court-martial. In a 1979 interview with researcher David S. †Lifton, Metzler described the coffin as "dark brown" with handles on the side.

See also AMBULANCE CONTROVERSY; BODY BAG CONTROVERSY.

📖 *Best Evidence*

MEXICO CITY

Much has been made of an October 10, 1963, †Central Intelligence Agency memo about Lee Harvey †Oswald's alleged activities at the Soviet and Cuban embassies in Mexico City during September 1963. The purpose of this trip was ostensibly for Oswald to arrange his return to the Soviet Union. There is overwhelming evidence that the CIA manufactured the bogus photographs and tape recordings that were supposed to prove Oswald had made the trip to Mexico City. Silvia †Duran, a Mexican national working at the embassy, is believed to have been pressured by the CIA, through its friends in the Mexico City police force, to testify that Oswald was there. E. Howard †Hunt was allegedly the senior CIA man in Mexico City during August and September 1963.

Although a surveillance camera at the Mexican consulate in New Orleans, where Oswald allegedly requested a Mexican visitor's card, produced film that was sufficiently clear to identify a bystander, the image of the man said to be Oswald was not clear enough to confirm his identity. Months after the assassination, and long after Oswald's belongings had first been thoroughly examined by federal agents, Marina †Oswald and Priscilla †Johnson discovered bus-ticket stubs for a round-trip journey to Mexico City in a Spanish-language magazine that they claimed to have found among Oswald's things. The †Warren Commission used this evidence to substantiate its conclusion that Oswald had traveled to Mexico City, but the belatedness of the discovery has led many researchers to question the ticket stubs' authenticity.

Many observers consider the entire story of Oswald's alleged Mexican trip an example of disinformation by the CIA.

See also ALVARADO, GILBERTO; BOWEN, JOHN "JACK"; GAUDET, WILLIAM GEORGE; LOPEZ, EDWIN J.; PHILLIPS, DAVID ATLEE; VECIANA, ANTONIO.

📖 *On the Trail of the Assassins*

MILLER, AUSTIN
According to researcher and author Mark †Lane, Austin Miller, who was standing on the overpass when the assassination occurred, signed an affidavit on the day of the assassination claiming he saw smoke coming from a "group of trees north of Elm," near the

railroad tracks. When Miller was questioned by lawyers from the ⁺Warren Commission, he was not asked about the smoke he saw.

See also OVERPASS WITNESSES; SMOKE FROM THE GRASSY KNOLL.

📖 *Rush to Judgment*

MILLICAN, A. J.

Millican was part of a crew that was fabricating plumbing piping for a building under construction just north of the ⁺Texas School Book Depository Building. The crew members were on their lunch break, and were standing near the Depository Building on Elm Street to watch the motorcade. Millican told sheriff's deputies he had no doubt where the shots came from. He told them that, just as the president's limousine passed him, he heard three shots that sounded as if they came from the area of the Book Depository Building. These were immediately followed by two additional shots that came from the area on the ⁺Grassy Knoll where the concrete pergola was located. Finally, according to Millican, another three shots came from the same direction (i.e., the Grassy Knoll), except a little farther back. Millican thought the gunfire came from either a high-powered rifle or perhaps a .45 automatic. Despite the thoroughness of his report of the shooting, Millican was never

interviewed by either the †Warren Commission or the †House Select Committee on Assassinations.
See also BRENNAN, HOWARD L.; SPEAKER, SANDY.
📖 *Crossfire*

MILLS, THOMAS

Mills was a hospital corpsman assigned to the office of President Kennedy's personal physician, Dr. George †Burkley. Two Secret Service agents, Floyd †Boring and Paul †Paterni, asked Mills to help them inspect the presidential limousine after it was flown back to the White House from Dallas. Paterni allegedly found a "metallic fragment in the front seat," and Mills another such fragment. Some observers have expressed suspicion that the fragments were "planted" to support the †single bullet theory.
See also MAGIC BULLET.
📖 *Best Evidence*

MILTEER, JOSEPH

A wealthy right-wing activist, Milteer belonged to a number of groups with links to †anti-Castro Cubans in Miami. He is alleged to have had advance knowledge of a plot to kill President Kennedy. A man resembling Milteer is said to appear in a photograph showing people standing in front of the †Texas School Book

Depository Building on November 22, 1963. Milteer supposedly told a police informant, in a conversation taped in Miami less than two weeks before the president was killed, that the assassination was "in the working." He even predicted it would be done with a high-powered rifle fired from an office building, although the venue for this assassination was supposed to be Miami (on November 18). After the assassination, Milteer told the informant that everything had gone according to plan, and then suggested that the informant had thought he was kidding. The informant, identified as William Somersett, asked Milteer whether he had been guessing when he made his prediction. Milteer's reply was that he didn't do any guessing. He then told Somersett he wasn't concerned about Lee Harvey †Oswald's being caught, because Oswald did not know anything. When questioned by the FBI, Milteer denied making any statements or predictions about the assassination.

📖 *Conspiracy*

MINSK

Lee Harvey †Oswald lived in the Soviet Union from late 1959 to June 1962, for the most part in the city of Minsk, where he met and married his Russian wife, Marina. The couple enjoyed an apartment that was

Marina and Lee Harvey Oswald, standing on a bridge in Minsk, U.S.S.R., in 1962

comfortable by Soviet standards and given them practically rent-free. Oswald was provided with a better-than-average job in a radio and television factory, suggesting that he received special treatment of a sort that was generally available only from the KGB, the Soviet State Security Committee. This suggests that Oswald was either in the employ or under the control of the KGB, or that the KGB was keeping an extra-close watch on him because it suspected he had been sent to the Soviet Union by the CIA. The KGB predictably denied any connection with Oswald, and the †Warren Commission found no such connection. Several photos taken of Oswald in Minsk by Ruth †Naman were provided to the Commission.
See also NOSENKO, YURI; OSWALD, MARINA.
📖 *Best Evidence*; *Crossfire*

MITCHELL, WILLIE
Mitchell was a prisoner at the Dallas County jail on Houston Street the day of the assassination. Mitchell's attorney claimed that his client saw nothing, but that other inmates witnessed the assassination.
See also POWELL, JOHN.
📖 *On the Trail of the Assassins*

MOLINA, JOE R.

Molina was the credit manager for the Texas School
Book Depository. He was standing in front of the
building with Buell Wesley †Frazier when the shots
were fired. When questioned by the †Warren
Commission, he said he thought the shots had come
from the "west side" of the building, toward the
†Grassy Knoll and overpass.
See also TEXAS SCHOOL BOOK DEPOSITORY BUILDING
EMPLOYEES.
📖 *Crossfire*

MONTGOMERY, L. D.

Detective Montgomery was the man standing directly
behind Lee Harvey †Oswald when Jack †Ruby shot
him. Montgomery testified that he was not informed
that the police and the FBI had received threats
against Oswald's life. In fact, he said Captain Will
†Fritz told him to make sure that Oswald did not get
away. It has been speculated that the detectives
escorting Oswald might have taken steps to protect
him had they been aware of such threats.
See also GRAVES, L. C.; LEAVELLE, JAMES R.
📖 *Rush to Judgment*

MOONEY, LUKE

Deputy Sheriff Mooney was on the sixth floor of the †Texas School Book Depository Building when the alleged murder weapon was found. Considering the confusion about whether the rifle that was discovered was a †Mannlicher-Carcano or a Mauser, it is surprising that the †Warren Commission failed to ask Mooney what make rifle he saw.

See also BOONE, EUGENE L.; CRAIG, ROGER D.; WADE, HENRY W.; WEITZMAN, SEYMOUR.

📖 *Rush to Judgment*

MOORMAN, MARY

Mary Moorman and her friend Jean †Hill had come to †Dealey Plaza to see a motorcycle police officer whom Hill wanted to date. As the presidential limousine approached their position, Hill called out to Kennedy, wanting him to look their way so Moorman could take his picture with her Polaroid camera. Moorman snapped away as the shots rang out and the president was mortally wounded. After the shooting, Moorman was taken to the sheriff's office for questioning, where most of her photographs were confiscated by a man identifying himself as a federal officer. One photo has survived, and close examination of an enlargement revealed what many believe is a man behind the stockade fence atop the †Grassy Knoll holding a rifle in the classic firing position.

See also "BADGEMAN."

📖 *Crossfire*

MORGAN, ROGER C.

Chief Warrant Officer Roger C. Morgan was allegedly the pilot who, according to former Marine navigator Larry Huff, flew a Marine investigation team to Japan immediately following the assassination to look into Lee Harvey †Oswald's background. Although the Marine Corps denied Huff's story, Morgan responded to questions from the †House Select Committee on Assassinations, verifying through his personal logbooks that he had commanded a flight to Japan on the dates Huff mentioned. Morgan explained that his personal record would not contain the names of crew members or passengers, but that this information should be in the official records. The congressional investigators were unable to locate Marine Corps records that would substantiate or refute Huff's allegations.

See also CAMP SMITH.

📖 *High Treason*

MORGAN, DR. RUSSELL H.

Dr. Morgan, a professor of radiology at Johns Hopkins

University, was a member of the medical panel
convened by Attorney General Ramsey Clark to
examine the Kennedy autopsy photographs and X rays.
See also CLARK PANEL.
📖 *Best Evidence*

MORITZ, DR. ALAN R.
A former professor of forensic medicine at Harvard,
Moritz was a member of the medical panel convened
by Attorney General Ramsey Clark to examine the
Kennedy autopsy photographs and X rays.
See also CLARK PANEL.
📖 *Best Evidence*

MORROW, ROBERT D.
A former CIA agent who had participated in actions
against Fidel †Castro, Morrow wrote a book titled
†*Betrayal,* published in 1976 by Regnery, in which he
claims to have purchased for the †Central Intelligence
Agency three †Mannlicher-Carcano rifles similar to the
one Lee Harvey †Oswald allegedly used to murder
President Kennedy. Morrow places responsibility for the
assassination on rogue elements in the Agency. He is
also the author of a book on the assassination of Robert
F. †Kennedy, *The Senator Must Die* (1988), and of *First*

Hand Knowledge: How I Participated in the CIA-Mafia Murder of JFK, published in 1992 by SPI Books.

MOSELEY, JACK
At the time of the assassination, Moseley was a reporter for the *Fort Worth Press*. He reported that he saw federal agents enter the embalming room in the funeral home where Lee Harvey †Oswald's body was stored. Moseley claimed the agents kept coming and going from the room, where they were alone with the body for an extended time, and that they had a crime lab kit for fingerprinting with them.
See also GROODY, PAUL; PALMPRINT ON RIFLE.
📖 *Best Evidence*

MOTORCADE ROUTE
The presidential motorcade through Dallas, Texas, on November 22, 1963, was a great success until it reached †Dealey Plaza. Critics of the †Warren Commission have argued, with justification, that the motorcade could easily have continued west on Main Street instead of turning north on Houston Street and making a sharp left turn onto Elm Street, forcing the cars to slow down considerably from the †Secret Service–prescribed speed of forty-four miles per hour.

The motorcade's destination was the Dallas Trade Mart, where the president was scheduled to give a luncheon speech. Anyone who has driven through Dealey Plaza will understand the questions raised about using Houston and Elm streets instead of continuing straight on Main Street. The only thing the turns accomplished was to put Kennedy in the sights of his assassin or assassins. According to the route published in the *Dallas Morning News* of November 22, 1963, the motorcade was originally scheduled to proceed straight through Dealey Plaza without turning or slowing down. No one in Dallas or Washington has accepted responsibility for altering the route.
📖 *High Treason; On the Trail of the Assassins*

MOYERS, BILL
Before joining the Kennedy administration as deputy director of the Peace Corps, Moyers, a native Texan, worked on the staff of then-senator Lyndon B. †Johnson. After Kennedy's assassination, he was named an aide to President Johnson. Moyers allegedly said that Kennedy did not want the protective bubble on his limousine during the Dallas trip, quoting Kennedy as saying, "Get that Goddamned bubble off unless it's pouring rain."
📖 *High Treason*

MUCHMORE, MARIE

Marie Muchmore was filming the motorcade from the grassy area to the left of the president's limousine when the shots were fired. Some researchers believe her film confirms that the president was hit by a shot fired from in front of him. The †Warren Commission disagreed.

See also NIX, ORVILLE.

📖 *High Treason*

MURPHY, THOMAS

Murphy was a railroad worker who watched the motorcade from the railroad overpass that borders †Dealey Plaza. He allegedly told assassination researcher Stewart Galanor that the shots "came from a tree to the immediate right [of the President]." He also said he saw smoke coming from a tree on the embankment near the fence on the †Grassy Knoll.

See also OVERPASS WITNESSES; SMOKE FROM THE GRASSY KNOLL.

📖 *Best Evidence*

NAGELL, RICHARD CASE

According to New Orleans district attorney Jim
†Garrison, Nagell's family arranged a secret meeting
between Garrison and Nagell in New York City. At the
time of their meeting, Nagell had just been released
from a federal prison on charges related to his firing a
gun into the ceiling of a bank in El Paso, Texas, a short
time before the assassination of President Kennedy.
Nagell claimed he did this to create an absolutely
foolproof alibi for himself the day of the assassination.
Nagell told Garrison that in the summer of 1963, he
was an intelligence agent employed by a federal agency
he refused to identify, and that he had been assigned to
investigate a project involving a group of individuals
that included Lee Harvey †Oswald. In the course of his
investigation, Nagell claimed he uncovered a "large"
operation aimed at killing the president. When his
superior was reassigned, and Nagell found himself
frozen out of his own agency, Nagell wrote a registered
letter to FBI director J. Edgar †Hoover, but received no
reply. Nagell said he understood what this meant, that

he was now on his own. Fearing that his contacts with Oswald might implicate him in the assassination if Oswald was ever arrested or investigated, he decided on the relative safety of a federal prison. Nagell said that after firing his gun into the bank ceiling, he walked outside and waited for the guard to arrest him. He was convicted of armed robbery and sentenced to ten years, but was released after three. The conviction was later overturned for lack of evidence that he ever intended to rob the bank.

Nagell was the subject of a book written by Dick Russell and titled, *The Man Who Knew Too Much,* published by Carroll & Graf in 1992.

📖 *On the Trail of the Assassins*

NAMAN, RITA

In the summer of 1961, Naman and a friend, Monica Kramer, traveled through the Soviet Union by car, an extraordinary experience at a time when few Westerners ventured behind the iron curtain. Pictures taken by tourists while visiting communist countries were routinely reviewed by the CIA. In Naman's case, the Agency looked at 150 snapshots she had taken and appropriated five, including a photo of Lee Harvey †Oswald she had snapped in a square in the city of †Minsk. Naman and Kramer claimed they had encountered Oswald as casual strangers twice on their trip within a span of ten days, once in Moscow and again, four hundred miles away, in Minsk. While in Moscow, the two women were approached by another American tourist, Marie Hyde, who claimed she had been separated from her tour group and wanted to join Naman and Kramer. Many researchers find it unlikely that a tourist to the Soviet Union in the 1960s could become separated from a group, since at the time the activities of such groups were tightly controlled by KGB agents or informants employed as Intourist guides. These guides were to keep a close watch on all tourists in the groups; the loss of any member would have been a serious offense.

The puzzling story of these tourists' encounters with Oswald, combined with the fact that the CIA held onto a photograph that included Oswald, has deepened some researchers' questions concerning Oswald's possible relations with the CIA.

📖 *Conspiracy*

NATIONAL ARCHIVES, DOCUMENTS MISSING FROM
The National Archives is the repository for many government documents of historic value. Despite excellent security arrangements, many documents and other items related to the assassination of President

Kennedy have vanished from the archives over the years. These include a large number of letters to and from members and staff of the †Warren Commission, some FBI laboratory reports, the †Dallas police dispatch tape, and a stainless steel receptacle believed to contain the president's brain.

📖 *High Treason*

NECK WOUND CONTROVERSY
See THROAT WOUND CONTROVERSY.

NELSON, DORIS
Nursing supervisor Nelson was one of the first people at †Parkland Memorial Hospital to learn that the president had been shot and was being brought to the hospital. Researcher Harrison Edward †Livingstone says that when he gave Nelson an autopsy picture of the back of the president's head showing a bullet entry wound at the rear of the head, she responded that there was no bone where the bullet hole allegedly was, that the portion of the skull containing the bullet hole had been blown away. Obviously, if Nelson is correct and there was no bone at the alleged site of a bullet hole, there could be no bullet hole.

See also PARKLAND MEMORIAL HOSPITAL STAFF.

📖 *High Treason 2*

NEWMAN, JEAN

Jean Newman was a twenty-one-year-old Dallas
resident who left her job to go to †Dealey Plaza to see
the presidential motorcade on November 22, 1963.
When the shots were fired, she was standing along the
sidewalk on Elm Street facing south. To her left was
the †Texas School Book Depository Building, and to
her right was the †Grassy Knoll and the railroad
overpass. When questioned by sheriff's deputies, she
told them that her impression was that the shots
"came from my right." The †Warren Commission did
not call Newman to testify.
See also DEALEY PLAZA WITNESSES.
📖 *Crossfire*

NEWMAN FAMILY

Bill and Gayle Newman both dropped to the ground
and covered their two children with their own bodies
during the shooting of President Kennedy. The
Newmans were standing in front of the †Grassy Knoll
along the curb on Elm Street watching the president
pass when shots were fired from "directly behind me,"
as Bill Newman stated. Interviewed within an hour of
the assassination, Newman said the president, of
whom he had a clear view, was struck in the side of
the temple by a bullet.

See also JACKS, HURCHEL; SITZMAN, MARILYN; TEMPLE WOUND CONTROVERSY.
📖 *Best Evidence*

NGO DINH DIEM

President of South Vietnam, Ngo Dinh Diem and his brother and close adviser, Ngo Dinh Nhu, were assassinated on November 2, 1963, during a coup that had the support of the United States government. It had been no secret that the Kennedy administration wanted to get rid of Diem and find a more pliable president. Many supporters of the Diem administration have charged that President Kennedy himself was involved in the decision to kill Diem, although there is no evidence of this. When Kennedy was killed twenty days later, some people viewed it as retribution for Diem's death. One of those who voiced this opinion was the new American president, Lyndon B. †Johnson, whom Hubert Humphrey quotes in his autobiography, *The Education of a Public Man,* as telling him a few days after assuming the presidency, "We had a hand in killing him [Diem]. Now it's happening here."

See also VIETNAM WAR.
📖 *High Treason*

NIELL, JAMES

James Niell was the Dallas attorney for Police Officer
Roy †Vaughn, who was guarding the Main Street
entrance ramp to the lower-level parking garage of
Police Headquarters when Jack †Ruby allegedly
walked past him on his way to kill Lee Harvey
†Oswald. Through Niell, Vaughn filed a suit to clear
himself of charges of misconduct on duty and any
involvement in a criminal conspiracy. Vaughn took
three lie-detector tests that showed he was telling the
truth when he stated Ruby did not enter the building
through the ramp he was guarding. Napoleon J.
†Daniels, a retired police officer who claimed he saw
Ruby walk past Vaughn as he entered the building,
failed a similar test. Niell maintains that Daniels was
pressured to lie in order to protect the person who
allowed Ruby in, who many suspect was Assistant
Police Chief Charles †Batchelor.
📖 *High Treason*

NITRATE TEST

Also known as a paraffin test, a nitrate test reveals
minute deposits of nitrate on the skin, the result of
burned gunpowder emitted by the firing of a gun.
When Lee Harvey †Oswald was given a nitrate test

following his arrest, deposits were found on his hand, but not on either cheek, where traces generally would exist on someone who had recently fired a rifle, especially one with a scope sight requiring the shooter to hold the weapon against one cheek while taking aim and firing.

📖 *On the Trail of the Assassins; Texas Connection*

NIX, ORVILLE

Nix was one of several people besides Abraham Zapruder who made a film that included frames taken at the moment when Kennedy was wounded. The Nix film, taken across the street from the †Grassy Knoll, clearly shows the president being knocked backward by the impact of the shot to his head. In the background there appears to be what many people believe is a gunman aiming a rifle at Kennedy, and the wisp of smoke many other witnesses claimed to have seen.
See also SMOKE FROM THE GRASSY KNOLL; ZAPRUDER FILM.

📖 *Best Evidence; High Treason*

NIXON, RICHARD M.

Some researchers have posited a link between the former president and the Kennedy assassination for several reasons, among them the fact that Nixon was

in Dallas on November 22, 1963, possibly meeting
with large oil interests that hated Kennedy. Nixon
himself, of course, disliked Kennedy for allegedly
stealing the 1960 election through ballot-box stuffing
in Texas and Chicago; Kennedy beat Nixon by the
smallest margin in U.S. history. It is alleged that
Nixon maintained ties with the Teamsters Union and
with members of the †Mafia, two groups that would
benefit from Kennedy's death. Nixon is also said to
have had ties with Jack †Ruby going back as far as
1947, when as a congressman he is believed to have
been instrumental in intervening on Ruby's behalf so
Ruby would not have to testify before the House
Committee on Un-American Activities. Marina
†Oswald testified before the †Warren Commission that
Lee Harvey †Oswald threatened to shoot Nixon in
April 1963.

📖 *Contract on America; Fatal Hour; High Treason;
Rush to Judgment*

NO-NAME KEY GROUP
This group consisted of CIA contract agents who
allegedly were training Cuban exiles for a second
invasion of their homeland, until President Kennedy
ordered FBI and other federal agents to raid their
camps in Louisiana and Florida. The group was part of

the CIA network investigated by New Orleans district attorney Jim †Garrison in his attempt to indict those responsible for Kennedy's assassination.

📖 *High Treason*

NORMAN, HAROLD D.

Harold Norman was one of three †Texas School Book Depository Building employees who watched the presidential motorcade from the fifth floor of the building. A †Secret Service report claims Norman said he heard the shots come from above him, that he also heard the expended shells fall to the floor, and could hear the bolt action of the rifle. The report was given great credibility by the †Warren Commission, even though Norman's testimony differed significantly from the impressions reported by his companions. Norman later denied making the statements attributed to him by the Secret Service.

See also CARTER, WILLIAM N.; JARMAN, JAMES, JR.; WILLIAMS, BONNIE RAY.

📖 *Rush to Judgment*

NOSENKO, YURI

Nosenko was a lieutenant colonel in the KGB section responsible for keeping tabs on British and American visitors to the Soviet Union. Among the subjects of his surveillance was Lee Harvey †Oswald during Oswald's stay in the U.S.S.R. (1959–1962). In 1962, Nosenko was recruited as an agent of the CIA. On January 20, 1964, while on a trip to Geneva, he contacted the CIA and said he wanted to defect. He allegedly told the American agent who met him that Oswald had no relations with Soviet intelligence, but that the KGB believed he was in the employ of an American intelligence agency. Richard †Helms, at the time deputy director for planning at the CIA, reportedly rejected Nosenko's request for asylum and told him to stay in Europe. Afraid his Soviet masters were on to him, Nosenko defected anyway. In the United States, Nosenko was treated to more than three years of imprisonment and physical abuse by the CIA. His requests to testify before the †Warren Commission were ignored. Nosenko was finally released, his silence allegedly purchased for an annual allowance of $30,000 and American citizenship.

See also ANGLETON, JAMES J.

📖 *Plausible Denial*

NSAM 273

National Security Action Memo 273, dated November 21, 1963, ordered a stepped-up program of U.S. covert activities against North Vietnam. NSAM 273 is considered by some observers as a reversal of President Kennedy's previously avowed decision to withdraw American troops from Vietnam. Kennedy never signed the document, and in fact never saw it, as he was killed the day after it was drafted by McGeorge Bundy, who was special assistant to the president. When Kennedy went to Texas, his order (NSAM 263) to reduce American military personnel in Vietnam by one thousand men before the end of the year was in effect. NSAM 273 would have reversed that policy. Some researchers and authors feel his efforts to wind down U.S. involvement in the war is the chief reason he was killed. A few days after Kennedy's death, his Vietnam policy was indeed reversed.

See also VIETNAM WAR.

📖 *High Treason 2*

O'BRIEN, LAWRENCE F.

A special assistant to the president, and a member of what the press called Kennedy's "Irish Mafia," O'Brien accompanied Kennedy to Texas and stayed with the coffin during the return trip to Washington aboard †*Air Force One.*

See also MCHUGH, GODFREY; O'DONNELL, KENNETH; POWERS, DAVE.

📖 *Death of a President*

O'CONNOR, PAUL K.

O'Connor was one of two laboratory technologists present during the autopsy of President Kennedy at †Bethesda Naval Hospital. A number of assassination researchers have interviewed him; the statements they report conflict. In 1990, Harrison Edward †Livingstone interviewed O'Connor twice. During these interviews, O'Connor described how he unzipped the body bag in which Kennedy's body was shipped; this conflicts with descriptions provided by medical personnel at

335

†Parkland Memorial Hospital who claim the body was wrapped in a sheet. O'Connor also insisted that the president's brain must have been blown out through the hole in his skull, because it was missing.
See also BODY BAG CONTROVERSY; BRAIN CONTROVERSY; JENKINS, JAMES C.
📖 *Best Evidence; High Treason 2*

ODIO INCIDENT

Sylvia Odio's father was a prominent, wealthy political prisoner in Cuba's infamous Isle of Pines. He had formerly supported Fidel †Castro in the struggle to overthrow Batista, but denounced the Cuban leader when Castro admitted he was a communist. Sylvia and her younger sister, Annie, lived in Dallas, where Sylvia worked for the Junta Revolucionaria Cubana (JURE), an anti-Castro group that, while opposed to Castro, was decidedly left of center.

In testimony she gave to a †Warren Commission attorney, Sylvia told of a visit to her Dallas apartment in late September 1963 by three men who said they were members of JURE. Odio said one of the three, an American who was introduced to her as Leon Oswald, had little to say during the visit. The two Latin-looking men with the man called Oswald sought her help in raising funds for anti-Castro operations. The trio's leader called himself "Leopoldo," while the other man was called either "Angel" or "Angelo." The leader seemed to have intimate knowledge of certain inside information about Odio's father that lent credence to his story, but Sylvia remained noncommittal. "Leopoldo" telephoned her the day after the visit, asking again for her help with fund raising. In the course of the conversation, he mentioned that the American who had been with him was an ex-Marine marksman who could be an asset to the cause, but that he was "loco." He then told her the American thought Cubans had no guts, that they should have shot Kennedy after the failure of the †Bay of Pigs invasion, and that killing Kennedy would be "so easy to do."

After the Kennedy assassination, when Sylvia saw pictures of Lee Harvey †Oswald, she recognized him as one of the three men who had visited her two months earlier. Fearing danger, the Odio sisters decided to say nothing. However, the story of Sylvia's visitors eventually became known to the FBI and the Warren Commission. In an effort to disprove Odio's story, the FBI produced a man named Loran †Hall, who said he was one of the three men who visited Sylvia. Hall's account of the incident fell apart when his alleged companions—William Seymour and Lawrence

Howard—called it untrue. When photos of these three men were shown to Sylvia, she said none of the individuals shown had visited her. A Warren Commission lawyer wrote that Sylvia "checked out thoroughly." He said the evidence of the visit was "unanimously favorable," and that she was the "most significant witness linking Oswald with the anti-Castro Cubans." Despite this opinion, the Commission chose to disregard Odio's story.

See also ANTI-CASTRO CUBANS.

[[*Conspiracy; Rush to Judgment*

ODOM, LEE

The name Lee Odom was found among other names and addresses in an address book belonging to Clay †Shaw, who had been arrested on charges brought by New Orleans district attorney Jim †Garrison of participating in the assassination of President Kennedy. Odom's address appeared in the book as P.O. Box 19106, Dallas, Texas. The same post office box number was found in Lee Harvey †Oswald's address book, even though in 1963 post office boxes had not yet been assigned numbers that high. Garrison challenged Shaw about this. Several days later, Shaw's lawyers turned up a man named Lee Odom who had rented post office box 174 in Irving, Texas, a Dallas suburb.

Odom said box 19106 had been used for several months by a barbecue company with which he had been associated. The relationship between Odom and Shaw was alleged to have concerned an idea for promoting a bullfight in New Orleans. Why Oswald had the same address in his book—and why he would have listed a post office box number that did not yet exist—are questions that remain unanswered.
📖 *On the Trail of the Assassins*

O'DONNELL, KENNETH

A special assistant to the president, and a member of what the press called Kennedy's "Irish Mafia," O'Donnell accompanied Kennedy to Texas and stayed with the coffin during the return trip to Washington aboard †*Air Force One.*
See also MCHUGH, GODFREY; O'BRIEN, LAWRENCE F.; POWERS, DAVE.
📖 *Death of a President*

ODUM, BARDWELL D.

Marguerite †Oswald, Lee Harvey †Oswald's mother, told the †Warren Commission that FBI agent Bardwell Odum visited her on November 23, 1963, the day before Jack †Ruby shot her son. During the visit, Agent Odum asked her to look at a photograph and identify the man

pictured. Marguerite said she did not know the man.
After her son was killed, she realized the man in the
photo Odum had shown her was Ruby. The FBI claims
the photograph originated with the CIA. According to
the FBI, the CIA said it was a man they suspected of
having ties with Oswald. The Agency denies that the
subject of the photograph was Ruby.
📖 *Rush to Judgment; Warren Report*

OFFICE OF NAVAL INTELLIGENCE (ONI)
Although there is no evidence to substantiate the
claim, some assassination researchers suspect that
Lee Harvey †Oswald was an agent for the Office of
Naval Intelligence. ONI's headquarters in New
Orleans was barely fifty feet from †544 Camp Street,
the address of Oswald's phony †Fair Play for Cuba
Committee and the building that housed the offices of
Guy †Banister, who was a former FBI and ONI agent.
📖 *High Treason; On the Trail of the Assassins*

OFFICE OF STRATEGIC SERVICES (OSS)
The Office of Strategic Services, the forerunner of the
†Central Intelligence Agency, was dissolved after
World War II by President Harry Truman. Truman
feared the OSS was involved in clandestine operations

that could lead the United States into trouble. When
the Central Intelligence Group, as it was first called,
was established, Truman expressly denied the new
agency license to engage in clandestine activities.
Following the assassination of Kennedy, Truman said
he was "disturbed" by what the CIA had become.
📖 *High Treason*

OGLESBY, CARL

Oglesby has spent years researching and writing about
the assassination of President Kennedy. Instrumental
in calling for a congressional investigation of the
matter, he was highly critical of the †House Select
Committee on Assassinations. He called its treatment
of Lee Harvey †Oswald's motivation for killing Kennedy
"confused and dogmatic," and said the Committee's
treatment of medical and technical evidence was
"shallow." Oglesby is the author of *Who Killed JFK?*
and *The JFK Assassination: The Facts and the
Theories,* both published by Signet in 1992.
📖 *High Treason*

O'LEARY, MUGGSEY

O'Leary was one of only five †Secret Service agents
present at the president's autopsy, according to

[†]Warren Commission records. According to James Curtis [†]Jenkins, a medical technologist who was also present, there were many unidentified civilians sitting in the gallery overlooking the autopsy room.

📖 *Best Evidence*

OLIVER, BETTY

Known to early researchers as the "Babushka Lady" because of the head covering she is seen wearing in photos of the assassination scene, Betty Oliver was filming the motorcade on her 8-millimeter movie camera when the shooting occurred. Her film was confiscated by an FBI agent she believes was Regis [†]Kennedy. The film disappeared without, as far as is known, ever being viewed by anyone. Oliver was familiar with many of the players involved (and allegedly involved) in the assassination. In addition to having been at the scene, she worked at the Colony Club, which was next door to Jack [†]Ruby's [†]Carousel Club, and knew Ruby. She is alleged to have claimed that Ruby once introduced her to a man named Lee [†]Oswald, who Ruby said was from the CIA. She also allegedly claimed she saw David [†]Ferrie in Ruby's club so often she thought he managed the place.

📖 *High Treason*

OLIVIER, DR. ALFRED G.

A veterinarian described by the †Warren Commission as "a doctor who had spent 7 years in wounds ballistics research with the U.S. Army," Olivier was one of the experts the Commission enlisted to conduct experiments designed to prove the †single bullet theory. Olivier testified that he did not believe the president's head wound was caused by a copper-jacketed bullet. Olivier examined a goat carcass into which a bullet was fired from the †Mannlicher-Carcano rifle alleged to be the murder weapon. He found the wounds "very similar" to the wound made in Governor John †Connally's chest, but reported that the bullet recovered from the test was "quite flattened." A second bullet was fired into the wrist of a human cadaver, causing a wound closely resembling the one to Connally's wrist. That bullet suffered a "severely flattened" nose from striking the bone. These experiments were conducted in an attempt to replicate the injuries to Governor Connally by a bullet that allegedly first wounded President Kennedy. Yet this, the so-called †magic bullet, was discovered in virtually perfect condition, not flattened as each of the test bullets was after causing only a portion of the damage the magic bullet is attributed with inflicting.
📖 *Rush to Judgment*

ONEAL, VERNON

The proprietor of a funeral home in Dallas, Oneal provided the four-hundred-pound bronze casket in which President Kennedy's body was allegedly taken from †Parkland Memorial Hospital and transported via †*Air Force One* to †Bethesda Naval Hospital. Two Oneal employees placed the body inside the casket, and Oneal closed it.

Rumors persist to this day that two large green oxygen tanks and a body bag were picked up at Oneal's Funeral Home, either by the hearse or by †Secret Service men in another vehicle, and that the tanks were used to simulate the president's weight in the casket while his body was transferred to another coffin.

President Kennedy was not buried in the casket and it was eventually returned to Oneal, who also allegedly received in payment a check for $13,495, an exorbitant amount for a casket in 1963. This suggests to some researchers that there may have been a payoff to Oneal; the amount is alleged to be $10,000 more than the fee that had been agreed on.

The same sources responsible for reports of the missing oxygen tanks claim that when the casket was returned to Dallas, it had chips of green paint inside, but no bloodstains.

See also BODY BAG CONTROVERSY; COFFIN

CONTROVERSY; McGUIRE, DENNIS "PEANUTS"; RIKE, AUBREY.
📖 *Best Evidence; High Treason 2*

O'NEILL AND SIBERT REPORT

FBI agent Francis X. O'Neill attended the president's autopsy with fellow FBI agent James Sibert. Although O'Neill and Sibert submitted a minutely detailed five-page report on which the official FBI summary of the autopsy appeared to be based, no mention of their role appears in the †Warren Report, or in the accompanying twenty-six volumes of testimony and evidence.

Three significant items in the O'Neill and Sibert report provide impressive evidence that belies the †single bullet theory. First, the report states that the bullet that entered the president's back did not travel through the body the way it was later described as doing when the wound was found to be caused by the †magic bullet. Second, the FBI agents described the wound as low in the back, not in the neck as stated by subscribers to the magic bullet theory. Finally, the report states that on examination of the body at the start of the autopsy, it was discovered that there had been "surgery of the head area, namely, in the top of the skull." Sibert later claimed that the statement concerning surgery to the top of Kennedy's head had been a mistake. The

questions raised by this report have never been dealt with adequately by an official investigative body.
See also AUTOPSY CONTROVERSY; THROAT WOUND CONTROVERSY.

📖 *Best Evidence*; *High Treason 2*

OPERATION 40

This was a CIA-organized and funded group of †anti-Castro Cubans described by Marita †Lorenz as an "assassination squad." CIA contract agent Frank †Sturgis admitted to playing a leadership role in the group. Lorenz claimed the men she accompanied on a trip to Dallas just before the Kennedy assassination were all members of Operation 40, and that they brought a small arsenal of weapons with them to the city. Lorenz charged the group with plotting the murder of Fidel †Castro as well as that of John F. Kennedy.
See also E. HOWARD HUNT.

📖 *High Treason*; *Plausible Denial*

OPERATION ZAPATA

Operation Zapata was the code name for the invasion of Cuba by Cuban exiles armed and trained by the CIA.
See also BAY OF PIGS.

ORGANIZED CRIME
See MAFIA.

ORTH, HERBERT
The photo chief at *Life* magazine in 1963, Orth edited the †Zapruder film for publication in the November 29, 1963, issue. CIA documents describing the time intervals between shots coincide exactly with the intervals set down in the *Life* article. This has given rise to speculation about whether the CIA supplied *Life* with the information, or whether the Agency had a copy of the film later and got its information from the *Life* data.
Best Evidence

"OSBORNE"
See ALIASES USED BY OSWALD.

OSBORNE, ALBERT
See BOWEN, JOHN "JACK."

OSBORNE, DR. DAVID
A Navy captain in 1963, and later an admiral, Osborne was present during the Kennedy autopsy in his role as chief of surgery at †Bethesda Naval Hospital. Osborne reportedly told investigators from the †House Select

Committee on Assassinations that when the president's
body was removed from the casket and placed on a table
for the autopsy, a "reasonably clean" and "unmarred"
bullet rolled out from under the body. Osborne insisted
to researcher David S. †Lifton that he actually picked
the bullet up and held it in his hand. Lifton claims that
Captain John †Stover, the commanding officer of the
U.S. Naval Medical School at the time, confirmed the
presence in the autopsy room of a complete bullet, but
that he thought it was the one found on a stretcher in
Dallas. The only complete bullet in this case is the
†magic bullet that was found in †Parkland Memorial
Hospital. Records demonstrate that this bullet traveled
from Dallas to the White House †Secret Service chief to
the FBI lab; it never went near Bethesda, and had no
reason to be sent there.
See also CUSTER, JERROL F.; TOMLINSON, DARREL C.
📕 *Best Evidence*

OSS
See OFFICE OF STRATEGIC SERVICES.

OSWALD, BACKYARD PHOTOGRAPH OF
This famous photograph, supposedly of Lee Harvey
†Oswald, was allegedly taken by Marina †Oswald in the
backyard of their home at 214 Neeley Street in Dallas.

The backyard photo of Lee Harvey Oswald

The photo, which shows "Oswald" holding copies of two militant communist newspapers—*The Worker* and *The Militant*—as well as a rifle resembling the †Mannlicher-Carcano rifle purported to be the assassination weapon, appeared on the cover of *Life* magazine's February 24, 1964, issue—as the †Warren Commission was still in the midst of its investigation. When questioned about the photograph by police while he was in custody after the assassination, Oswald said that it was a fake. Subsequent statements by photographic analysts, including John †Pickard and Malcolm †Thompson, have supported Oswald's claim. Analysts have pointed out, for example, that the photograph shows a man with a square chin, whereas Oswald's chin was somewhat pointed, and that the shadows cast by the facial features of the man in the photograph do not correspond, directionally, with other shadows in the photograph—leading to the supposition that the photo may represent a montage in which part of Oswald's face has been superimposed on a photograph of someone else. In February 1992, the *Houston Post* reported that the Dallas Police Department had released several copies of the backyard photo; the *Post* claimed that the photo "shows clear evidence of darkroom manipulation."

An interesting strand of the lore surrounding this photograph involves Roscoe †White, who allegedly

claimed to have been the actual assassin of President
Kennedy. It has been reported that, in 1975, the home
of White and his wife, Geneva, was burglarized; the
thieves were apprehended, and among the Whites'
belongings that were discovered in their possession was
a theretofore unknown print of the backyard photograph. How the Whites came by the photograph has not
been explained.
See also BOOKHOUT, JAMES W.
📖 *High Treason 2; Rush to Judgment*

OSWALD, LEE HARVEY

Twenty-four-year-old Lee Harvey Oswald was identified
by the †Warren Commission as the †lone assassin of
President Kennedy, despite the fact that no motive for
the killing could be discovered. When Oswald was
arrested, he cried out that he was a "patsy," a cry that
is still heard today by researchers and writers who
continue to challenge the Commission's findings.

For a young man, Oswald had a crowded and
bizarre past. He served in the Marine Corps from 1956
to 1959, and there is evidence to support the
contention that his Marine Corps assignments may
have supplied him with knowledge concerning the
secret missions of †U-2 spy planes (*see also* ATSUGI
AIR BASE). In 1959, Oswald defected to the Soviet

Union, where he remained until 1962. While in the U.S.S.R. he lived mostly in the city of †Minsk, where he met and married his Russian wife, Marina (*see* OSWALD, MARINA, *below*). Many researchers consider Oswald's defection a ruse cloaking an operation of U.S. intelligence agencies. It has been clearly demonstrated that Oswald had ties to the †Central Intelligence Agency, and possibly to the †Federal Bureau of Investigation and the †Office of Naval Intelligence.

On returning to the United States in 1962, Oswald and his family lived first in Fort Worth, Texas, later moving to Dallas, where he took a job with the graphic arts firm of †Jaggers-Chiles-Stovall. In the summer of 1963, leaving Marina behind in Dallas, Oswald moved to New Orleans, where he lived with relatives and worked for the †William Reily Coffee Company. While in New Orleans, Oswald was closely involved with †anti-Castro Cubans and Americans— even though he was photographed and arrested while distributing pro-Castro propaganda, ostensibly for the †Fair Play for Cuba Committee, a phony branch of which he had established at †544 Camp Street.

Returning to Dallas in the early fall of 1963, Oswald continued to live separately from his wife and daughter (a second daughter was born in October),

who were staying in the home of Ruth †Paine in the
Dallas suburb of Irving. Oswald lived in a series of
rented rooms in Dallas. According to the Warren
Commission, Oswald made a mysterious trip to
†Mexico City in late September and early October,
apparently visiting the Soviet and Cuban embassies
there in an effort to arrange passage back to the
U.S.S.R. Many assassination researchers have
doubted the veracity of this story, construing elements
of it as CIA disinformation promulgated to cover up
the Agency's role in the president's assassination.

Two weeks prior to the assassination, Oswald took
a job as a warehouseman at the †Texas School Book
Depository Building. It was from a †sniper's nest
constructed of cardboard boxes behind a window on the
sixth floor of that building that the Warren
Commission concluded Oswald had fired three shots at
the presidential motorcade passing through †Dealey
Plaza at 12:30 P.M. on November 22, 1963. According to
the Commission's widely disputed determinations, one
of these bullets struck the pavement, one delivered
nonfatal wounds to both President Kennedy and Texas
governor John †Connally, and a third struck the
president in the head, killing him. The Commission
also reached the equally disputed conclusion that, after
leaving the assassination scene, Oswald shot and

killed Dallas police officer J. D. †Tippit in the Oak Cliff section of Dallas at 1:15 P.M. According to the official version of events, it was for Tippit's murder that Oswald was first picked up by police, who discovered him hiding out in the †Texas Theatre.

In an incredibly dramatic event witnessed by millions watching on TV, Oswald was himself killed two days after the assassination, when he was shot by Jack †Ruby in the basement garage of Dallas Police Headquarters.

Many researchers believe that Oswald had no direct part in the assassination of President Kennedy, while others suspect he was just one of the assassins in Dallas on November 22, 1963.

See also ALIASES USED BY OSWALD.

OSWALD, MARGUERITE
Mother of Lee Harvey †Oswald, Marguerite obtained the services of attorney Mark †Lane to protect her son's rights before the †Warren Commission. Lane also

Lee Harvey Oswald is murdered by Jack Ruby in the basement of Dallas Police Headquarters on the morning of Sunday, November 24, 1963.

tried to represent the alleged assassin in the role of defense attorney, but was refused by the Commission. Marguerite, along with Oswald's wife, Marina, and their two children were taken into "protective custody" by the †Secret Service on November 24, 1963, despite Marguerite's objections. When she finally forced her own release on November 28, she claimed the Secret Service would not release Marina and the children, and refused to allow her to see them to say goodbye. Marguerite Oswald never wavered from her conviction that her son was innocent of the charge of killing President Kennedy.

See also ODUM, BARDWELL D.

📖 *Rush to Judgment*

OSWALD, MARINA

Lee Harvey †Oswald's young, Russian-born wife was considered a more reliable witness by the †Warren Commission than his mother, despite Marina's often conflicting testimony. Perhaps this was because unlike Marguerite †Oswald, who continued to believe in her son's innocence, Marina, evidently under the influence of †Secret Service and FBI agents who held her in isolated "protective custody" for months, changed her mind about her husband and agreed with the federal officers that he was guilty. In addition to possibly

Marina Oswald in 1988

influencing her story, federal officials found her an attorney and a business manager, James H. †Martin, to look after her financial interests. Many suspect that the threat, stated or implied, that if she failed to cooperate, she might be deported back to the Soviet Union, was constantly hanging over her head.

Examples of her conflicting testimony include a statement to the Secret Service in December 1963 that she never saw Lee with a pistol; then, the following February, she identified the pistol allegedly used to kill Police Officer J. D. †Tippit as her husband's. At first she called Lee a "good family man," but later claimed he beat her. The tone of her responses to questioning, and the alterations in her answers, have led many observers to suspect she was coached by federal authorities.

See also PAINE, RUTH.

📖 *Best Evidence; Plausible Denial; Rush to Judgment*

OSWALD, ROBERT

Robert, Lee Harvey †Oswald's brother, testified to the †Warren Commission that Lee and Jack †Ruby knew each other. After he visited his brother in jail, Robert reported that Lee told him not to be taken in by the "so-called evidence."

📖 *Best Evidence; High Treason*

O'TOOLE, GEORGE

Author of *The* †*Assassination Tapes* (Penthouse Press, 1975), and a former CIA computer analysis specialist, O'Toole believes certain people in the Dallas Police Department could have helped frame Lee Harvey †Oswald for both the Kennedy and J. D. †Tippit murders. He charges, among other things, that the handgun allegedly taken from Oswald was never proven to be the Tippit murder weapon. He claims that tapes of Oswald's statement that he didn't shoot anybody were examined in a "psychological stress evaluator" test and showed he was telling the truth. O'Toole raises several questions about the veracity of statements made by various individuals involved in the assassination and its aftermath.

OVERPASS WITNESSES

In November 1963 work was being performed on the railroad tracks that pass over Commerce, Main, and Elm streets as they head west out of †Dealey Plaza. Many of the workmen on the overpass stopped to watch the presidential motorcade move through the plaza and head directly under them. Only a few of these men were questioned by the FBI and the †Warren Commission. Every one of them reported sounds or sights that led them to believe the shots were fired from the area of the †Grassy Knoll. The testimony or statements of these men are included in individual entries for Richard C. Dodd; Sam Holland; Clemmon Johnson; Austin Miller; Thomas Murphy; Frank Reilly; James Simmons; Royce G. Skelton; and Walter Winborn. Also on the overpass were Dallas police officers J. M. Foster and J. C. White.

OWENS, ERNEST JAY

According to Jim †Marrs, Owens reported to the Dallas police that while driving on Wood Street, not far from the assassination scene, he saw a heavyset man in a dark suit carrying a "foreign-made rifle." After the arrest of Lee Harvey †Oswald, the police seemed no longer interested in chasing down other leads.
📖 *Crossfire*

OXFORD, J. L.

Oxford was a Dallas deputy sheriff who, when he heard the shots, ran across †Dealey Plaza in the direction of the †Grassy Knoll, apparently in the belief that that was where the shots originated. Oxford encountered a bystander who told him he had seen †smoke near the wooden fence atop the Grassy Knoll. *See also* CRAIG, ROGER, D.
📖 *Best Evidence; Rush to Judgment*

P

PAINE, RUTH

Ruth Paine met Lee Harvey †Oswald and Marina
†Oswald at a social gathering in Dallas in February
1963. Two months later, Oswald decided to go to New
Orleans to seek work, and Ruth, who spoke some
Russian, invited Marina, who spoke little English, to
bring her small daughter and stay with her in her
home in Irving, Texas, a Dallas suburb. Ruth and her
husband, Michael, were separated at the time. Both
Paines belonged to a local chapter of the †American
Civil Liberties Union, and Michael took Lee to at least
one meeting of the organization.

In May 1963, Ruth drove Marina and her
daughter to New Orleans to join Lee, who had found
work there. In September Ruth once again drove to
New Orleans, this time to pick up Marina, who was
pregnant with the couple's second child, and her
daughter, to take them back to Irving, where they
again lived in the Paine home. Marina continued to

live with Ruth Paine until after the assassination, even though Lee had moved back to Dallas prior to that. During this time Lee would visit his family at the Paine home only on weekends. The one exception was his stay there the night before the assassination.

According to a report by Dallas County sheriff's deputy Roger D. †Craig, when Oswald was confronted with Craig's charge that he had seen Oswald run from the †Texas School Book Depository Building and jump into a waiting station wagon, Oswald blurted out that the car belonged to Mrs. Paine, and that the cops should not try to get her involved in the assassination.

📖 *Conspiracy; Crossfire; Death of a President; Warren Report*

PALMPRINT ON RIFLE

The †Mannlicher-Carcano rifle allegedly found on the sixth floor of the †Texas School Book Depository Building was turned over to Dallas police lieutenant J. Carl †Day, who examined it for fingerprints. Day claimed that he removed a palmprint from the underside of the barrel before he sent the weapon on to the FBI lab in Washington on the night of the assassination. According to Sebastian Francis †Latona, head of the FBI's Latent Fingerprint Section, there were no prints of value on the rifle. The weapon was then returned to the Dallas police. Several days later, on November 26, Day acknowledged that he had taken a palmprint from the weapon. The print matched Lee Harvey †Oswald's right hand.

According to reports by both Paul †Groody, a funeral director at the Miller Funeral Home in Dallas, and Jack †Moseley, a Fort Worth reporter, it seems probable that a group of men they believed were federal agents took fingerprints and palmprints from Oswald's body during the predawn hours of November 25 while the body lay in a room at the funeral home and before it was prepared for burial. Because this incident took place one day before it was announced that Oswald's palmprint had been found on the weapon, there has been much speculation about the real source of the palmprint.

According to Lieutenant Day, the palmprint was lifted from a section of the gun's barrel that is covered by the wood stock. He had to remove the stock to locate the print. All the palmprint establishes, provided its discovery was as reported, is that at some point Oswald held the weapon's barrel in his hand while the rifle was dismantled.

See also DRAIN, VINCENT.

📖 *Best Evidence; Rush to Judgment*

PARKLAND MEMORIAL HOSPITAL

In 1963, Parkland was one of the primary-care hospitals in Dallas, as it is today. It was the scene of the deaths of President John F. Kennedy, and Lee Harvey †Oswald. The hospital is located approximately four miles from †Dealey Plaza.

PARKLAND MEMORIAL HOSPITAL STAFF

When news reached the hospital via the police dispatcher that President Kennedy had been wounded and was being rushed to Parkland, nurses and doctors prepared for the most important patient the emergency room had ever admitted. Critics of the autopsy performed at †Bethesda Naval Hospital rely on the statements of the Parkland medical staff because they were more spontaneous, less inclined to political influence, and less colored by the pressure of individuals who might not want certain information made public. The descriptions of the president's head wounds made by Parkland staff differ so strikingly from those made by the doctors at Bethesda who performed the autopsy that one might be led to believe the two teams were describing different patients.

Among the medical staff at Parkland who worked on President Kennedy and Governor John †Connally were the following idividuals, each of whom is

discussed in an entry in this book under his or her name: Dr. Gene C. Akin; Dr. Fouad A. Bashour; Dr. Charles R. Baxter; Audrey Bell; Diana Bowron; Dr. Kemp Clark; Dr. Charles A. Crenshaw; Dr. Richard Dulaney; Dr. Adolph Giesecke; Dr. Charles Gregory; Dr. Robert Grossman; Margaret Henchcliffe; Dr. Jackie Hunt; Patricia Hutton; Dr. Marion Jenkins; Dr. Ronald Jones; Dr. Robert N. McClelland; Dr. Malcolm Perry; Dr. Paul Peters; and Dr. Philip Williams.
📖 *Best Evidence; High Treason 2*

PARKLAND PRESS CONFERENCE
In response to demands for information from reporters gathered in and around †Parkland Memorial Hospital following the announcement of the president's death, a press conference was held at about 3:00 P.M. on November 22, 1963, at which Dr. Malcolm †Perry and Dr. Kemp †Clark presided. The information these two men conveyed to the press at this time is important because it was spontaneous and described exactly what they had seen. It was unmarred by the pressures that later seemed to influence testimony. For example, as the press conference transcript shows, Dr. Perry was unequivocal in his description of the president's †throat wound as a bullet entry wound. Subsequently,

in testifying before the †Warren Commission, Perry wavered in his assessment of the wound after receiving an admonition about "false rumors" from Commission member and former CIA director Allen W. †Dulles.

The following is an excerpt from the official transcript of the press conference:

> QUESTION: Where was the entrance wound?
> DR. PERRY: There was an entrance wound in the neck.
> QUESTION: Which way was the bullet coming on the neck wound? At him?
> DR. PERRY: It appeared to be coming at him? . . .
> QUESTION: Doctor, describe the entrance wound. You think from the front in the throat?
> DR. PERRY: The wound appeared to be an entrance wound in the front of the throat; yes, that is correct. . . .

Critics find support for their skepticism toward the Warren Commission in these and other remarks by the medical team at Parkland.
📖 *Best Evidence*

PARTIN, EDWARD
See DANIELS, HAWK.

PATERNI, PAUL

Paterni was one of the †Secret Service agents who inspected the presidential limousine after it was returned to the White House. He reportedly found a metal fragment on the front seat of the car, which some believe to have come from the †magic bullet. Another fragment was allegedly found in the rear seat by Thomas †Mills.

📖 *Best Evidence*

PATTERSON, B. M.

Patterson was an employee of the Reynolds Motor Company on East Jefferson Boulevard in the Oak Cliff section of Dallas. He was one of three employees who claimed to have seen a man with a handgun running from the scene of the shooting of J. D. †Tippit. Patterson was later questioned by the FBI. When he learned that the FBI report of his interview said that he had been shown a picture of Lee Harvey †Oswald, he signed an affidavit requesting that the report be changed because he had never been shown a picture of Oswald. The original FBI report was included in the †Warren Commission documents without the changes Patterson requested.

See also LEWIS, L. J.; REYNOLDS, WARREN.

📖 *Rush to Judgment*

PAUL, RALPH

Ralph Paul was a Dallas restaurant owner and longtime friend and financial backer of Jack †Ruby's. Paul held an interest in Ruby's †Carousel Club. Paul and Ruby dined together the night before Kennedy was killed at a restaurant owned by their mutual friend Joseph †Campisi. Campisi allegedly had ties with the †Mafia organizations of Carlos †Marcello and Santos †Trafficante, both considered suspects in the assassination by many researchers.

The night before he killed Lee Harvey †Oswald, Ruby made a series of telephone calls, including four to Paul. A waitress at Paul's restaurant, The Bull Pen, said she heard Paul say something about a gun during the first call he received from Ruby that evening. Paul also had an interest in another restaurant, Austin's Bar-B-Cue, where Police Officer J. D.†Tippit moonlighted as a security guard.
📖 *Conspiracy*

PELLICANO, ANTHONY

An assassination researcher, Pellicano criticized the acoustical work done by Dr. James †Barger on the †Dallas police dispatch tape. Pellicano believes there was a conspiracy to kill Kennedy and suspects that the disruption in police radio communications

supposedly caused by an unintentionally open microphone on a policeman's motorcycle was actually someone's attempt to jam police communications during the assassination.
See also ACOUSTICAL EVIDENCE.
📖 *High Treason*

PENA, OREST

According to researcher and author Mark †Lane, Pena requested that Lane represent him in a criminal case following his arrest by the New Orleans Police. In return for Lane's legal services, Pena promised to tell him all he knew about Lee Harvey †Oswald's connections to the †Federal Bureau of Investigation. Pena operated a bar and house of prostitution and allegedly provided temporary living quarters for Cuban exiles in the employ of the †Central Intelligence Agency. Pena also claimed to be working for a local FBI agent, Warren †deBrueys.

According to Lane, Pena told him that Oswald worked for the FBI and reported to deBrueys, whom he met on a regular basis. DeBrueys is alleged to have introduced Oswald to local CIA contacts. When Texas attorney general Waggoner †Carr informed the †Warren Commission that he had learned Oswald was an "undercover agent" employed by the FBI, the

Commission asked J. Edgar †Hoover for a statement to the contrary. With that, the matter was dropped.
📖 *Plausible Denial*

PENN, MRS. LOVELL
Mrs. Penn is reported to have discovered three men firing a rifle illegally on her property in the Dallas area. This supposedly occurred in October 1963. After chasing them away, she found an empty cartridge case allegedly stamped with the name †Mannlicher-Carcano, the brand of rifle Lee Harvey †Oswald supposedly used to kill the president.
📖 *On the Trail of the Assassins*

PERMINDEX
Permindex was a sister organization of the Centro Mondiale Commerciale in Italy, allegedly an organization of pro-Fascists through which the †Central Intelligence Agency funneled funds to paramilitary and intelligence groups. Clay †Shaw, who was charged with, but not convicted of, participation in the Kennedy assassination served on the boards of directors of both organizations. Jim †Garrison was unaware of this when he failed to convince a New Orleans jury of Shaw's links to the CIA.
📖 *On the Trail of the Assassins*

PERRY, DR. MALCOLM

Dr. Perry was an attending surgeon at †Parkland
Memorial Hospital when President Kennedy was
brought in after the shooting. Perry was the second
doctor to examine Kennedy, and he almost immediately performed a †tracheotomy in an attempt to
improve the patient's breathing. The tracheotomy cut
was made over what Perry and virtually everyone else
in the emergency room described as a bullet entry
wound in the throat. After Kennedy died, Perry
described the wound to reporters as an entry wound.
This same wound was described by the †Warren
Commission as an exit wound.
See also PARKLAND MEMORIAL HOSPITAL STAFF;
PARKLAND PRESS CONFERENCE.
📖 *Best Evidence*

PETERS, DR. PAUL

A physician at †Parkland Memorial Hospital, Dr.
Peters arrived in the emergency room shortly after
President Kennedy was brought in. He noticed what
he called "the wound of entry in the throat." Later a
professor and chairman of the Urology Department at
Southwestern Medical School, Dr. Peters was shown
the official autopsy pictures of the president's head
wound. He is reported as saying, "I don't think it's

consistent with what I saw." When he viewed the drawing of the wound made by another Parkland doctor, Robert N. †McClelland, his reported response was, "It's not too far off." The controversy over what the doctors in Dallas report they saw and what the Bethesda autopsy pictures show continues.
See also AUTOPSY CONTROVERSY; HEAD WOUND CONTROVERSY; PARKLAND MEMORIAL HOSPITAL STAFF; THROAT WOUND CONTROVERSY.
◻ *Best Evidence; High Treason*

PETTY, DR. CHARLES

Dr. Petty was a member of the Forensic Pathology Panel created by the †House Select Committee on Assassinations to review the Kennedy autopsy report, X rays, and photographs. On September 16, 1977, the panel met with the autopsy team of Dr. James J. †Humes and Dr. Thornton †Boswell. Dr. Petty's first question appeared to set the tone for this meeting. In view of the widely discussed reports that Kennedy had Addison's disease, which is a failure of the adrenal glands, and the fact that "normally we examine the adrenals in the general course [of an] autopsy," he asked Dr. Humes whether he had looked at the adrenals, because no mention of having done so appeared in the autopsy report. Humes's response was, "Since I don't think it bore directly on the death of the president, I'd prefer not to discuss it with you, Doctor."

Although five of the six panel members supported the †Warren Report—the exception was Dr. Cyril H. †Wecht—many observers regard the autopsy with suspicion, judging that at best it was ineptly performed.

See also AUTOPSY CONTROVERSY.

📖 *Best Evidence*

PHILLIPS, DAVID ATLEE

Phillips's lengthy career with the †Central Intelligence Agency culminated in his appointment in the 1960s as head of operations in the Western Hemisphere. He was a covert operative in Havana from 1958 to 1961 and bitterly blamed Kennedy for the †Bay of Pigs failure. Phillips was working out of †Mexico City at the time of Lee Harvey †Oswald's alleged visits to the Cuban and Soviet embassies there. In 1977, he explained to the †House Select Committee on Assassinations that no intelligence photos of Oswald's Mexico City trip were available because a photographic capability was not in operation on a twenty-four-hour-a-day basis and Oswald visited the embassies while the cameras were off.

CIA operative David Atlee Phillips

Virtually everyone familiar with the claim that Oswald visited Mexico City in September 1963 finds it strange that not even one photograph of him during any of his alleged five visits to the embassies was captured by CIA surveillance cameras. Few researchers believe the person who made these visits was Oswald.

Phillips, who is believed by some researchers to have used the alias "Maurice †Bishop," is suspected of having tried to foment a confrontation between the United States and the Soviet Union over Cuba. He also told the Assassinations Committee that when Lee Harvey Oswald was in Mexico City, his reason for visiting the Cuban and Soviet embassies was to try to arrange for his return to the Soviet Union.

📖 *Conspiracy; High Treason; Plausible Denial*

PICKARD, JOHN

Army major Pickard was the commanding officer of the Canadian Defense Department's photographic division. In 1977, the Canadian Broadcasting Corporation asked him to study the famous photographs of a man alleged to be Lee Harvey †Oswald holding a rifle and a newspaper while standing in the backyard of a home. Largely because of the inconsistencies of the shadows caused by the figure's nose and those of his body, Pickard decided the pictures had the "earmarks of being faked." Pickard claimed that the body in one photo is larger than that in the other, yet the heads match perfectly in size. The shadows of the nose and the torso fall in different directions, indicating that those portions of the body were photographed at different times of the day. This supports Oswald's charge, made while he was being questioned at Dallas Police Headquarters, that a picture of his head had been superimposed on the body of someone else who was holding the rifle. That the photos were faked is also supported by Malcolm †Thompson.

See also OSWALD, BACKYARD PHOTOGRAPH OF.

📖 *Conspiracy*

PITZER, WILLIAM B.

A trained X-ray technician at †Bethesda Naval Hospital, Navy commander Pitzer is believed to have filmed the Kennedy autopsy from the gallery overlooking the room. According to Dennis †David, Pitzer had in his possession a movie of the autopsy and slides that were presumably made from the film. Pitzer's name, however, does not appear on the official list of those who attended the autopsy.

Commander Pitzer was found dead of a gunshot
wound to the head in his Bethesda office on October
29, 1966. The death was ruled a suicide. After years of
delay, the Navy finally released the report of Pitzer's
autopsy, which revealed no gunpowder burns to the
head, evidence that would be present had he held the
gun in his own hand. The bullet that killed Pitzer was
fired into the right side of his head, although friends
claim he was left-handed. In addition, both his wife
and David, who was a close friend, claim there was no
reason for him to kill himself. They believe he was
murdered to prevent his film—now vanished—from
becoming public, and as a warning to anyone else who
might possess evidence concerning the autopsy.
See also AUTOPSY CONTROVERSY.
📖 *High Treason; High Treason 2*

PIZZO, FRANK
Pizzo was Albert G. †Bogard's boss at †Downtown
Lincoln-Mercury in Dallas. While Bogard's memory of
the man calling himself Lee Oswald was not that good,
Pizzo's was much stronger. When shown photos of Lee
Harvey †Oswald by the †Warren Commission, he
described a man who looked similar to, but not exactly
like, Oswald. When pressed to identify the man in the
picture as the man who had visited the dealership on

November 9, 1963, and had remarked that he would
be coming into money soon to buy a new car, Pizzo
responded, "I have to say that he is not the one."
📖 *On the Trail of the Assassins*

PLAUSIBLE DENIAL

Written by Mark †Lane and published in 1991 by
Thunder's Mouth Press, *Plausible Denial: Was the CIA
Involved in the Assassination of JFK?* tells the
fascinating story surrounding a lawsuit brought by
former CIA operative and Watergate conspirator
E. Howard †Hunt against the right-wing publication
†*Spotlight*. Lane acted as the attorney for the
defendants in the suit, *Spotlight* and its publisher,
†Liberty Lobby, Inc.

Hunt's suit was based on his charge that he had
been defamed in an article published by *Spotlight* in
September 1978. Titled "CIA to Admit Hunt Involved
in Kennedy Assassination," the article was written by
another former CIA operative, Victor †Marchetti. In
the piece, Marchetti alleged that the †Central Intelligence Agency was about to engage in what is known
as a "limited hangout"—a strategy used when the
Agency can no longer cover up some misdeed and so
releases a small part of the truth to the public in an
effort to satisfy people's demand to know without the

Agency's having to reveal too much damaging information. In the "limited hangout" Marchetti wrote about, the CIA was going to provide the †House Select Committee on Assassinations with evidence that Hunt's alibi concerning his whereabouts on the day of the assassination was a lie and that he was indeed in Dallas on November 22, 1963.

The case permitted Lane to submit a long list of CIA-related individuals to searching questions about their knowledge of or involvement in the assassination. When the trial concluded—with a decision in *Spotlight's* favor—the jury forewoman, Leslie †Armstrong, told reporters that Lane had convinced her that the CIA had indeed killed President Kennedy.

See also HELMS, RICHARD; LORENZ, MARITA; STURGIS, FRANK.

POE, J. M.

At the scene of the murder of Police Officer J. D. †Tippit, Officer Poe was handed two spent cartridges picked up by one of the witnesses, Domingo †Benavides. Poe scratched his initials, JMP, into the cartridges as a way of later confirming their identity. When the †Warren Commission showed him four cartridges allegedly from the bullets used to kill Tippit,

Poe was unable to identify them because none bore his initials. Sergeant Willie E. †Barnes, who also scratched his initials into cartridges found at the scene, had similar difficulty in precisely identifying them when the Warren Commission presented him with the cartridges it claimed had been found at the scene.
📖 *Rush to Judgment*

PONTCHARTRAIN, LAKE

A large lake north of New Orleans, Lake Pontchartrain was the site of a CIA-supported training camp for Cuban exiles who were being prepared for an invasion of Cuba. When the Kennedy administration learned of the camp, the FBI was ordered to raid it and destroy all equipment found there. The raid was heavily publicized, as was Director J. Edgar †Hoover's habit, but its actual results in breaking up the groups engaged in training were questionable. Among those connected to the camp were David †Ferrie and Guy †Banister.
📖 *On the Trail of the Assassins*

POST OFFICE BOX 2915

When he moved from Fort Worth to nearby Dallas, Lee Harvey †Oswald rented post office box 2915 under

the name Lee H. Oswald. This box is the one
identified as the address of the recipient who ordered
the †Mannlicher-Carcano rifle allegedly found on the
sixth floor of the †Texas School Book Depository
Building after the assassination. It was also the
address of the recipient of the handgun allegedly used
to kill Police Officer J. D. †Tippit. The rifle was
shipped to the name A. Hidell by †Klein's Sporting
Goods Company of Chicago.
See also ALIASES USED BY OSWALD; HOLMES, HARRY D.
□ Conspiracy

POWELL, JAMES
James Powell, an Army intelligence officer, was locked
inside the Dal-Tex Building overlooking †Dealey Plaza
when the building was sealed immediately after the
assassination. Also inside the building was a †Mafia
courier named Eugene Hale Brading, who was using
the alias Jim †Braden. Powell's appearance at the
scene, and the suspected presence of other Army
intelligence agents, has led to speculation that
military intelligence officials may have been
responsible for the assassination and for setting up
Lee Harvey †Oswald as the scapegoat.
□ High Treason

POWELL, JOHN

John Powell, jailed for a minor infraction, occupied a sixth-floor cell of the Dallas County Jail, which was across the street from the †Texas School Book Depository Building. Years after the assassination, Powell said that he and many other prisoners saw two men in the "assassin's window" adjusting the telescopic sight on a rifle. According to Powell, one of the men he observed had dark-colored skin and appeared to be Latin. *See also* DARK-COMPLEXIONED MAN (OR MEN); MITCHELL, WILLIE.

📖 *Conspiracy; High Treason*

POWERS, DAVE

Powers was an assistant to President Kennedy and had joined him on the Texas trip. Powers was riding in the car directly behind the presidential limousine and witnessed both Kennedy's and John †Connally's reactions to the shots. He told the †Warren Commission that although his first impression was that the shots came from overhead and to the right, he also had a "fleeting impression that the noise appeared to come from in front in the area of the Triple Underpass." Powers returned to Washington in the rear of †*Air Force One* with Mrs. Kennedy and the casket.

See also MCHUGH, GODFREY; O'BRIEN, LAWRENCE F.;
O'DONNELL, KENNETH.
📖 *Best Evidence*; *Crossfire*

POWERS, GARY
See U-2 SPY PLANE.

POWERS, JACQUIE
A staff correspondent for the *Wilmington* [Del.]
Sunday News Journal, Powers and fellow
correspondent Joe Trento wrote an article published in
the August 20, 1978, issue of the paper exposing the
existence of a 1966 CIA memo written by William
Corson that definitely placed E. Howard †Hunt in
Dallas on the day of the assassination. The article
offers speculation that some CIA investigators may
have theorized that Hunt's purpose for being in Dallas
was to murder Lee Harvey †Oswald on orders from a
KGB mole who had infiltrated a high-level CIA post.
See also MARCHETTI, VICTOR.
📖 *Plausible Denial*

PREYER, RICHARDSON
A former federal judge, Preyer was a congressman
from North Carolina when he was appointed to the

†House Select Committee on Assassinations. After a period of turmoil that saw the original chief counsel, Richard †Sprague, forced out and Committee chairman Henry †Gonzalez resign in disgust, Preyer and the new chief counsel, G. Robert †Blakey, became de facto cochairmen. The new chairman, Louis †Stokes, showed little inclination to assume firm control over the Committee and its staff. Preyer concurred with the Committee's finding that the president's murder was probably the result of a conspiracy.
📖 *High Treason*

PRICE, JESSE C.
Jesse Price was watching the presidential motorcade from the roof of the Terminal Annex Building located across †Dealey Plaza from the †Grassy Knoll. Within an hour of the assassination, he gave the Dallas sheriff's office an affidavit stating that he heard a "volley" of shots, and saw a man running behind the fence on the Grassy Knoll toward some passenger cars on the railroad siding. Despite his vivid eyewitness testimony, Price was never questioned by the †Warren Commission. When author Mark †Lane interviewed him in 1966, Price said the man was carrying something that "could have been a gun."
📖 *Rush to Judgment*

PRICE, MALCOLM H.

Malcolm Price told the †Warren Commission he had seen a man he believed was Lee Harvey †Oswald practicing with a rifle at the Sports Drome Rifle Range in Dallas only weeks before the assassination. The other witnesses at the rifle range had mixed reactions to the identification; some of the patrons thought the man had been Oswald, while others did not.

See also SLACK, GARLAND G.

☐ *Rush to Judgment*

PROUTY, L. FLETCHER

Colonel Prouty was the liaison officer between the Air Force and the †Central Intelligence Agency in their cooperative †U-2 spy plane operation during the time Lee Harvey †Oswald served in the Marines and during his subsequent defection to the Soviet Union. Prouty said Oswald was no ordinary Marine, and that he was probably on a cover assignment when he went to the Soviet Union.

Prouty is the author of *The Secret Team: The CIA and Its Allies in Control of the United States and the World,* published by Prentice-Hall in 1973, and *JFK: The CIA, Vietnam and the Plot to Assassinate John F. Kennedy,* published by Birch Lane in 1992. He is outspoken in his opinion that the assassination was a coup by what he terms the "secret team." He identifies this "secret team" as a powerful group of wealthy men who formed the military-industrial complex that wanted to keep the †Vietnam War going for personal profit. Prouty has also said that Kennedy was indeed engaged in breaking up the CIA and was intent on ending U.S. involvement in Vietnam.

📖 *Conspiracy; High Treason*

PRUSAKOVA, ILYA

Ilya Prusakova was Marina †Oswald's uncle, with whom she was living when Lee Harvey †Oswald met her at a dance in †Minsk. Prusakova was a colonel in the Soviet Ministry of Internal Affairs, which had a secret police component. When Oswald applied for the return of his U.S. passport (which he had relinquished when he had defected), J. Edgar †Hoover objected, fearing that the KGB would substitute one of its agents for Oswald.

📖 *Crossfire; High Treason*

PURDY, D. ANDREW

D. Andrew Purdy, an attorney, supervised the medical portion of the investigation of Kennedy's death by the †House Select Committee on Assassinations. Purdy was involved in a controversy concerning whether or not he had shown autopsy pictures to the †Parkland Memorial Hospital doctors to get their reactions. According to researcher Harrison Edward †Livingstone, Purdy claimed he had, but none of the doctors remembered his doing so. Only one of the Dallas doctors could recall seeing any of the visual record of the autopsy: Dr. Malcolm †Perry, who claims he was shown an autopsy drawing of the wound to the president's throat, but not an actual photograph. Livingstone claims that Purdy was not given access to the autopsy photographs, which were kept in the Committee's safe.

📖 *High Treason 2*

PUTERBAUGH, JACK

Assassination researcher Penn Jones claims that †Secret Service agent Puterbaugh was responsible for ignoring Secret Service regulations that prescribe a minimum speed of forty-four miles per hour for the presidential limousine and for revising the motorcade route, forcing the car to make two turns in †Dealey Plaza instead of going straight on Main Street. The circuitous route that took the car from Houston Street onto Elm Street required it to slow down to seven miles per hour.

📖 *High Treason*

QUIGLEY, JOHN

John Quigley worked in the †Federal Bureau of
Investigation's New Orleans office. When Lee Harvey
†Oswald was arrested in that city for creating a
disturbance while distributing †Fair Play for Cuba
Committee literature, he demanded to see an FBI
agent. His request granted, he met with Special Agent
Quigley in a lengthy private interview. Later, Quigley
claimed he destroyed his notes from that interview, an
act that does not square with usual Bureau procedure.

Oswald has been suspected of being a paid
informant for the FBI, a charge the †Warren
Commission decided to handle by requesting a
statement from J. Edgar †Hoover saying that Oswald
had never worked for him.
See also CARR, WAGGONER; PENA, OREST.
📖 *On the Trail of the Assassins*

QUIROGA, CARLOS

Quiroga was a Cuban exile leader whom a New

Orleans private investigator named David L. Lewis reportedly saw in the company of David †Ferrie and a "Leon Oswald." Lewis later claimed that "Leon Oswald" was Lee Harvey †Oswald. (Ferrie and Oswald were seen together at least twice in the offices of Guy †Banister.)

📖 *High Treason 2*

RACHLEY, VIRGIE

By the time she testified before the †Warren Commission, Miss Rachley had become Mrs. Donald Baker. Rachley was a bookkeeper in the †Texas School Book Depository Building in 1963. On the day of the assassination, she was standing outside the building watching the motorcade pass. When the shots were fired, at first she thought they were firecrackers being set off by kids, because she saw something hit the pavement just behind the presidential limousine and throw up sparks as it struck. Rachley told an attorney from the Warren Commission that she thought the shots came from "close to the underpass."
See also BULLETS FIRED, NUMBER OF; TEXAS SCHOOL BOOK DEPOSITORY BUILDING EMPLOYEES.
📖 *Crossfire; Rush to Judgment*

RAGANO, FRANK

In the January 14, 1992, issue of the *New York Post,* Ragano, who claimed to have been Jimmy †Hoffa's attorney and confidant, was reported as saying that he carried a message from Hoffa to mob bosses Carlos †Marcello and Santos †Trafficante asking them to kill President Kennedy. Ragano says he delivered the message in early 1963, with Hoffa's admonition, "This must be done." Ragano's statement created a furor among former Hoffa associates and detractors, who expressed doubt that Ragano was close enough to Hoffa for the Teamsters leader to trust him with such a confidential message. In the 1992 edition of their book *Fatal Hour,* authors G. Robert †Blakey and Richard N. †Billings report that Ragano claims to have had a deathbed talk with Trafficante in which Trafficante admitted involvement in the Kennedy assassination. 📖 *Contract on America; Fatal Hour*

RAMSEY REPORT
Dr. Norman Ramsey, a Harvard physics professor, was asked by the National Academy of Sciences to study the †Dallas police dispatch tape. The †House Select Committee on Assassinations had asked the Justice Department to continue its investigation of the alleged four gunshots on the tape when the Committee's term expired, and Justice passed the request to the National Academy of Sciences. The result was the creation of the †Committee on Ballistics Acoustics.

The ballistics committee's report, generally known as the Ramsey Report, concluded that the acoustics examinations done for the House Select Committee on Assassinations were incorrect, that the tape does not reveal that a shot was fired from the †Grassy Knoll. Needless to say, this caused an uproar among assassination researchers, who charged that the Ramsey group had been given not the original police recording but a poor copy.
📖 *Final Disclosure; High Treason*

RANDLE, LINNIE MAE
Randle was Buell Wesley †Frazier's sister. Frazier drove Lee Harvey †Oswald, his colleague at the Texas School Book Depository, to work the day of the assassination. Randle, who lived with Frazier in Irving, Texas, across the street from Ruth †Paine's house, where Marina †Oswald was living and where Lee had spent the previous night, told the †Warren Commission she saw Lee place a package in her brother's car before they left for work. When Frazier asked what was inside the package, Oswald told him, "Curtain rods."

In each of two experiments conducted more than three months apart, FBI agents showed Randle a package whose length they asked her to fold to match the approximate length of the package she had seen Oswald carrying. The first time, she identified a package that was 27 inches long. The second time, she selected a package that was 28.5 inches long. Frazier measured the approximate length of the package as he remembered it resting on the rear seat of his car at 27 inches. When the †Mannlicher-Carcano rifle, allegedly the murder weapon, was dismantled, the largest piece was 34.8 inches long. If the package Oswald carried that day contained the murder weapon, as claimed by the †Warren Commission, it could not have been shorter than approximately 35 inches.

📖 *Rush to Judgment*

RANKIN, J. LEE

A former solicitor general of the United States, Rankin was the general counsel for the †Warren Commission. In that post, he set the tone for the work done by the attorneys working under him. Rankin is accused by assassination researchers of skillfully guiding the Commission's investigation toward its desired conclusion that Lee Harvey †Oswald was guilty and that he worked alone; he is also accused of using a double standard in assessing evidence and statements by witnesses.

📖 *Best Evidence*

J. Lee Rankin, chief counsel to the Warren Commission

RATHER, DAN

When television news anchor Rather discussed Oliver
†Stone's film †*JFK* on the "CBS Evening News," he
described it as mixing "fact, fiction, and theory."
Rather himself was guilty of doing the same thing
decades earlier when he told TV viewers that the
†Zapruder film showed the president's head moving
forward as the fatal bullet hit it. Years later, Rather
admitted this was wrong. As anyone who has seen the
film can testify, the president's head snaps backward
and his entire body falls back and to his left.
📖 *High Treason; High Treason 2*

REBENTISCH, DONALD

A Navy petty officer at †Bethesda Naval Hospital in
1963, Rebentisch is quoted as saying that he and five
other petty officers took the president's coffin from the
ambulance to the room where the autopsy was to be
performed. This conflicts with the Military District of
Washington, D.C., †Casket Team's report, which states
that the team brought the coffin into the hospital.
Rebentisch claims he was told by a chief petty officer
that the ambulance parked in front of the hospital was
carrying an empty coffin. Assassination researcher
Harrison Edward †Livingstone believes the casket
Rebentisch carried into the hospital contained the

remains of an Air Force major awaiting burial.
See also COFFIN CONTROVERSY.
📖 *High Treason 2*

REDLICH, NORMAN

Norman Redlich, a †Warren Commission attorney, was
General Counsel J. Lee †Rankin's special assistant.
Redlich was a main contributor to the text of the
†Warren Report, which frequently ignored or even
denied compelling facts that ran counter to the
Commission's insistence on the †single bullet theory
and the †lone assassin theory. Redlich summed up his
unshakable support for the single bullet theory with
words to this effect: to admit that Kennedy and
Governor John †Connally were hit with separate
bullets is synonymous with saying there were two
assassins.
📖 *Best Evidence*

REED, EDWARD F.

An X-ray technician at †Bethesda Naval Hospital,
Reed was present during the Kennedy autopsy.
According to author David S. †Lifton, Reed assumed,
based on the location of the head wound, that the
president had been shot from the front. It was almost
six months before it dawned on him that his opinion

differed from the official autopsy report.

See also AUTOPSY CONTROVERSY; CUSTER, JERROL F.; HEAD WOUND CONTROVERSY.

📖 *Best Evidence*

REID, MRS. ROBERT A.

Mrs. Reid was a clerical supervisor at the †Texas School Book Depository Building. She had joined Depository vice president Ochus V. †Campbell and superintendent Roy †Truly to watch the presidential motorcade from the sidewalk in front of the building. They heard what they thought were firecracker explosions, and Mrs. Reid turned to Campbell and said she thought they came from "our building." Campbell replied that they came from the direction of the †Grassy Knoll. Mrs. Reid then encountered Lee Harvey †Oswald, whom she said was drinking a Coke, on the second floor of the Book Depository, just two minutes after the assassination.

See also TEXAS SCHOOL BOOK DEPOSITORY BUILDING EMPLOYEES.

📖 *Crossfire*

REILLY, FRANK

An electrician at Union Terminal, Reilly joined coworkers to watch the presidential motorcade pass

through †Dealey Plaza from the vantage point of the railroad overpass. He substantiated the testimony of others on the overpass that they had seen puffs of †smoke rise above the †Grassy Knoll moments after the shots were fired. Reilly testified that "the shots come [*sic*] out of the trees" near the top of the knoll.
See also OVERPASS WITNESSES.
▢ *Best Evidence*

REILY, WILLIAM
Owner of the †William Reily Coffee Company, where Lee Harvey †Oswald was employed while he lived in New Orleans, Reily is said to have been an active supporter of †anti-Castro Cuban groups.
▢ *On the Trail of the Assassins*

REVILL, JACK
On the afternoon of the assassination, after Lee Harvey †Oswald's arrest, Dallas police lieutenant Revill wrote a memorandum about Oswald that gave his address as 605 Elsbeth Street. Oswald had no identification with him that included an address, and the police claim they had no previous file on Oswald, so the question is, where did Revill get that address? In November 1963, Oswald did not live on Elsbeth Street, but he had lived at 602 Elsbeth Street until

March of that year. Evidently an old file on Oswald existed and was given to the Dallas police immediately on his arrest.

According to researchers, the Texas state intelligence agency had a file on Oswald that was nothing more than several newspaper clippings. Many observers suspect that the address came from an unidentified U.S. Army intelligence officer who was allegedly riding in Revill's car soon after the assassination. If so, to produce the Oswald information so quickly, the man must have been carrying it with him prior to the assassination.

📖 *High Treason*

REYNOLDS, WARREN

Reynolds heard the shots that killed Police Officer J. D. †Tippit. He said that a man with a gun in his hand ran south on Patton Avenue and that he gave chase but lost the man after a block or so. Reynolds was not questioned about what he saw that day by any law enforcement agency until January 21, 1964, even though he had discussed what he witnessed previously on television and radio news programs. Reynolds was unable to identify the man he chased as Lee Harvey †Oswald.

Things began going badly for Reynolds after his

refusal to identify Oswald. He was shot in the head; Darrell Wayne †Garner, the boyfriend of Betty Mooney †MacDonald, one of Jack †Ruby's strippers, was arrested for the attempted murder but released when MacDonald corroborated his alibi. Then someone attempted to abduct Reynolds's ten-year-old daughter, and someone purposely unscrewed the light that illuminated the front porch of his home. By July 1964, Reynolds had had enough, and he identified Oswald as the man he had chased. The †Warren Commission could find no connection between Reynolds's original testimony and the events that followed it, or the reason he changed his testimony.

See also LEWIS, L. J.; PATTERSON, B. M.

📖 *High Treason; Rush to Judgment*

RICH, NANCY PERRIN

Nancy Perrin Rich was a bartender at Jack †Ruby's †Carousel Club. Rich testified to the †Warren Commission that Ruby had standing orders that any police officers who came to the club were to be served liquor at no charge. The Commission chose to ignore this testimony and claimed that Ruby offered only coffee and soft drinks to visiting cops. Rich claimed that when she first came to town, the Dallas police got her the job at Ruby's club.

Despite the fact that Rich told the Commission that Ruby knew virtually every cop in Dallas, and that every police officer on the Dallas force visited Ruby's club, with the exception of Captain Will †Fritz, the Commission decided to rely on Police Chief Jesse E. †Curry's guess that Ruby knew less than twenty-five cops.

Rich's testimony, which did not square with the Commission's image of Ruby as a friendly police groupie who knew more cops than the average citizen, does not even appear in the †Warren Report. Also ignored were Rich's allegations that Ruby had been involved with anti-Castro elements and that he had helped run guns into Cuba for anti-Castro guerillas. 📖 *Rush to Judgment*

RIEBE, FLOYD A.

A medical photographer at †Bethesda Naval Hospital, Riebe was present during the autopsy performed on President Kennedy. As recently as May 1992, Riebe continued to insist that the official autopsy photographs could not be the ones he took because they show head wounds that are substantially different from the wounds he photographed. Riebe is also said to have claimed, along with others who were in the autopsy room, that some of the photographs appear to have been shot elsewhere, because certain walls and floors in the background do not resemble those at Bethesda.

See also AUTOPSY CONTROVERSY; AUTOPSY PARTICIPANTS; CUSTER, JERROL F.; HEAD WOUND CONTROVERSY.

📕 *Best Evidence; High Treason 2*

RIFLE IDENTIFICATION

The Italian-made †Mannlicher-Carcano rifle allegedly linked to Lee Harvey †Oswald through the Chicago mail-order house †Klein's Sporting Goods Company was eventually designated the weapon that was used to kill President Kennedy. It is allegedly the weapon discovered on the sixth floor of the †Texas School Book Depository Building, although the four law enforcement officers connected with finding the rifle all state clearly that the one they found was a 7.65-caliber Mauser. These officers are Deputy Constable Seymour †Weitzman, Deputy Sheriff Luke †Mooney, Deputy Sheriff Roger D. †Craig, and Deputy Sheriff Eugene L. †Boone. The Mannlicher-Carcano has the following inscription clearly stamped on it: *Made in Italy, Cal. 6.5.*

When Army marksmen attempted to fire the Mannlicher-Carcano, they found that the sight was off so much they had to send it to an expert, who had to put shims under the scope to align it with the trajectory of the shots it fired. Rifle experts appear to agree virtually unanimously that this particular gun is a remarkably poor choice of weapon for an assassination. 📖 *On the Trail of the Assassins*

RIGHT-WING EXTREMISTS

Researchers Robert J. †Groden and Harrison Edward †Livingstone, among others, have raised the possibility that right-wing hate groups were involved in President Kennedy's assassination. On November 22, 1963, the *Dallas Morning News* carried an ad, paid for by the †American Fact-Finding Committee, accusing Kennedy of being a "fellow traveler," i.e., a communist sympathizer. From the point of view of groups such as the Ku Klux Klan, the Minutemen, and the White Citizens' Council, Kennedy was anathema not only because he was soft on communism but also because he supported civil rights. These violent groups flourished in the South and did especially well in Texas.

Kennedy's policies were also despised by conservative businessmen. For example, in 1963, the oil business was threatened with a substantial loss of revenue because of Kennedy's proposed retraction of the oil-depletion allowance.

See also FERRIE, DAVID; HUNT, H.L.; MILTEER, JOSEPH.

RIKE, AUBREY

An employee of Oneal's Funeral Home, Aubrey ("Al") Rike supervised placing the president's body in the coffin at †Parkland Memorial Hospital. Although some witnesses at †Bethesda Naval Hospital claim Kennedy was inside a body bag, Rike says he lined the coffin with a plastic bed liner to prevent blood from spilling on the satin lining. He said he did not use a body bag.

See also BODY BAG CONTROVERSY.

📖 *Best Evidence*; *High Treason 2*

ROBERTS, DELPHINE

Roberts was Guy †Banister's secretary in his office at †544 Camp Street in New Orleans. At first hesitant to discuss what she had seen there, she later confirmed that both Lee Harvey †Oswald and David †Ferrie were frequent visitors. She also confirmed that Banister, a leader among anti-Castro elements, was fully aware that Oswald was distributing pro-Castro literature on the streets of New Orleans.

📖 *Conspiracy*

ROBERTS, EMORY

A †Secret Service agent riding in the car following the president's, Roberts was one of two men seated in

front of agent Glen [†]Bennett, who reported seeing a
bullet strike the president four inches below the right
shoulder.

📖 *Best Evidence*

ROBERTS, EARLENE

Earlene Roberts was the housekeeper at the rooming
house where Lee Harvey [†]Oswald was living at the
time of the assassination. Roberts told the [†]Warren
Commission that Oswald returned home about 1:00
P.M., thirty minutes after the shooting in [†]Dealey
Plaza, put on a dark blue jacket, and left immediately.
She said that several minutes later, observing him
from the front window of the house, she saw Oswald
standing at a bus stop. Roberts claimed that while
Oswald was in his room, a police car with two men
inside stopped in front of the house and sounded its
horn twice, as if signaling someone, then pulled away.
The identity of the car has never been established.

Roberts's testimony was not accepted by the
Commission on two counts: First, the time frame in
which she claims to have seen Oswald, especially her
report that he was standing at a nearby bus stop, does
not allow him to get to the scene of the J. D. [†]Tippit
shooting in time to be the murderer; and, second, she
claims Oswald was wearing a dark blue jacket, while

witnesses to the Tippit murder said the shooter wore a
light-colored jacket and the police reported finding a
white jacket that was allegedly discarded by the killer
as he made his escape. Mark †Lane has also pointed
out that a bus stopping where Roberts saw Oswald
standing would have taken him in a direction away
from the place where Tippit was shot.

📖 *Conspiracy; Rush to Judgment*

ROSE, DR. EARL

Dr. Rose was the Dallas County medical examiner in
1963. When the Kennedy party decided to remove the
president's body from †Parkland Memorial Hospital,
Dr. Rose told them they should not break "the chain of
evidence." Rose insisted that the body not be taken
from the hospital until an autopsy had been performed.
He called on a local police officer, who stood next to
him in an attempt to prevent the †Secret Service and
Kennedy's aides from taking the body. It was Rose's
position that the president's death was a homicide and
that under Texas law a homicide required a thorough
autopsy before the body could leave the state.

When Justice of the Peace Theron †Ward gave his
approval to the Secret Service request to remove the
body, Rose was pushed aside and the president's body
taken away to †Bethesda Naval Hospital outside

Washington, where the autopsy, perhaps the most criticized in history, was performed. One cannot help but wonder whether all the tales of wound alterations, evidence tampering, body switching, and falsified autopsy photographs and X rays might have been avoided had Dr. Rose prevailed and performed the autopsy at Parkland instead.
📖 *Death of a President*

ROSE, GUS
Dallas police detective Rose reportedly claimed that a Minox camera containing exposed film was found among Oswald's possessions following the assassination. The police property report lists the camera as item #375. When the property inventory was issued by the FBI, item #375 had become a Minox light meter. Rose reportedly said that the FBI attempted to get him to alter the police report so it would conform with the FBI report.
📖 *Conspiracy; High Treason*

ROSELLI, JOHNNY
Roselli was a Las Vegas–based †Mafia figure and a link in the CIA-Mafia chain. He had close ties to three Mafia bosses associated with the Kennedy assassination: Sam †Giancana of Chicago, Santos

†Trafficante of Florida, and Carlos †Marcello of New Orleans.

According to columnist Jack †Anderson, Roselli told him that mob leaders had ordered Jack †Ruby to kill Lee Harvey †Oswald because they were afraid he might crack and reveal their part in the conspiracy to kill President Kennedy.

In July 1976, shortly before Roselli was to be questioned by the Senate Intelligence Committee, his body was discovered floating in Dumfoundling Bay in Miami. He had been strangled and stabbed; his legs had been sawed off and stuffed into an empty oil drum along with the rest of his body. It is believed that Roselli was killed by someone working for Trafficante because he was talking too much about the Kennedy assassination.

📖 *Conspiracy*

ROWLAND, MR. AND MRS. ARNOLD

Arnold Rowland and his wife and son were across from the †Texas School Book Depository Building awaiting the arrival of the presidential motorcade. At approximately 12:15 P.M., Rowland noticed a man with a high-powered rifle standing a few feet back from the southwest corner window of the sixth floor of the building. He thought the man was a presidential security guard and pointed him out to his wife. Mrs. Rowland did not see the man, who her husband said had stepped back, but she was "very nearsighted" and did not have her glasses on. But what about the southeast corner, where Lee Harvey †Oswald supposedly fired from? Rowland said he saw a black man lean out that window minutes before the shooting.

The †Warren Commission treated Rowland as if he were a liar. Commission lawyers even got his wife to admit that he had once exaggerated his school grades. The problem was, the Commission had apparently already concluded that the assassination was carried out by one man. Thus, any testimony, like Rowland's, that supported the possibility of more than one shooter, was likely to be dismissed.

See also DARK-COMPLEXIONED MAN (OR MEN); DEALEY PLAZA WITNESSES.

📖 *Conspiracy; Rush to Judgment*

ROWLEY, JAMES J.

†Secret Service Chief Rowley was sent the †magic bullet from Dallas and forwarded it to the FBI lab. He also called †Bethesda Naval Hospital and told Agent Roy †Kellerman, who was watching the autopsy, about the discovery of a bullet. Rowley reported to the

†Warren Commission that he had reviewed all
materials from the local Dallas television and radio
stations, as well as the three national television
networks, but was unable to locate a transcript of the
press conference in Dallas at which Dr. Macolm †Perry
had described the president's †throat wound as a
bullet entry wound. A copy of that transcript had been
made by the White House because it was considered a
presidential press conference, and a copy was
available to researchers who requested it.
See also PARKLAND PRESS CONFERENCE.
📖 *Best Evidence*

RUBY, JACK

To the horror of millions of Americans who watched
the event on a live television broadcast, Jack Ruby
shot and killed Lee Harvey †Oswald at 11:21 A.M.
(CST) on Sunday, November 24, 1963. Ruby shot
Oswald as Oswald was being taken, under guard,
through the basement garage of Dallas Police
Headquarters en route to the Dallas County jail, to
which he was being transferred. Ruby delivered one
shot to Oswald's abdomen at point-blank range using
a .38 snub-nosed revolver. Ruby had no business being
in the garage, and it is widely suspected that his close
police contacts gave him entree to the building.

Jack Ruby

Ruby, who in 1963 was the owner of a Dallas striptease club called the †Carousel, had had close ties to underworld organizations, including the †Mafia, for most of his life. Born Jacob Rubenstein in Chicago in 1911, Ruby had moved to Texas in 1947. There is ample evidence that Ruby participated in Mafia-backed gun-running schemes to Cuba in 1959 in an effort to help Fidel †Castro overthrow the regime of Cuban dictator Batista—an episode that Ruby and others involved later regretted when Castro banished the mobsters, who were heavily invested in Havana's hotel and casino business, from the island.

Ruby's motive for killing Oswald remains obscure. There is evidence to suggest that he and Oswald were acquainted with one another, a conclusion discounted by both the †Warren Commission and the †House Select Committee on Assassinations. Some evidence also leads to the speculation that Ruby knew Dallas police officer J. D. †Tippit, whom the Warren Commission concluded Oswald killed early in the afternoon on November 22, 1963, shortly after having presumably assassinated President Kennedy.

In statements shortly after Oswald's death, Ruby claimed not to have premeditated his act, but to have killed Oswald in high passion, wanting, he said, to spare Jacqueline †Kennedy the pain of having to return to Dallas for Oswald's trial. Later, however, Ruby claimed to have been framed into committing Oswald's murder. In letters smuggled out of his prison cell, Ruby implicated Lyndon B. †Johnson in the plot to kill Kennedy. And in one of his last public statements on the subject, Ruby said, "The world will never know the true facts of what occurred—my motive, in other words."

Ruby seems to have been present in a number of key places on the day of President Kennedy's assassination. Witnesses have alleged that Ruby was at †Dealey Plaza both before and at the time of the assassination *(see below),* that he was at †Parkland Memorial Hospital while doctors there were vainly attempting to save the president's life *(see below),* and that he elbowed his way into a news conference given by Oswald at police headquarters after midnight that night. All these reported appearances have led researchers to suppose that Ruby was somehow involved in the death of the president.

Ruby was indicted for Oswald's murder by a Dallas grand jury on November 27, 1963. His trial began on February 17, 1964, and lasted until March 3. The jury delivered its guilty verdict and sentenced him to death on March 14. Ruby's conviction, however, was reversed by the Texas Court of Appeals on October 5, 1966, because of irregularities in the murder trial, over which Judge Joe †Brown had presided. Before a new trial could occur, Ruby suddenly died of cancer on January 3, 1967. Some researchers remain unsatisfied that Ruby died of "natural" causes—raising suspicions that Ruby had been injected with cancer-producing cells or that he had been subjected to heavy doses of cancer-causing X rays.

📖 *Crossfire; Ruby Cover-up*

RUBY IN DEALEY PLAZA
Jack Ruby claimed he was in the offices of the *Dallas Morning News* at the time of the assassination, a statement that was only partially corroborated by witnesses there. Several witnesses, however, claimed they saw Ruby near the †Texas School Book Depository Building moments after the shooting; these witnesses include Victoria †Adams, Philip L. †Willis, and Wes †Wise. Julia Ann †Mercer claims that on the morning of the day of the assassination, she saw Ruby behind the wheel of an illegally parked truck on Elm Street near the railroad overpass.

RUBY AT PARKLAND MEMORIAL HOSPITAL
Jack Ruby denied that he was anywhere near †Parkland Memorial Hospital during the time the

president's body was there. The †Warren Commission
chose to believe him in spite of testimony from two
witnesses who said they saw him inside the hospital
at that time. Reporter Seth †Kantor told the
Commission that he not only saw Ruby, whom he had
known for several years, but actually spoke to him
briefly while the doctors were still working to save
Kennedy's life in the emergency room. Wilma †Tice
told the Commission that she saw a man, who she
later realized was Ruby when she saw his picture on
television, in the hospital while the president was
there. She said Ruby was talking to another man who
was probably Kantor, based on the portions of their
conversation she overheard.

📖 *Rush to Judgment*

RUDNICKI, JAN GAIL

Rudnicki was Dr. Thornton †Boswell's lab assistant
and was called to duty by Boswell to help with the
president's autopsy. Researcher Harrison Edward
†Livingstone asked Rudnicki if he recalled whether a
complete bullet was found in the sheets on which
Kennedy's body had been lying. He explained that he
was in the autopsy area for the entire procedure, but
was going back and forth to the adjoining tissue room
to prepare slides. He said he might have been in the

tissue room at the time, "but I remember some conversation concerning" what he assumed was a "bullet."
See also OSBORNE, DR. DAVID.
📖 *High Treason 2*

RUSH TO JUDGMENT
Published in 1966 by Holt, Rinehart & Winston and reissued (with two new sections) in 1991 by Thunder's Mouth Press, this book by attorney Mark †Lane remains the landmark work on the assassination and the investigation conducted by the †Warren Commission. Lane, who tried unsuccessfully to represent Lee Harvey †Oswald before the Commission, examines the evidence provided by witnesses never questioned by Commission representatives and also reviews testimony taken but ignored. *Rush to Judgment* was a runaway best-seller that convinced many people that the Warren Commission investigation was incomplete and its conclusions wrong.

RUSSELL, RICHARD B.
A Democrat from Georgia, Russell was one of two senators appointed to the †Warren Commission. According to Commission insiders, Russell objected to signing a report stating that one bullet—the †magic bullet—struck both Kennedy and John †Connally.

Russell also raised questions about Lee Harvey
†Oswald's alleged trip to †Mexico City in the fall
of 1963.
📖 *Best Evidence*; *Plausible Denial*

RUSSO, PERRY
Russo was an acquaintance of David †Ferrie's who
testified before a New Orleans grand jury that he had
been present at a meeting in which Ferrie, Clay †Shaw
(known to him as "Clay Bertrand") and another man,
called Leon Oswald, discussed reasons for killing
President Kennedy. According to Russo, Ferrie favored
the idea because it would lead to war with Cuba if
they could place the blame for the assassination on
Fidel †Castro.
📖 *On the Trail of the Assassins*

RYDER, DIAL D.
Ryder was a repairman at the †Irving Sports Shop.

S

SANDERS, DAVID

Sanders was the orderly on duty in the emergency room at †Parkland Memorial Hospital while the president was being treated. According to William †Manchester's report of how Kennedy's body was placed in the coffin, Sanders was instructed by funeral director Vernon †Oneal to line the inside of the coffin with a plastic sheet. This plastic sheet has become the focus of controversy because some technicians in the autopsy room at †Bethesda Naval Hospital reported that the president's body arrived inside a zippered bag. *See also* BODY BAG CONTROVERSY.

📖 *Death of a President*

SAWYER, HERBERT J.

Police inspector Sawyer provided the initial description of the assassination suspect to the police dispatcher for broadcast: a white man about thirty years old, five feet ten inches in height, and weighing about 165 pounds.

Yet witnesses who had seen a man or men at the sixth-floor window of the †Texas School Book Depository Building gave descriptions that varied from a young white man to an elderly black man. Controversy rages around the speed with which the Dallas police identified the suspect as Lee Harvey †Oswald. When the †Warren Commission questioned Sawyer about the source of the information he gave the dispatcher, Sawyer couldn't identify the witness who had supplied it. He could only recall that the man was white and that "he wasn't young and he wasn't old." The Commission eventually concluded that Sawyer's source was Howard L. †Brennan. However, the identity of the man who actually gave Sawyer Lee Harvey Oswald's description remains a mystery. Some critics suspect the unidentified man was part of a conspiracy to make Oswald the "patsy" for the assassination.
📖 *Best Evidence; Rush to Judgment*

SCHEIM, DAVID E.
Scheim is the author of *Contract on America: The Mafia Murder of President John F. Kennedy,* published by Zebra Books in 1988. This book deals with Jack †Ruby's ties to organized crime and connotes that the †Mafia had the "motive, means, and opportunity" to kill the president.

SCOGGINS, WILLIAM

Scoggins was a taxi driver who was parked not far from the scene of the shooting death of Police Officer J. D. †Tippit. He reported that he saw a man walk away from the scene, but he ducked down behind his cab so the man would not see him. In a lineup that another taxi driver, William †Whaley, called unfair to the suspect, Scoggins selected Lee Harvey †Oswald as the man he had seen. Later, when asked to pick the man out from a number of photographs shown him by an FBI or Secret Service agent, Scoggins chose someone other than Oswald.

📖 *Rush to Judgment*

SCOTT, FRANK

Scott was responsible for preparing a report for the †House Select Committee on Assassinations dealing with the question of the authenticity of the autopsy photographs. He concluded that the photos were authentic, but left ample room for debate when he added a disclaimer saying he assumed "that the object photographed is, indeed, the body of President Kennedy."

📖 *High Treason 2*

SECRET SERVICE

Charged with protecting the life of the president, the

Secret Service failed to do a professional job during Kennedy's visit to Dallas. The Service made four major errors. First, it never made a thorough investigation of the motorcade route to identify and neutralize potential sniper locations. Second, there were no Secret Service agents on the ground in Dallas; they were all riding in the motorcade, where they could react only after an assassination attempt, not take preventive action to avert one. Third, there was no order mandating the closing of windows in buildings overlooking the motorcade route, such as the †Texas School Book Depository Building; such an order could have reduced the risk of someone firing at the president through an open window. Finally, the president's car was permitted to slow down to only a few miles per hour as it passed through †Dealey Plaza—in direct violation of Secret Service regulations requiring the car to maintain a speed of at least forty-four miles per hour.

Additionally, some researchers have charged that a group of Secret Service agents responsible for the president's protection spent the night before the assassination getting drunk at a Fort Worth, Texas, after-hours club, The †Cellar.

The extremely poor performance of the president's bodyguards has led some people to suspect the Secret

Service was somehow involved in a conspiracy to kill Kennedy, although there has never been any proof that this was so.

In 1992, St. Martin's Press published *Mortal Error: The Shot That Killed JFK,* whose author, Bonar Menninger, maintains that Kennedy's death resulted from a shot fired accidentally by Secret Service agent George †Hickey, who was riding in the follow-up car following the presidential limousine. Hickey did not answer the publisher's request for a response to the charge, but another Secret Service agent, Samuel †Kinney, denied that Hickey had fired a shot.
📖 *Crossfire*

SECRET SERVICE AGENTS, UNKNOWN
According to the Secret Service, no agents were assigned to the area around †Dealey Plaza on November 22, 1963. Yet Police Officers D. V. †Harkness and Joe M. †Smith report having encountered men who identified themselves as Secret Service agents behind the †Grassy Knoll and behind the †Texas School Book Depository Building.

SEIZURE INCIDENT
See BELKNAP, JERRY B.

SELZER, ROBERT

A photographic expert, Selzer was a member of a panel created by the †House Select Committee on Assassinations to examine photographs and films made of the assassination. The panel members held varied opinions concerning what some believe was movement in more than one window of the sixth floor of the †Texas School Book Depository Building. Selzer concluded that there was movement that could mean there was a person in more than one window.
See also BRONSON FILM; HUGHES, ROBERT.
📖 *Conspiracy*

SENATOR, GEORGE

Senator shared an apartment with Jack †Ruby in Dallas. Senator told the †Warren Commission that he was genuinely shocked when he learned that Ruby had shot and killed Oswald, because Ruby had not indicated to him that he had planned to take any steps against Kennedy's assassin.
📖 *Rush to Judgment*

SEWALL, FRED

Sewall was a salesman at the Bolton Ford dealership in New Orleans. Jim †Garrison reported Sewall as claiming that he was approached by two men who

wanted the dealer to give them a bid on the price of ten Ford pickup trucks. The men said they were from a group called †Friends of Democratic Cuba. One of the men was powerfully built and of Latin heritage. He identified himself as "Joseph Moore." The second man was a thin Anglo-Saxon who said his name was Oswald and explained that he was the one paying for the trucks. This incident took place on January 20, 1961, while Lee Harvey †Oswald was in the Soviet Union and three months before the †Bay of Pigs invasion. Garrison charges that this was just one of many instances when Oswald's name was used by intelligence agencies, and he suspects the trucks were intended for the Cuban forces engaged in the Bay of Pigs attack. Garrison claims that one of the persons named in the incorporation papers for the Friends of Democratic Cuba was Guy †Banister.
📖 *On the Trail of the Assassins*

SEYMOUR, WILLIAM
See ODIO INCIDENT.

SHANEYFELT, LYNDAL
A photographic analysis expert employed by the FBI, Shaneyfelt examined the †Zapruder film. He testified that †Secret Service agent Clinton †Hill placed one

foot on the rear step of the presidential limousine at frame 368, which, according to researcher David S. †Lifton, would be approximately three seconds after the fatal shot was fired at Kennedy. Hill testified that the car did not accelerate until he had stepped on it, meaning that the car remained relatively still until after the head shot was fired. Lifton argues that this means that Kennedy's head could not have been thrown backward—a motion that is clearly visible in the Zapruder film—by the acceleration of the automobile. That the limousine did not immediately speed up lends credence to the claim that Kennedy's head was propelled backward by the impact of a bullet that had been shot from somewhere in front of the limousine.

📖 *Best Evidence*

SHANKLIN, L. GORDON
Agent-in-charge of the FBI office in Dallas during November 1963, Shanklin has come under fire from numerous quarters for allegedly ordering Agent James †Hosty to destroy a note Lee Harvey †Oswald wrote him. The †House Select Committee on Assassinations called this act a "serious impeachment" of Shanklin's credibility.

📖 *Conspiracy*

SHAW, CLAY

Clay Shaw was a well-known business leader in New Orleans during the 1960s. He was also a member of a small clique of gay men that included David †Ferrie. Shaw used the alias Clay Bertrand when he spent his evenings in the seedier bars of the French Quarter, but many people there knew his real identity. Shaw had close ties to Guy †Banister and his ring of †anti-Castro Cubans, and knew Lee Harvey †Oswald. In January 1969, New Orleans district attorney Jim †Garrison charged Shaw with conspiracy in the murder of President Kennedy. He also charged that Shaw was a secret †Central Intelligence Agency operative, a charge Shaw denied, but that was later confirmed as true. Shaw was acquitted of the conspiracy charge, but in interviews following the trial, jurors conceded that Garrison had convinced them that a conspiracy was behind the assassination of President Kennedy. Shaw died on August 14, 1974, and was quickly buried. When the New Orleans coroner, Dr. Frank Minyard, wanted to exhume the body to perform an autopsy, he was assailed by the local press and decided to leave the issue alone. The trial of Clay Shaw is the major focus of Oliver †Stone's film †*JFK*.

See also PERMINDEX.

📖 *On the Trail of the Assassins*

Clay Shaw (left), with his attorney Edward Wegmann

SHAW, J. GARY

Shaw has spent years researching and writing about the assassination. He has interviewed hundreds of people with connections to Kennedy's death. He is the author of *Cover-up: The Governmental Conspiracy to Conceal the Facts About the Public Execution of John Kennedy,* which he self-published in 1976. He is also the coauthor, with Dr. Charles A. †Crenshaw, of *JFK: Conspiracy of Silence,* published by Signet in 1992.

SHAW, JACK

Reverend Shaw was with alleged CIA hitman and former Dallas police officer Roscoe †White when White died following a mysterious fire. Shaw claimed that White made a deathbed confession to a number of murders. In 1991, Shaw told researcher and author Harrison Edward †Livingstone that he believed White told the truth when he said he killed Kennedy. White is also believed to have shot and killed J. D. †Tippit.
📖 *High Treason 2*

SHAW, DR. ROBERT

Dr. Shaw was a †Parkland Memorial Hospital surgeon who worked on the chest wound Governor John †Connally received during the assassination. Dr. Shaw told †Warren Commission member John J. †McCloy that

when a bullet hits "a bony substance such as a rib, usually the reaction is quite prompt." This testimony damages the †single bullet theory, because the †Zapruder film shows that Connally's reaction to being shot occurs substantially later than Kennedy's reaction to his †throat wound, indicating that both men were not shot with the same bullet. Shaw also testified that based on the amount of metal fragments in Connally's wrist, he found it "difficult to believe" that the so-called †magic bullet inflicted the governor's wounds. He also said the Parkland doctors were confused when they were told that the assassin had been behind the president when they were under the impression the bullet had "entered at the front of his neck."
See also FINCK, DR. PIERRE; MCCLELLAND, DR. ROBERT N.
📖 Best Evidence

SHELLEY, WILLIAM
A †Texas School Book Depository Building employee, Shelley was standing in front of the building when the motorcade passed by. He told the †Warren Commission that the shots "came from the west." The †Grassy Knoll is to the west of the Book Depository Building.
See also LOVELADY, BILLY NOLAN.
📖 Rush to Judgment

SHERIDAN, WALTER
An employee of the National Broadcasting
Corporation, Sheridan was instrumental in the
development of an NBC "White Paper" program called
"The †Case of Jim Garrison," which the New Orleans
district attorney viewed as an attack on his
investigation of the Kennedy assassination. The show
relied heavily on the testimony of convicted felons,
among others, to smear Garrison's ethical practices.
According to a report by an investigator on Garrison's
staff, Perry †Russo claimed that Sheridan had
promised to move him to California and protect his job
with the Equitable Life Insurance Company, as well as
guarantee he would not be extradited to Louisiana if
he helped "bust up the Garrison probe."
📖 *On the Trail of the Assassins*

SIBERT, JAMES
See O'NEILL AND SIBERT REPORT.

SIMILAS, NORMAN
Similas was a businessman from Toronto, Canada,
visiting Dallas on the day of the assassination. He was
standing on the left side of Elm Street taking
photographs of the approaching motorcade when the
shots were fired. In an article written for a Canadian

magazine, Similas claimed that when he had the photos developed, he could clearly see a rifle sticking out of a sixth-floor window of the †Texas School Book Depository Building, with two figures standing over it. He said that he sent the negatives to a Toronto newspaper, which paid him handsomely for them but did not publish the photos. According to Similas, the paper later said it had lost the negative of the photo that Similas says showed the two figures with the rifle. Similas is also quoted as saying that he was within ten feet of the President when he was shot and could clearly see a hole in Kennedy's left temple. By coincidence, Similas, who was in Dallas for a soft-drink bottlers' convention, spent part of the evening before the assassination at the †Carousel Club, where he had a long chat with its owner, Jack †Ruby.
See also TEMPLE WOUND CONTROVERSY.
📖 *Best Evidence; Crossfire*

SIMMONS, JAMES

A railroad worker who watched the presidential motorcade from the overpass above Elm Street, Simmons is reported to have said the shots came from the "wooden fence" atop the †Grassy Knoll. He saw a puff of smoke from the same area. Simmons also reported having seen hundreds of footprints in the muddy ground behind the wooden fence, where he and other railroad workers rushed in the minutes following the shooting.

See also FOSTER, J. W.; HOLLAND, SAM; JOHNSON, CLEMMON; MILLER, AUSTIN; REILLY, FRANK; SMOKE FROM THE GRASSY KNOLL.

📖 *Rush to Judgment*

SIMMONS, RONALD

Simmons was one of three "master" marksmen the †Warren Commission used to test fire the †Mannlicher-Carcano rifle allegedly found on the sixth floor of the †Texas School Book Depository Building following the assassination. Simmons estimated that the tower from which he and his colleagues fired their test shots was about thirty feet off the ground, only half the estimated sixty-foot height of the Depository Building's sixth floor. He reported numerous complaints about the rifle's operation, including the difficulty one man had in operating the bolt during his firing exercise. Simmons also told the Commission that the stationary target they fired at was not as far from them nor at the same angle as it would have been for someone taking aim from the sixth floor of the Depository Building.

See also FIRING SEQUENCE CONTROVERSY.

📖 *Rush to Judgment*

SINGLE BULLET THEORY

†Warren Commission Assistant Counsel Arlen †Specter is credited with originating the single bullet theory. The theory is believed to have been devised as a result of evidence that the Commission could not ignore concerning one of the bullets fired at President Kennedy. This was the bullet that hit the pavement halfway across †Dealey Plaza from the president's limousine, kicking up debris that injured a bystander named James T. †Tague. That left two other bullets, according to the Commission's conviction that only three shots were fired, to cause all the wounds President Kennedy and Texas governor John †Connally received. One of these hit Kennedy's head and fragmented, leaving the other to do the rest. According to the Commission, this one bullet hit the president in the back, exited through his throat, passed through Connally's body, breaking a rib, then shattered a bone in his wrist, and finally entered his left thigh. All of these injuries were attributed to a bullet in near-perfect condition allegedly found in †Parkland Memorial Hospital— what became known as the †magic bullet (Warren Commission exhibit #399). Virtually all Warren Commission critics charge that the single bullet

theory requires the bullet in question to make several sharp turns during its travels through both men—a highly improbable, if not utterly impossible, route. Rejecting the single bullet theory means accepting that more than three bullets were fired, and therefore that more than one gunman took part in the assassination, since Lee Harvey †Oswald— whom the Commission identified as the assassin— could not possibly have gotten off more than three rounds during the specified time.

See also BULLETS FIRED, NUMBER OF; LONE ASSASSIN THEORY.

📖 *Crossfire; High Treason 2*

SITZMAN, MARILYN

Marilyn Sitzman was standing alongside Abraham Zapruder on the concrete pergola on the †Grassy Knoll when the president was shot. She reportedly had an unobstructed view of Kennedy when he was hit, and is quoted as saying that the head shot struck him just above his ear. Despite her proximity to the scene, she was never questioned by either the police or the †Warren Commission.

See also GRASSY KNOLL WITNESSES; ZAPRUDER FILM.

📖 *Best Evidence*

SKELTON, ROYCE G.

Along with a group of others, Skelton watched the presidential motorcade and the assassination from the vantage of the railroad overpass that borders the west side of †Dealey Plaza. Skelton told the †Warren Commission that he thought there had been four shots fired and that either the third or fourth shot had struck the roadway near "the left front of the President's car."

See also BULLETS FIRED, NUMBER OF; DECKER, J. E. (BILL); FOSTER, J. W.; OVERPASS WITNESSES.
📖 *Warren Report*

SLACK, GARLAND G.

Slack told the †Warren Commission that at some time during the weeks preceding the assassination, he had had an argument at the Sports Drome Rifle Range in Dallas with a man he later believed was Lee Harvey †Oswald. Other patrons of the Sports Drome, including Malcolm †Price, also testified that they had encountered someone calling himself Oswald there that day. The man Slack thought was Oswald fired at Slack's target, resulting in a confrontation between them. The Warren Commission decided that Oswald could not have been at the range on the day in question. It also never pursued the reason someone whose appearance

was similar to Oswald's was demonstrating his marksmanship publicly and clearly calling attention to himself.
📖 *Rush to Judgment*

SLAWSON, DAVID
Slawson was a lawyer with the Justice Department in 1966 when J. Lee †Rankin, general counsel for the †Warren Commission, received a letter from Wesley J. †Liebeler, who had been an assistant counsel for the Commission. In the letter, Liebeler questioned some of the medical evidence the Commission had been given. Slawson allegedly wrote to Ramsey Clark, then acting attorney general, explaining that there was still a "chance of spiking" a full-scale investigation of the autopsy by conducting a limited investigation. This may have resulted in the creation of the †Clark Panel.
📖 *Best Evidence*

SMITH, JOE M.
Dallas police officer Smith was directing traffic at the intersection of Houston and Elm streets when he heard the shots that killed the president. He raced up the †Grassy Knoll, where he thought the shots had originated, pulling his handgun from its holster as he ran. Behind the fence at the top of the knoll, he smelled

gunpowder, and ran into a man who identified himself as a Secret Service agent by showing Smith his ID card and shield. This is but one of numerous instances in which an individual encountered a Secret Service agent behind the Grassy Knoll or the †Texas School Book Depository Building, yet the Secret Service insisted that no agents were on foot in the area that day, that they were all riding in the motorcade.

See also SECRET SERVICE AGENTS, UNKNOWN

📖 *Conspiracy; Crossfire; Rush to Judgment*

SMITH, L. C.

Deputy Sheriff Smith was standing in front of the Dallas County jail when he heard three shots ring out. He dashed to Elm Street, where a woman told him the president had been shot in the head by someone firing from the fence on the †Grassy Knoll. Smith joined several other police officers and deputies racing up the grass slope to the wooden fence, but found no shooters there.

📖 *Crossfire*

SMOKE FROM THE GRASSY KNOLL

The kind of ammunition still manufactured in 1963 produced a puff of smoke that rose above the shooter's head when a rifle was fired. Several people in or around †Dealey Plaza at the time of the assassination reported seeing smoke rising from the stockade fence near the top of the †Grassy Knoll during the seconds after the shots were fired. These witnesses include Richard C. †Dodd, Sam †Holland, Clemmon †Johnson, Austin †Miller, Thomas †Murphy, Frank †Reilly, James †Simmons, and Walter †Winborn.

SNIPER'S NEST

Some forty boxes were stacked around a sixth-floor window inside the †Texas School Book Depository Building, effectively blocking the view from the remainder of the floor. Each box was full of books and weighed about fifty pounds. Three spent cartridges were allegedly found inside this protected area. The †Warren Commission claimed that Lee Harvey †Oswald built this protection around himself so other employees would not stumble across him while he was preparing the kill the president. The boxes were examined for fingerprints, but only three partial prints belonging to Oswald were found on them. Oswald was, however, employed in the building to handle such boxes. According to the time frame established by the Commission, Oswald had less than fifteen minutes to construct his nest, yet when a six-foot seven-inch former football tackle attempted to re-

create the sniper's nest, the job took him twenty-one minutes and he was left exhausted.
📖 *Texas Connection*

SORRELS, FORREST V.

Sorrels was the agent-in-charge of the Dallas †Secret Service office. He rode in the first car of the motorcade with Police Chief Jesse E. †Curry and Sheriff J. E. (Bill) †Decker. According to Orville †Nix, who claims to be a friend of Sorrels's, the agent told him that at the time of the assassination, he thought the shots had come from the †Grassy Knoll. Sorrels, who then traveled with the motorcade directly to †Parkland Memorial Hospital, was the only Secret Service agent to return to †Dealey Plaza after the shooting. He reported having walked in through the back door of the †Texas School Book Depository Building without being stopped or questioned one hour after the assassination, by which time the building had supposedly been "secured." He denied Howard L. †Brennan's claim of having given Sorrels an accurate description of Lee Harvey †Oswald as the killer within ten minutes of the shooting. Sorrels claimed that Brennan never said any such thing, and that he couldn't have returned from Parkland Memorial Hospital in that short a time.
📖 *Best Evidence; Crossfire*

SOUETRE, JEAN

A Frenchman who had once attempted the murder of French president Charles de Gaulle, Souetre was reportedly in the United States at the time of the Kennedy assassination. According to CIA documents uncovered in 1977 by assassination researcher Mary †Ferrell, a French intelligence agency was searching for Souetre five months after the assassination and claimed that he had been picked up by U.S. authorities somewhere in Texas within two days of President Kennedy's death and then expelled from the country. Dr. Lawrence †Alderson, a dentist and resident of Houston, Texas, who had known Souetre in the early 1950s, claimed to have been put under FBI surveillance during the month after the assassination and to have been subjected to FBI questioning in December 1963 concerning his relationship with Souetre.
📖 *Reasonable Doubt*

SPEAKER, SANDY

According to author Jim †Marrs, Speaker, who was the construction foreman on a project near †Dealey Plaza on November 22, 1963, reports hearing at least five shots coming from different directions. Speaker told Marrs that his experience as a combat Marine fighting behind enemy lines during World War II made him

sure he had heard more than three shots.
See also BRENNAN, HOWARD L.; MILLICAN, A. J.
📖 *Crossfire*

SPECTER, ARLEN

An assistant counsel to the †Warren Commission, and later a United States Senator from Pennsylvania, Specter is said to have been responsible for developing the †single bullet theory. Specter has often been attacked by Warren Commission critics for, among other things, attempting to get members of the †Parkland Memorial Hospital medical staff to change their testimony regarding their initial belief that President Kennedy's †throat wound was an entry wound, not an exit wound as the autopsy concluded.
📖 *Best Evidence*

SPORTS DROME RIFLE RANGE

See PRICE, MALCOLM H.; SLACK, GARLAND G.

SPOTLIGHT

The †Liberty Lobby, which publishes *Spotlight,* was sued by CIA agent E. Howard †Hunt over an article written by Victor †Marchetti charging that Hunt was in Dallas the day of the assassination, and that he had ties to the president's murder. The suit was rejected by a jury whose foreperson, Leslie †Armstrong, later told reporters that she had been convinced by the evidence presented during the trial that the CIA was behind the assassination. The trial is the basis of lawyer-author Mark †Lane's best-seller †*Plausible Denial,* (Thunder's Mouth Press, 1991).

SPRAGUE, RICHARD A.

Sprague was the first chief counsel for the †House Select Committee on Assassinations. Sprague was practically given carte blanche by the Committee's first chairman, Congressman Thomas Downing. After fighting with the Committee's second chairman, Henry †Gonzalez, over control of the investigation, Sprague ran what Gonzalez called a "put-up job" of an investigation. Sprague quickly came under fire from members of Congress and was finally forced out.
📖 *High Treason*

STOKES, LOUIS

The third chairman of the †House Select Committee on Assassinations, Stokes is quoted by authors Robert J. †Groden and Harrison Edward †Livingstone as telling the Committee's staff, "We all know that the fatal head shot came from the front."
📖 *High Treason*

Oliver Stone, director of the film JFK

STONE, OLIVER

Stone's 1991 film †*JFK* (which he wrote, produced, and directed) came under fire from the establishment press in this country even before he began shooting it. Once the darling of the liberal/left media, the Oscar-winning movie maker was, thanks to *JFK,* turned into a pariah in virtually all quarters, except in the eyes of the millions of people who paid to see the film. While almost everyone who is familiar with the conflicting details of President Kennedy's assassination may argue this or that point with Stone, as many researchers do over what they see as Stone's deification of Jim †Garrison, one fact is certain: His film brought the assassination back to the American consciousness.

STOVER, JOHN

Captain Stover was the commanding officer of the U.S. Naval Medical School at Bethesda, Maryland, on November 22, 1963. Following the autopsy performed on President Kennedy, at which he was present, Stover issued a written order confirming the verbal instructions all military personnel in attendance had received: that, under threat of court-martial, nothing was to be said to anyone about what happened in the autopsy room.

See also AUTOPSY CONTROVERSY; HEAD WOUND
CONTROVERSY.
📖 *Best Evidence*

STRINGER, JOHN
Stringer was a Navy medical photographer with
twenty years' experience in photographing the human
body during an autopsy. He photographed President
Kennedy's body during the autopsy at †Bethesda Naval
Hospital. (The authenticity of the autopsy photographs
as they now exist has been widely disputed.) Significantly, on November 1, 1966, Stringer went to the
National Archives, where most of the available autopsy
material is kept, and signed a statement affirming that
the pictures on file were the ones he had taken. When
researcher David S. †Lifton asked what test he applied
to the photos before he signed the statement, Stringer
told him there was none, because he had never seen
the pictures developed. He had simply shot them and
handed the film holder to a †Secret Service agent.
See also NATIONAL ARCHIVES, DOCUMENTS MISSING
FROM; RIEBE, FLOYD A.
📖 *Best Evidence*

STROUD, MARTHA JO
An assistant United States attorney in Dallas, Stroud

wrote to †Warren Commission General Counsel J. Lee †Rankin about evidence concerning a bullet that went wild and struck a curb opposite the †Grassy Knoll. Stroud's insistence that the Commission interview James T. †Tague, who was struck in the face by a piece of the curb thrown up by the bullet, forced the Commission to conclude that only two of the three bullets it claimed Lee Harvey †Oswald fired had caused all the wounds—fatal and nonfatal—to President Kennedy and Governor John †Connally. The result was the Commission's creation of what has come to be called the †magic bullet, or †single bullet, theory.

See also FIRING SEQUENCE CONTROVERSY; SPECTER, ARLEN.

📖 *Crossfire*

STURGIS, FRANK

Sturgis was a CIA contract employee who worked with the Agency's anti-Castro groups before and after the †Bay of Pigs Invasion. He is closely linked with E. Howard †Hunt, and with the Watergate burglary that brought down the presidency of Richard M. †Nixon. Sturgis was identified by Marita †Lorenz, whom he recruited into the service of the CIA, as one of a group of heavily armed men she accompanied on a

trip to Dallas shortly before the assassination.
📖 *Plausible Denial*

STYLES, SANDRA

Styles was on the fourth floor of the †Texas School
Book Depository Building when the shooting took
place. She was unable to judge where the shots came
from, but told FBI agents she and Victoria †Adams
descended the back stairs to the street level moments
after the shots were fired. Neither woman saw or
heard anyone else while they were on the stairs; this
would have been the same time Lee Harvey †Oswald
is alleged to have been running down the stairs from
the sixth floor to the second-floor cafeteria, where he
was seen minutes later by Police Officer Marrion
L. †Baker.
See also DORMAN, ELSIE; GARNER, DOROTHY ANN;
HOBSON, MRS. ALVIN.
📖 *Crossfire*

SULLIVAN, WILLIAM

Sullivan was a top aide to FBI director J. Edgar
†Hoover, and led the FBI investigation into Kennedy's
assassination. It is reported that within two weeks of
the assassination, Sullivan wrote a memo in which he
said there was no evidence that Lee Harvey †Oswald

was an agent for a foreign power, including Cuba. This was in direct conflict with the stories being circulated, allegedly by "rogue" elements in the CIA, that Oswald was either a Soviet or a Cuban agent. On July 16, 1978, shortly before he was to be questioned by the †House Select Committee on Assassinations, Sullivan was shot to death in what was described as a hunting accident.
📖 *High Treason 2*

SWEATT, ALLEN
Head of the Dallas Sheriff's Criminal Division, Deputy Sweatt reportedly received from Deputy John Wiseman the missing Polaroid photograph snapped by Mary †Moorman. Sweatt then turned it over to the †Secret Service, and it has never been seen again. A second Moorman photo, taken within seconds of the missing one, shows what many believe is a rifleman behind the fence atop the †Grassy Knoll.
See also HILL, JEAN.
📖 *High Treason*

SWINNEY, MRS.
See TROON, MRS.

SZULC, TAD
Tad Szulc, a reporter for the *New York Times,* claims

that during a 1961 interview with the president, Kennedy raised the subject of attempts on Fidel †Castro's life. Szulc said the president expressed grave concern about pressure he was receiving from the intelligence community to have Castro killed, but that he was "violently opposed" to political assassinations. Sources that are believed to be connected to the †Central Intelligence Agency have tried to link Lee Harvey †Oswald with Castro's government. Oswald, they claim, killed Kennedy on orders from Castro because the president had ordered Castro's assassination. Szulc also maintained that E. Howard †Hunt was in †Mexico City at the time of Oswald's alleged visit there in the fall of 1963.

📖 *Conspiracy*

T

TAGUE, JAMES T.

Tague was stopped in traffic on Commerce Street on
the side of †Dealey Plaza opposite the †Grassy Knoll.
He got out of his car and watched the presidential
motorcade. When the shooting, which he believed
came from the Grassy Knoll, started, a bullet struck
the curb in front of him and a piece of concrete hit him
in the cheek, causing a small wound. Deputy Sheriff
Eddy †Walthers saw the wound and immediately
searched the area where Tague had been standing. He
filed a report in which he stated that he found a place
"where a bullet had splattered on the top edge of the
curb," causing damage to the concrete. At first the
†Warren Commission ignored this information,
probably because it did not correspond with its
assessment that only three shots were fired, all by Lee
Harvey †Oswald, from the †Texas School Book
Depository Building. Under pressure apparently
created by a letter from Assistant U.S. Attorney
Martha Jo †Stroud about a bullet mark on the curb,

the Commission had a staffer interview Tague. The FBI removed the section of curb and reported that it contained metal smears of lead. Unable to ignore this evidence of a wild shot, the Commission nonetheless held to its belief that only three shots were fired at Kennedy and created the †single bullet theory to account for the nonfatal †throat wound of the president and the multiple wounds suffered by Governor John †Connally.

See also FIRING SEQUENCE CONTROVERSY; HAYGOOD, CLYDE A.; MAGIC BULLET; SPECTER, ARLEN.

📖 *Crossfire; Rush to Judgment*

TATUM, JACK

Tatum, who was driving in the Oak Cliff section of Dallas on the afternoon of November 22, 1963, claims he saw a young white man near the police car of J. D. †Tippit when he heard three shots fired. When Tatum looked toward the car, he saw the officer on the ground and the young man standing over him. He said the man ran toward the rear of the police car, stopped, and fired one more shot at the officer, who was lying in the street in front of the car. Tatum sped off when the gunman ran in his direction.

See also TIPPIT MURDER SCENE WITNESSES.

📖 *High Treason*

TEAMSTERS, INTERNATIONAL BROTHERHOOD OF
See HOFFA, JIMMY.

TEMPLE WOUND CONTROVERSY
According to the †Warren Commission, President
Kennedy was shot only from the rear. Critics of the
Commission's conclusions, however, have maintained
that shots were fired from other locations as well—
including the †Grassy Knoll and possibly the railroad
overpass. Important evidence that Kennedy may have
been shot from the front appears to have been ignored
by the official investigators of the assassination. One
piece of evidence involves the †throat wound that
members of the †Parkland Memorial Hospital staff
identified as a bullet entry wound (but which the
Commission described as an exit wound). Another
involves a hole in the front of the president's head
that, if caused by a bullet, could only have resulted
from a gun fired from in front of him.

Four people reported having seen a hole in the
president's temple. Father Oscar †Huber, who
administered last rites to Kennedy minutes after his
death, has been quoted as telling reporters that he saw
a "terrible wound" over the president's left eye. Dr.
Marion †Jenkins told the Warren Commission that
while attempting to take Kennedy's pulse he noticed

what he thought was a wound in "the left temporal area, right in the hairline." Pages 526 and 527 of the †Warren Report reproduce a written report prepared at 4:45 P.M. on November 22, 1963, by Dr. Robert †McClelland. The report states, "The cause of death was due to massive head and brain injury from a gunshot wound of the left temple." A †Dealey Plaza witness to the shooting, Norman †Similas, who was about ten feet from the presidential limousine, reported he could clearly see a hole in Kennedy's left temple.
📖 *Best Evidence; Warren Report*

TERRY, L. R.
According to an interview conducted by Jim †Marrs, Terry claims he was standing across the street from the †Texas School Book Depository Building. When the motorcade passed him, he noticed two men at an upper-floor window and then saw a rifle barrel appear from the same window. He said the man holding the rifle was not wearing a white shirt, as others have described him.
See also BRENNAN, HOWARD L.
📖 *Crossfire*

THE TEXAS CONNECTION
This best-selling 1992 book, written by Scottsdale,

Arizona, attorney Craig I. Zirbel and self-published by the Texas Connection Company, is billed as "the criminal investigation . . . against Lyndon B. †Johnson," who the author charges was involved in the assassination of President Kennedy. The book's thesis is founded on what Zirbel calls "The right-hand-man theory" of political assassinations.

TEXAS SCHOOL BOOK DEPOSITORY BUILDING
According to the †Warren Commission, it was from a sixth-floor window of the Texas School Book Depository Building that Lee Harvey †Oswald, on November 22, 1963, fired three shots at the presidential motorcade passing below, killing President Kennedy and wounding Governor John †Connally. A nondescript, worn-looking tan brick building at the corner of Houston and Elm streets, at the northeast corner of †Dealey Plaza, the Depository had seen better days by 1963. Originally built to house the offices of a railroad company, the seven-story building later was occupied by the John Deere Company. The next occupant was a grocery wholesaler. In the early 1960s, it became a warehouse for the Texas School Book Depository, a depot that distributed textbooks to schools throughout the state. Some of its offices were rented to publishers of textbooks that were purchased for the Texas school

*The Texas School Book Depository Building in 1964,
one year after the assassination*

456

systems. During the 1980s, there was talk that Dallas County was going to sell the building, until it was learned that the prospective buyer planned to dismantle it and sell the bricks as souvenirs. Today it serves as an annex for the county. Open to the public on the sixth floor (which in 1963 was used as a textbook storeroom) is a re-creation of the so-called †sniper's nest.

TEXAS SCHOOL BOOK DEPOSITORY BUILDING EMPLOYEES

The †Texas School Book Depository Building housed offices for several textbook publishers as well as the Depository. Some building employees were outside the building at the time of the assassination, while others were inside watching from office or warehouse windows. Still others were not watching the motorcade and therefore saw nothing of the assassination. Among employees were: Victoria †Adams; Carolyn †Arnold; Mrs. Avery †Davis; Jack E. †Dougherty; Buell Wesley †Frazier; Dorothy Ann †Garner; Mrs. Alvin †Hobson; James †Jarman, Jr.; Dolores A. †Kounas; Billy Nolan †Lovelady; Harold D. †Norman; Lee Harvey †Oswald; Virgie †Rachley; Mrs. Robert A. †Reid; Roy †Truly; Bonnie Ray †Williams; and Steven F. †Wilson.

TEXAS THEATRE
This movie house in the Oak Cliff section of Dallas
was the scene of Lee Harvey †Oswald's arrest shortly
after the murder of Dallas police officer J. D. †Tippit
several blocks away. A patron, George J. †Applin, later
claimed that one of the other patrons at the time was
Jack †Ruby.
📖 *Crossfire*

THOMPSON, MALCOLM
A retired Scotland Yard superintendent with extensive
experience in photographic evidence analysis,
Thompson examined a now-famous photograph of Lee
Harvey †Oswald that shows him standing near a fence
holding a rifle and a newspaper. When Oswald was
shown this photo by Police Captain Will †Fritz, he
commented that someone had put his face on the
photograph of another man. Thompson is reported to
have identified several areas of the photo that were
retouched. Apparently agreeing with Oswald,
Thompson said the photograph was a "fake," and that
it was a composite of several pictures pieced together.
He called it a "montage," noting that although Oswald
had a pointed chin, the chin of the man in the
photograph is square. The opinion that the photo was

faked was shared by John †Pickard.
See also OSWALD, BACKYARD PHOTOGRAPH OF.
□ *Conspiracy*

THROAT WOUND CONTROVERSY
When President Kennedy, nearing death, was brought
into †Parkland Memorial Hospital, Dr. Malcolm †Perry
almost immediately performed a †tracheotomy—a
procedure in which a small opening is made in the
patient's throat and a tube is inserted to improve
breathing. The tracheotomy incision was made over a
wound that Perry later described to reporters as a
bullet entry wound (*see* PARKLAND PRESS CONFER-
ENCE). In his account of the assassination, Dr. Charles
A. †Crenshaw, who was present in the emergency
room, described the wound as "an entry bullet hole."

When the autopsy was performed on President
Kennedy's body at †Bethesda Naval Hospital, the
doctors failed to realize that the tracheotomy had been
performed over a bullet wound. They concluded that
the bullet hole in the president's back was caused by a
bullet that had failed to penetrate the body and that
had fallen out while he was being moved. When they
were later told about the throat wound, they
concluded that the bullet that entered Kennedy's back

had exited through his throat, although this would have required the bullet to have traveled along an incredibly convoluted path.

Virtually every member of the medical team that worked on the president at †Parkland Memorial Hospital described the hole in his throat as an entry wound, yet the †Warren Commission chose to identify it as an exit wound made by the so-called †magic bullet that allegedly wounded both Kennedy and Texas governor John †Connally. Obviously, if the doctors and nurses in the Parkland emergency room were correct in their original assumption (and there is no reason to doubt they were, given their extensive experience in treating gunshot wounds), an entrance wound in the president's throat could only have been caused by a bullet fired at him from the front.

In addition to the debate regarding whether the wound represented a bullet's entry or exit point, another controversy swirls around the condition of the wound when the body left Parkland. According to those at the scene, the tracheotomy and bullet hole were not closed before Kennedy's body was removed by the †Secret Service for the trip to Washington. Yet in March 1978, the Lancaster, Pennsylvania, *Intelligencer-Journal*, in an interview with Dr. John †Ebersole, who had X-rayed the body at Bethesda, reported that Ebersole said that when examining the body he had discovered a "very neatly sutured" opening in the throat that was identified as a surgical incision for a tracheotomy. According to Dr. Kemp †Clark, who was interviewed by researcher David S. †Lifton, no suturing was performed before Kennedy's body left Parkland hospital. As with so many other controversies associated with the president's murder, this one remains unresolved.

See also HENCHCLIFFE, MARGARET.

📖 *Best Evidence; High Treason*

TICE, WILMA

Tice was at †Parkland Memorial Hospital when the president's death was announced. She claimed that she saw Jack †Ruby in the hospital at that time. She said Ruby was greeted by a man who said to him, "How are you doing, Jack?" Ruby turned and spoke to him, giving Tice a clear view of his face. Ruby denied he was at the hospital while the president was there. The transcript of Tice's testimony before the †Warren Commission's counsel gives the impression that the lawyer did not want her to testify about Ruby's presence in the hospital. Tice insisted that the man she saw was either Ruby "or his twin brother." Tice was so upset by the way the Commission's lawyer

treated her that she later called and visited Ruby's sister, Eva †Grant, and confirmed her own identification of the clothing Ruby was wearing that day. *See also* RUBY AT PARKLAND MEMORIAL HOSPITAL.
📖 *Rush to Judgment*

TILSON, JOHN
Dallas police officer John Tilson was off duty when President Kennedy was assassinated. He was driving near the area with his daughter when, as he approached the railroad overpass that borders †Dealey Plaza, he saw a man "slipping and sliding" down the railway embankment. The man threw something into a black car parked at the bottom of the embankment, ran around the car and jumped into the driver's seat, and sped off. Tilson, who had been a police officer for seventeen years, well understood that a man running from a scene to which everyone else he could see was drawn was suspicious, so he decided to give chase. Unable to overtake his quarry, Tilson noted the car's tag numbers. He later gave this information to the Dallas Police Homicide Division, but in the chaos of reports that flooded in, this vital piece appears to have been lost, and as far as is known, the license plate number was never checked.
📖 *Conspiracy*

TIPPIT, J. D.

Jefferson Davis Tippit, a Dallas police officer, was
murdered in the Oak Cliff section of Dallas
approximately forty-five minutes after President
Kennedy was shot. According to witnesses, Tippit
stopped his squad car along the curb and spoke briefly
to a man who the †Warren Commission concluded was
Lee Harvey †Oswald. Tippit then got out of his car and
walked around the front of the car toward the man,
who pulled out a handgun and fired. Tippit was shot
four times and died instantly. Oswald was apprehended at the †Texas Theatre, a few blocks away, and
charged with Tippit's murder but never stood trial
because he, in turn, was murdered by Jack †Ruby just
two days later. Various assassination researchers have
speculated that Tippit had connections with Oswald,
Ruby, or both, as well as with Roscoe †White, who is
said to have claimed he was the actual assassin. It is
possible that Tippit knew Ruby, since it was Ruby's
habit to ingratiate himself with police officers. Tippit
could also have known Oswald through innocent
connections. It was never established why Tippit
stopped to speak with Oswald (if his murderer really
was Oswald); perhaps the encounter began as a
friendly conversation. Or perhaps the connections
between Tippit and Oswald and/or Ruby were more

Dallas police officer J. D. Tippit

sinister than will ever be known. It is even possible that Tippit had no connection with Ruby or Oswald, that his murder was committed by an unknown person for reasons entirely unconnected with the president's assassination, and that the murder charge was pinned on Oswald. The meaning of Tippit's murder remains one of the important mysteries surrounding the assassination of President Kennedy.

📖 *Reasonable Doubt; Rush to Judgment*

TIPPIT MURDER SCENE WITNESSES

Almost as much controversy rages around the scene of Dallas police officer J. D. †Tippit's murder as around the scene of President Kennedy's assassination in †Dealey Plaza. People who claim to have witnessed the death of officer Tippit or to have seen his killer run away include Domingo †Benavides; Acquilla †Clemmons; Barbara †Davis; Virginia R. †Davis; Helen Louise †Markham; B. M. †Patterson; Warren †Reynolds; and Frank and Mary †Wright.

TOMLINSON, DARREL C.

Tomlinson was the senior engineer at †Parkland Memorial Hospital in 1963. He is credited with discovering the one piece of evidence that allowed the †Warren Commission to "prove" that a lone gunman

shot President Kennedy and Governor John †Connally: the †magic bullet. During the afternoon of November 22, Tomlinson moved a gurney that was blocking an elevator door against a corridor wall. As it bumped against the wall, a bullet rolled out from under a mat. Tomlinson gave the bullet to the hospital's chief of security, former Dallas deputy police chief O. P. †Wright, who turned it over to the †Secret Service. Tomlinson reported that on the night following the assassination he received a telephone call from the FBI warning him not to talk about his discovery. After repeated questioning by Arlen †Specter of the Warren Commission, Tomlinson was still unable to say whether the stretcher on which he found the bullet was the one used for Governor Connally. Wright reportedly told someone from *Life* magazine that the bullet he turned over to the Secret Service had a sharp, pointed nose, not the rounded nose of the magic bullet the Warren Commission claims Tomlinson found. *See also* LONE ASSASSIN THEORY; OSBORNE, DR. DAVID; SINGLE BULLET THEORY.
📖 *Best Evidence; Reasonable Doubt*

TONAHILL, JOE
Tonahill was Jack †Ruby's defense lawyer when he was tried for the murder of Lee Harvey †Oswald. Ruby's

defense was based on the premise that his shooting of Oswald was not premeditated, but an impulsive act. Tonahill emphasized this point in his closing remarks to the jury, telling them that it was up to the state to prove that Ruby had conspired with someone in the Dallas Police Department to murder Oswald.
📖 *Rush to Judgment*

TORRES, MIGUEL

A convicted burglar, Torres was confined to the state prison at Angola, Louisiana, when NBC television investigators questioned him about his knowledge of New Orleans district attorney Jim †Garrison's investigation of Clay †Shaw. On an NBC "White Paper" program titled "The †Case of Jim Garrison," Torres said Garrison's office had attempted to bribe him with a Florida vacation and a supply of heroin if he testified that Shaw was also known as Clay Bertrand. When a grand jury asked Torres to repeat under oath what he had said on television, he refused. Torres was found guilty of contempt and received additional prison time.
📖 *On the Trail of the Assassins*

TRACHEOTOMY

When President Kennedy was brought into †Parkland Memorial Hospital after the shooting, he was barely clinging to life. Dr. Charles †Carrico inserted an endotracheal tube into Kennedy's mouth and down his throat in an effort to improve his breathing. This was removed when Dr. Malcolm †Perry made a small incision in the patient's throat to insert a tracheotomy tube. He made his incision directly through a small, clean, round opening that those present described as a bullet entry wound. Questioned by researcher David S. †Lifton about the size of the incision, Dr. Perry responded that it was 2 to 3 centimeters long. According to the autopsy report prepared by Dr. James J. †Humes at †Bethesda Naval Hospital, and published as part of the †Warren Report, the incision Humes found in the president's throat was 6.5 centimeters, or more than twice and perhaps three times as long as the incision made by Dr. Perry. The autopsy doctors considered this opening to be the exit wound for the bullet entry wound they found in the president's back.

See also AUTOPSY CONTROVERSY; BAXTER, DR. CHARLES R.; CLARK, DR. KEMP; CRENSHAW, DR. CHARLES A.; DUDMAN, RICHARD; HENCHCLIFFE, MARGARET; JONES, DR. RONALD; THROAT WOUND CONTROVERSY.

📖 *Best Evidence*

Mafia boss Santos Trafficante

TRAFFICANTE, SANTOS

This Florida †Mafia boss is reported to have made several threats on President Kennedy's life. Trafficante was deeply involved with the †Central Intelligence Agency in plans to assassinate Fidel †Castro. The mobster reportedly told José †Aleman that Kennedy would not survive to the next election, that he was going to be "hit" before then. Trafficante sought the protection of the Fifth Amendment clause against self-incrimination when asked by the †House Select Committee on Assassinations whether he had ever discussed plans to kill the president and whether Jack †Ruby had visited him after he was imprisoned by Castro along with other gangsters and gamblers. *See also* MCWILLIE, LEWIS J; MARCELLO, CARLOS; ROSELLI, JOHNNY.

📖 *Conspiracy*

TRIPLE UNDERPASS (OR OVERPASS)

See OVERPASS WITNESSES.

TROON, MRS.

Troon was a telephone operator on duty at Dallas Police Headquarters while Lee Harvey †Oswald was being held there the night following the assassination.

she allegedly reported that another operator, Mrs. Swinney, possibly under instructions from two †Secret Service agents waiting in another room, prevented Oswald from placing a telephone call to someone named Hurt in Raleigh, North Carolina. According to Troon, Swinney told Oswald the number he called did not answer, even though she never attempted to put the call through.

📖 *Conspiracy*

TRULY, ROY

Roy Truly was the superintendent of the †Texas School Book Depository Building and the man who had hired Lee Harvey †Oswald. He told the †Warren Commission that the shots came from the "vicinity of the railroad or the WPA project." The "WPA project" to which Truly referred is the concrete pergola near the top of the †Grassy Knoll. Truly assisted motorcycle patrolman Marrion L. †Baker in his search of the building when they observed building employee Oswald in the second-floor cafeteria calmly drinking a Coke.

See also TEXAS SCHOOL BOOK DEPOSITORY BUILDING EMPLOYEES.

📖 *Crossfire; Rush to Judgment*

TUTEUR, WERNER
Werner Tuteur was Jack †Ruby's prison psychiatrist.
Shortly after he was granted a new trial, and before
he died of cancer, Ruby allegedly told Tuteur that he
knew who had ordered the assassination of President
Kennedy, and that he had been "framed" to kill Lee
Harvey †Oswald.
📖 *High Treason*

"UMBRELLA MAN"

The †Zapruder film and several photographs taken at the time of the assassination show two mysterious men at the edge of the curb close to where the presidential limousine passed. One man had a light complexion and carried a black umbrella. The other was dark-skinned, possibly Hispanic. As the limousine entered Elm Street the man with the umbrella stood up, opened the umbrella, and held it over his head as if it were raining, which it wasn't. Just at the moment the shots were fired, he raised the umbrella almost two feet over his head, then lowered and closed it. He then sat back down on the curb. The second man appeared to be speaking into a hand-held radio unit. When the limousine sped away after the shooting, both men rose and walked away in opposite directions. Neither followed the large group of people heading toward the †Grassy Knoll.

Following years of speculation about the "umbrella man," who many suspect used his umbrella to signal the assassin or assassins, a warehouse manager named Louis Steven Witt appeared before the †House Select Committee on Assassinations claiming to be the man. He testified that he thought the open umbrella would somehow annoy Kennedy. His testimony about his actions at the assassination scene is inconsistent with the photographs, and critics consider Witt's story unconvincing.

📖 *Crossfire*

UNDERPASS

See OVERPASS WITNESSES.

UNDERWOOD, JAMES

Underwood was the assistant news director for the Dallas television station KRLD. He interviewed a fifteen-year-old black boy named Amos L. †Euins, who had told a motorcycle police officer just minutes after the assassination that he had seen "a colored man lean out of the window upstairs and he had a rifle." Underwood then asked the witness if he was certain the man was black. Euins responded that the man he saw was "colored." When pressed by Underwood whether he was sure the man was "colored," Euins replied, "Yes, sir." After Euins reportedly received threatening telephone calls to his home, he changed his testimony and told the †Warren Commission he wasn't sure whether the man was white or black.

□ *Rush to Judgment*

UNDERWOOD, MARTY

A Kennedy advance man, Marty Underwood was with the president during the entire Texas trip. In an interview with Harrison Edward †Livingstone in 1991, Underwood was told that some people believed the autopsy photos of President Kennedy were fake. He replied, "Oh, I'm sure they were forged." He then explained that he was sure Lyndon B. †Johnson knew who killed Kennedy, although he felt strongly that Johnson was not behind it.

□ *High Treason 2*

U-2 SPY PLANE

During the late 1950s the U.S. Air Force and the †Central Intelligence Agency jointly conducted regular surveillance of military operations in the Soviet Union using the supersecret, high-flying U-2 spy plane. In May 1960 the Soviets shot down a U-2 aircraft piloted by Gary Powers, an incident that caused then-President Dwight D. Eisenhower serious embarrassment and that undermined his chances of success at an upcoming summit meeting with the

U.S.S.R. Powers's plane, which should have been
invulnerable to Soviet attack because of the altitude
at which it flew, was shot down a few months after Lee
Harvey †Oswald defected to the U.S.S.R.

In a CIA-authorized book Powers wrote after his
release from a Soviet prison, the pilot expressed the
suspicion that Oswald might have given the Soviets
new technical data that he could have acquired while
stationed at †Atsugi Air Base in Japan, where several
U-2s were based. According to Soviet defector Yuri
†Nosenko, the KGB never had more than a passing
interest in Oswald, which is remarkable considering
his stint at Atsugi and the Soviet desire for
information about the U-2s. If the CIA did suspect
that Oswald was responsible for the downing of
Powers's plane, it is also remarkable that the Agency
never attempted to debrief Oswald on his return to the
United States.

📖 *Conspiracy*

VAUGHN, ROY

Dallas Police Officer Vaughn was stationed at the top of the Main Street car ramp leading to the garage level of Dallas Police Headquarters, where Jack †Ruby shot and killed Lee Harvey †Oswald. Despite Vaughn's testimony that Ruby did not enter the building by way of the ramp, as well as corroborating testimony by others who were there at the time, the †Warren Commission chose to believe the testimony of Napoleon J. †Daniels, who claimed he saw someone resembling Ruby pass Vaughn and enter the ramp. Vaughn later took three polygraph tests that indicated he was telling the truth. According to researcher Harrison Edward †Livingstone, Vaughn's attorney professed that Police Officer Red †Davis told Vaughn that Ruby was taken to the basement by Assistant Police Chief Charles †Batchelor.

See also NEILL, JAMES.

📖 *High Treason*

VECIANA, ANTONIO
A founder of the †anti-Castro group called †Alpha 66,
Veciana was backed by the †Central Intelligence
Agency. His contact was a man known to him only as
"Maurice †Bishop." Veciana claims that in either late
August or early September 1963, he witnessed "Bishop"
speaking to a man whose picture was broadcast
around the world on November 22 of that year, Lee
Harvey †Oswald. Regarding Veciana's testimony, a
†House Select Committee on Assassinations report
concluded that "There was absolutely no doubt in his
mind that the man was Oswald. . . ." Veciana further
stated that after the Kennedy assassination, "Bishop"
asked him to persuade a cousin who worked in the
Cuban Embassy in †Mexico City to verify a fabricated
report that Oswald had visited the embassy.
See also ALVARADO, GILBERTO; ANTI-CASTRO
CUBANS; BOWEN, JOHN "JACK"; DURAN, SILVIA;
GAUDET, WILLIAM GEORGE; PHILLIPS, DAVID ATLEE.
📖 *Conspiracy*

VIETNAM WAR
Proponents of the theory that Kennedy was killed
because of his alleged plans to pull out of Vietnam
ignore very strong historical evidence that if Kennedy
had lived, the war might well have continued just as it

did under Lyndon B. †Johnson. John Kennedy was not the "peacenik" many attempt to paint him as. Throughout his Senate career, he was always considered a hard-liner against the communist bloc. Many of the men who advised Johnson to expand the war were Kennedy's closest advisers while he was in the White House, and there is every reason to believe he would have followed their advice just as Johnson did.

On the other hand, many foreign policy experts believe that Kennedy genuinely intended to pull out of Southeast Asia after the 1964 election. In late 1961, tensions between hawks and doves in Washington were intensifying. In November, the president ordered a massive reorganization—later referred to as the "Thanksgiving Day Massacre"—of both the State Department and the †Central Intelligence Agency. In 1963, Kennedy further angered interventionists in his own government by signing NSAM 263 on October 2. The measure called for the withdrawal of one thousand U.S. military advisers from Vietnam by the end of the year and also included a timetable for total withdrawal. That policy would have been reversed by NSAM 273, dated the day before Kennedy's assassination but never signed by him.

That members of the so-called military-industrial complex were dismayed over Kennedy's likely reduction of U.S. forces in Indochina is one of the prime motivations for the assassination explored in Oliver †Stone's film †*JFK*.

See also NGO DINH DIEM.

WADE, HENRY W.

Dallas County district attorney Wade held a formal
press conference at midnight November 22, 1963,
nearly eleven hours after the alleged assassination
weapon was recovered on the sixth floor of the †Texas
School Book Depository Building. When asked about
the identification of the weapon, Wade said it was a
7.65-caliber Mauser. The weapon sent to the FBI lab
for examination as the official assassination weapon,
however, was a 6.5-caliber †Mannlicher-Carcano rifle.
Despite the fact that the weapon remained in police
custody, it continued for a time to be identified as a
Mauser, not a Mannlicher-Carcano.
See also BOONE, EUGENE L.; MOONEY, LUKE;
WEITZMAN, SEYMOUR.
📖 *Reasonable Doubt*

WALKER, EDWIN A.

General Walker was a highly controversial figure
during the early 1960s. He had been relieved of

command of the Twenty-fourth Division of the U.S.
Army in 1961 for distributing right-wing materials to
his troops. As a civilian living in Dallas, he was active
in right-wing organizations, and a speaker at
gatherings around the country. In April 1963, someone
fired a shot through a window of his home, narrowly
missing his head. The testimony of Marina †Oswald to
the †Warren Commission as well as evidence found
among Lee Harvey †Oswald's possessions implied that
Oswald was Walker's would-be assassin. The Commission concluded that Oswald was indeed the gunman.
□ *Conspiracy*

WALTER, WILLIAM S.
A former employee at the New Orleans office of the
FBI, Walter told assassination researcher and author
Mark †Lane that on November 17, 1963, his office
received a telex message from FBI headquarters
alerting him to a possible plot to kill the president
while he was in Dallas. Walter claimed that after the
assassination, the two office copies of the message
vanished, though he made a handwritten copy of the
message.
See also FBI TELEX MESSAGE.
□ *On the Trail of the Assassins*

WALTER REED ARMY MEDICAL CENTER
Judging from taped transcripts of radio conversations
between †*Air Force One,* as it returned to Washington
from Dallas with President Kennedy's coffin aboard,
and various military officers on the ground, the
original intent of those in Washington was to transfer
the president's body to Walter Reed Medical Center for
the autopsy once the plane landed at †Andrews Air
Force Base. The destination of the body was changed
to †Bethesda Naval Hospital. Researcher David S.
†Lifton says that in 1980 he inquired into this
decision, speaking with, among others, the president's
naval aide, Captain Tazwell Shepherd, whom some
believed was responsible for the change in plans.
Lifton reported that Shepherd had no recollection of
making arrangements for transporting the body or for
the autopsy. Lifton theorizes that the change in
venues to Bethesda required that the president's body
be secretly removed from *Air Force One* and taken to
Walter Reed, where it was possible to alter the
wounds before sending the body to Bethesda, where
the start of the autopsy was delayed for several hours.
See also AMBULANCE CONTROVERSY; COFFIN
CONTROVERSY.
📖 *Best Evidence*

WALTHER, CAROLYN

Carolyn Walther worked in a dress factory in the Dal-Tex Building on the east side of †Dealey Plaza. She and another worker went to the street to watch the presidential motorcade. Moments before the president's limousine turned onto Elm Street, she noticed two men at an open upper-floor window of the †Texas School Book Depository Building. One man was holding a rifle, which he pointed down toward the street. She assumed the men were guards stationed there to protect the president. Later, she also insisted that she had heard four shots fired.

See also ROWLAND, MR. AND MRS. ARNOLD.

📖 *Crossfire*

WALTHERS, EDDY

A Dallas County deputy sheriff, Walthers encountered James T. †Tague, a bystander at the scene of the assassination who was hit by flying debris when a stray bullet struck the ground near where he was standing. Walthers reported that he "found where a bullet had splattered on the top edge of the curb on Main Street." The †Warren Commission decided that only three bullets had been fired, all of them by Lee Harvey †Oswald, so when it was forced to admit the existence of this bullet, it had to find a way to explain

how only two bullets had caused all the wounds (fatal
and nonfatal) to President Kennedy and Governor
John †Connally. This resulted in the creation of the
†magic bullet theory, which permitted the Commission
to stand by its †lone assassin theory.

See also FIRING SEQUENCE CONTROVERSY; HAYGOOD,
CLYDE A.; SINGLE BULLET THEORY; SPECTER, ARLEN;
STROUD, MARTHA JO.

📖 *Crossfire*

WARD, THERON

Ward, a local Dallas justice of the peace (justices of
the peace are elected magistrates in Texas), was called
to †Parkland Memorial Hospital to mediate a dispute
between the †Secret Service and the presidential party,
on one side, and Dallas medical examiner Dr. Earl
†Rose, on the other. Rose demanded that the
president's body not be removed until an official
autopsy was done. He insisted that the chain of
evidence must be maintained and that Texas law
required an autopsy before the deceased could be
removed from the state. Under pressure from the
representatives of the president and the federal
government, and with the acquiescence of District
Attorney Henry W. †Wade, Ward gave his permission
to remove the body. In view of the puzzle surrounding

the †ambulance and the †autopsy controversies, one can't help but wonder what the result would have been had Dr. Rose been permitted to conduct his autopsy before the president's body was taken from Parkland.

📖 *Death of a President*

WARNER, ROGER C.

Author and assassination researcher David E. †Scheim reports that Warner, a †Secret Service agent, interviewed Karen †Carlin on November 24, 1963. Carlin was a stripper at Jack †Ruby's †Carousel Club. Ruby sent Carlin a Western Union money order on the morning of November 24, just before going to Dallas Police Headquarters, where he shot Lee Harvey †Oswald. Carlin allegedly told him that she feared she would be killed if she gave the authorities any information. But it was her impression that Ruby and Oswald were part of a plot to kill the president.

📖 *Contract on America*

WARREN, EARL

Chief Justice of the United States Supreme Court, Warren at first refused President Lyndon B. †Johnson's request that he serve on the commission to investigate President Kennedy's assassination. It was only after

Chief Justice Earl Warren

receiving a summons to the White House that he accepted the post as the commission's chairman. The leader of the "Warren Court" would from that time on have his name irrevocably linked with what many Americans regard as a cover-up of one of the worst crimes in history.

Warren was a purely political animal who, as governor of California and heavyweight at the 1952 Republican national convention, had been instrumental in winning the party's nomination for General Dwight D. Eisenhower. His reward was a promise of the next Supreme Court seat. As it turned out, the next seat was that of chief justice, but Eisenhower kept his promise and Warren was appointed.

Like many other politicians, Warren had his own dirty laundry to keep out of the public eye. This was revealed in that, at the same time the Kennedy brothers were part of a Senate investigation of labor union ties to organized crime, with special emphasis on the Teamsters, Warren often expressed his "admiration" for the Teamsters, calling the corrupt union "not only something great of itself, but splendidly representative of the entire labor movement."

📖 *Conspiracy; Plausible Denial*

WARREN COMMISSION
On November 29, 1963, President Lyndon B. †Johnson
issued Executive Order No. 11130, creating a
commission to investigate the assassination of
President Kennedy, the wounding of Governor John
†Connally, and the murder of Police Officer J. D.
†Tippit. Officially known as the President's
Commission on the Assassination of President
Kennedy, it quickly became referred to popularly as
the Warren Commission, after its chairman, Earl
†Warren, chief justice of the United States Supreme
Court. The Commission collected testimony from 552
individuals. Of these, 94 appeared before members of
the Commission, 395 were questioned by Commission
lawyers, and 63 supplied either affidavits or
statements. Before the Commission's report, known
as the †Warren Report, was even published, critics
charged that important witnesses whose information
differed from the Commission's findings—that Lee
Harvey †Oswald alone killed Kennedy and that no
conspiracy was involved in the assassination—were
not called to testify, or their testimony was ignored or
altered. Following publication of the Report, the
Commission released twenty-six volumes containing
the testimony, affidavits, and statements of witnesses

The members of the Warren Commission, presenting President Lyndon B. Johnson with a copy of the Warren Commision Report (September 24, 1964). From left to right: John J. McCloy; J. Lee Rankin, counsel; Senator Richard B. Russell (D-Ga.); Representative Gerald R. Ford (R-Mich.); Chief Justice Earl Warren, commission head; President Johnson; Allen Dulles; Senator John Sherman Cooper (R-Ky.); and Representative Hale Boggs (D-La.).

as well as other related material. Many early
Commission critics used the twenty-six volumes to
build their cases against its findings.

WARREN COMMISSION MEMBERS
The members of the Warren Commission, selected by
President Lyndon B. †Johnson, were its chairman,
Earl †Warren, chief justice of the United States
Supreme Court; Hale †Boggs, the Democratic
representative from Louisiana, whose death
Commission critics consider mysterious; Gerald †Ford,
the Republican representative from Michigan and
future appointed president, who continues to defend
the Commission; John Sherman †Cooper, the
Republican senator from Kentucky, who is said to
have opposed the †single bullet theory in the
Commission's findings; Richard B. †Russell, the
Democratic senator from Georgia, who helped force
the Commission staff to investigate the link between
Lee Harvey †Oswald and the †Central Intelligence
Agency; Allen W. †Dulles, who was fired as CIA
director by President Kennedy following the †Bay of
Pigs invasion failure; and John J. †McCloy, a former
chairman of Chase Manhattan Bank.

It has been reported that with the exception of
Allen Dulles, each member chosen to serve on the

Commission initially refused the appointment, finally giving in to Johnson's plea for help in resolving a national emergency.

📖 *Plausible Denial*

WARREN REPORT

On September 24, 1964, ten months after the murder of President Kennedy, the †Warren Commission presented the results of its investigation to President Lyndon B. †Johnson. Officially titled *The Report of the President's Commission on the Assassination of President John F. Kennedy*, the Report is an 888-page summary of the investigation and the conclusions reached by the Commission; it was presented to Johnson along with twenty-six volumes of exhibits and records of the Commission's hearings. The Report, first issued by the Government Printing Office, was reprinted by at least half a dozen publishers within a week of its release, and millions of copies of both the hardcover and paperback editions were sold. In 1992, twenty-nine years after the assassination, at least two publishers issued new editions of the Report.

Before the Warren Report was even released, the Commission's work had come under attack by critics. Since its release, the Report and the accompanying volumes of testimony and exhibits have been minutely examined in scores of books and hundreds of magazine articles. Most of these have been critical of the way the investigation was conducted and of the Commission's interpretation of the physical evidence and the testimony of various witnesses.

📖 *Warren Report*

WEATHERFORD, HARRY

A Dallas County deputy sheriff, Weatherford was standing in front of the sheriff's office on the east side of †Dealey Plaza with approximately twenty other deputies when the shots were fired. In a report filed later that day, he said he thought the first shot was a railroad torpedo, because the sound came from the "railroad yard." When he recognized the shots that followed for what they were, he ran across the plaza toward the railroad yard behind the †Grassy Knoll, "where the sound seemed to come from."

See also CRAIG, ROGER D.

📖 *Rush to Judgment*

WEBERMAN, ALAN J.

Alan Weberman is coauthor, with Michael L. †Canfield, of †*Coup d'Etat in America,* published in 1975 by The Third Press. The book claims the CIA had assassination squads in Dallas the day Kennedy was killed.

WECHT, DR. CYRIL H.

Dr. Wecht has been a critic since at least 1967 of the autopsy performed on President Kennedy at †Bethesda Naval Hospital. He has condemned the autopsy report and the †single bullet theory. Dr. Wecht, a forensic pathologist with extensive experience performing autopsies on victims of gunshot wounds, was the coroner of Allegheny County in Pennsylvania. He has also been president of the American Academy of Forensic Sciences.

Wecht was a member of the panel of nine pathologists asked by the †House Select Committee on Assassinations to review the autopsy X rays and photographs. He was the only critic of the †Warren Report to serve on the panel. In May 1992, Dr. Wecht appeared on television on the CNN program "Larry King Live" to discuss an article published in the May 1992 issue of the *Journal of the American Medical Association* that professed to reveal "new" evidence supporting the Warren Report, but was nothing more than a rehash of the autopsy report prepared by Dr. James J. †Humes, who performed the procedure.

Wecht is one of the most articulate and knowledgeable critics of the medical evidence produced by the autopsy.
See also BOSWELL, DR. THORNTON; CUSTER, JERROL F.; LUNDBERG, DR. GEORGE; RIEBE, FLOYD A.
📖 *Best Evidence*

WEHLE, PHILIP C.
Commanding officer of the Military District of Washington, D.C., General Wehle accompanied the Military District †Casket Team to †Bethesda Naval Hospital to ensure that the president's body had a proper honor guard at all times. In a 1967 interview reported by researcher David S. †Lifton, General Wehle denied that he had been present in the autopsy room when the Dallas coffin was opened, as reported in William †Manchester's book *The †Death of a President*. Wehle confirmed the information supplied by members of the team that two Navy ambulances were used when the president's body was brought to Bethesda and that the team was sent in pursuit of the wrong ambulance. According to official records, there was no "decoy" ambulance, contrary to what team members claim. The alleged presence of a second ambulance has given rise to charges that the

president's body was not in the ambulance bearing the Dallas coffin.

See also AMBULANCE CONTROVERSY.

📖 *Best Evidence*

WEIGMAN, DAVE

Weigman, an NBC television cameraman, was filming the motorcade from his position in the seventh car in line. After the shots were fired, with his camera rolling, he ran up the †Grassy Knoll in pursuit of the many police officers who had done likewise. According to researcher Jim †Marrs, one frame from Weigman's film clearly shows the remains of a puff of smoke hanging in the air near the top of the knoll. This is the same smoke reported by other witnesses.

See also OVERPASS WITNESSES; SMOKE FROM THE GRASSY KNOLL.

📖 *Crossfire*

WEISBERG, HAROLD

Considered by many to be the "grandfather" of assassination researchers, Weisberg has spent years pressuring the federal government to release documents related to the murder of President Kennedy. The basement of Weisberg's home is filled with dozens of metal filing cabinets containing thousands of assassination documents. He is the author of several books on the subject, including the*Whitewash* series and *Oswald in New Orleans* (Canyon Books, 1967), as well as a book on the assassination of Martin Luther King, Jr.

WEISS, MARK

An acoustics expert, Mark Weiss was called on by the †House Select Committee on Assassinations to review earlier acoustics studies of the shooting, along with Dr. James †Barger and Ernest †Aschkenasy. These experts analyzed a recording of the sounds of what appeared to be four gunshots that were picked up by the open radio microphone of a police motorcycle near the scene of the shooting. They concluded that there was a 95 percent or better probability that the third shot was fired from the area of the †Grassy Knoll. *See also* ACOUSTICAL EVIDENCE; BELL LABORATORY; DALLAS POLICE DISPATCH TAPE; RAMSEY REPORT. ⌐ *Fatal Hour; High Treason*

WEISSMAN, BERNARD

Bernard Weissman, in collaboration with Joseph P. †Grinnan and Larrie H. Schmidt, placed an advertisement in the *Dallas Morning News* the day of the assassination attacking President Kennedy's policies. *See also* AMERICAN FACT-FINDING COMMITTEE.

WEITZMAN, SEYMOUR

Deputy Constable Weitzman raced to the †Grassy Knoll from his post at the corner of Main and Houston streets when he heard the shots fired at the president. One of the first officers to reach the fence atop the knoll, Weitzman climbed over it and searched for the source of the shots. He found a railroad yardman, who told Weitzman he had seen a man throw something into a bush and run off.

Later, Weitzman assisted other officers in recovering a rifle on the sixth floor of the †Texas School Book Depository Building. On the following day, he signed an affidavit that appears on page 228 of volume 24 of the Warren Commission Hearings. In the affidavit, Weitzman said that at 1:22 P.M. he and Deputy Sheriff Eugene L. †Boone found a rifle on the sixth floor of the Depository Building. "That rifle was a 7.65 Mauser bolt action rifle equipped with a 4/18 scope, a thick leather brownish-black sling on it." Weitzman had once been in the sporting-goods business and was extremely knowledgeable about rifles. The rifle the †Warren Commission identified as the murder weapon is clearly stamped "Made in Italy" and "Cal. 6.5," distinguishing it unmistakably, even for someone with no more than a cursory knowledge of rifles, from a German-made 7.65 Mauser.

Deputy Boone told the Warren Commission that he thought the weapon he found was a 7.65 Mauser, and claimed that Captain Will †Fritz had also given the rifle the same identification. When the Commission showed Boone the †Mannlicher-Carcano rifle in its possession, Boone said he could not identify it as the rifle he had found.

📖 *Rush to Judgment*

WEST, JOE

A private detective, West announced in May 1990 that there had been a gunman on the †Grassy Knoll. He identified the gunman as †Mafia figure Johnny †Roselli, who in 1976 had been killed in a gangland-style execution.

📖 *High Treason 2*

WEST, ROBERT H.

West, A Dallas County surveyor, was standing on

Main Street watching the president's limousine slowly head west on Elm when he heard what he thought was a motorcycle backfiring. He reports that he then heard three more of what now sounded like "rifle fire" noises. He claimed the shots originated in the "northwest quadrant" of †Dealey Plaza, which is the location of the wooden fence on the †Grassy Knoll. *See also* DEALEY PLAZA WITNESSES.

📖 *Crossfire*

WHALEN, EDWARD

According to former New Orleans district attorney Jim †Garrison, Whalen was a professional criminal whom David †Ferrie and Clay †Shaw attempted to hire to kill Garrison before he could begin his investigation of the Kennedy assassination. Shaw supposedly offered Whalen $25,000 plus expert medical care for his daughter, who had cancer, if Whalen would accept the job. Whalen decided he didn't want to kill a district attorney, so he turned down the offer.

📖 *On the Trail of the Assassins*

WHALEY, WILLIAM

Whaley was a Dallas cabdriver. The †Warren Commission claimed that Lee Harvey †Oswald used

Whaley's cab to escape from the assassination scene, following a brief bus ride. Whaley provided the Commission with his trip log, which showed that he had picked up a passenger near the Greyhound Bus Station at 12:30 P.M. and dropped him off at 12:45. Since the president was shot at 12:30 P.M., the Commission decided that Whaley picked up Oswald at 12:47 or 12:48, but recorded the time as 12:30 because he kept his log in fifteen-minute intervals. The Commission did not explain why Whaley did not write 12:45 instead of 12:30, nor did it acknowledge that the trip log contained start and stop times in other than fifteen-minute intervals. Other times recorded in the log include 8:10, 10:50, and 9:40.
See also MCWATTERS, CECIL J.
📖 *Rush to Judgment*

WHITE, GENEVA
See WHITE, ROSCOE.

WHITE, J. C.
On the day of the assassination, Dallas police officer White was assigned to the west side of the railroad overpass that borders the west end of †Dealey Plaza. White claims he saw nothing of the assassination because a train crossed the overpass at the time of the

shooting. He appears to be the only person who reported this train.

See also OVERPASS WITNESSES.

📖 *Crossfire*

WHITE, JACK

White is an assassination researcher who attempted to convince the †House Select Committee on Assassinations that the various photographs of the alleged murder weapon do not match one another. He claimed that after careful study, he found that the length of the weapon differed in at least two photos.

See also "BADGEMAN."

📖 *High Treason*

WHITE, RICKY

See WHITE, ROSCOE.

WHITE, ROSCOE

Roscoe White was a Dallas police officer who was close to Jack †Ruby. In fact, White's wife, Geneva, was employed by Ruby as a B-girl. In August 1990, shortly before she died from lung cancer, Mrs. White claimed that her husband, who had died earlier in a mysterious fire, had been a professional hitman. She further said that at one time, she overheard Ruby and her husband discuss a plan to assassinate President Kennedy. She said that Roscoe and Lee Harvey †Oswald had been friends and had used a nearby firing range together.

Ricky White, son of Roscoe and Geneva, claims he found a secret diary his father had kept containing evidence, including CIA cables, that the CIA had ordered his father to kill Kennedy. The diary and cables vanished soon after Ricky's revelation. There is no hard evidence to support Geneva and Ricky White's claims, although one interesting incident does point to the possibility that they were telling the truth. In 1975, a burglary occurred at the White's Texas home. When the burglars were arrested in Arizona, among the White possessions they had stolen was a never-before-seen version of the famous backyard photograph of Oswald. The FBI obtained the photo and turned it over to the Senate Intelligence Committee. It finally came into the possession of the †House Select Committee on Assassinations, but it was never determined how the White family came to have the photograph in their home.

See also OSWALD, BACKYARD PHOTOGRAPH OF; SHAW, JACK.

📖 *High Treason 2*

WHITMEYER, GEORGE

Lieutenant Colonel Whitmeyer, commander of the Dallas area's Army Intelligence reserve unit, rode in the pilot car that traveled the motorcade route, but maintained a distance of about one-quarter of a mile in front of the car preceding the president's limousine. 📖 *Crossfire; High Treason*

WHITWORTH, EDNA

Edna Whitworth operated the Furniture Mart in Irving, Texas. The store was less than two blocks from the †Irving Sports Shop. She told the †Warren Commission that a man she later identified as Lee Harvey †Oswald, accompanied by a woman she identified as Marina †Oswald and two small children, came into her store one day in November 1963. Oswald asked about a part for a gun, but Whitworth told him the gunsmith's shop was no longer located there, even though his sign was still outside the building. Whitworth's testimony appeared to lend credibility to the testimony of Dial D. †Ryder concerning a repair tag at the Irving Sports Shop for work done on a rifle owned by someone named "Oswald." The Commission discounted Whitworth's testimony for trivial reasons, obviously wanting to discredit the implications of the

rifle repair tag, because the work was not done on the
†Mannlicher-Carcano, which the Commission claimed
was Oswald's only rifle.

📖 *Rush to Judgment*

WILCOTT, JAMES

In March 1978, Wilcott, who had been employed by the
†Central Intelligence Agency for several years, told the
†House Select Committee on Assassinations that
shortly after the Kennedy assassination, a CIA case
officer told him that Lee Harvey †Oswald was an
undercover CIA operative when he defected to the
Soviet Union, but was brought home because the
Soviets never believed in his defection. Wilcott claimed
that the CIA had a hold over Oswald because of some
major crime he had once committed, possibly a murder.

📖 *Conspiracy*

WILLIAM REILY COFFEE COMPANY

Lee Harvey †Oswald worked for a short period at this
New Orleans company. It was next door to the
†Crescent City Garage, where several government
agencies kept their cars parked. It is curious that
Oswald, who was distributing pro-Castro literature in
the streets, worked for William †Reily, who was an

outspoken supporter of the anti-Castro groups in New Orleans. An unusually high number of Reilly employees left the company to work at nearby aerospace companies and at the facilities of the National Aeronautics and Space Administration, raising questions about a possible preexisting—and continuing—link among the employees of the Reily Coffee Company.

📖 *On the Trail of the Assassins*

WILLIAMS, BONNIE RAY

An employee of the †Texas School Book Depository Building, Williams ate lunch near a sixth-floor window on the day of the assassination. When he finished, he joined two coworkers on the fifth floor. He testified that he left the sixth floor about ten minutes before the shooting. He claimed he did not see Oswald or anyone else on the sixth floor while he was there. Williams and his coworkers, James †Jarman, Jr., and Harold D. †Norman, originally reported that they thought the shots came from the right side of the building, toward the †Grassy Knoll. When they appeared before the †Warren Commission, they said the shots came from above them.

📖 *Rush to Judgment*

WILLIAMS, HAROLD

Harold Williams is one of several people, including
George †Arnett, who said that Jack †Ruby and J. D.
†Tippit knew one another. In April 1966, researcher
and author Mark †Lane interviewed Williams in
Arlington, Texas, a Dallas suburb. Lane had heard
that Williams knew from personal experience that
Ruby knew Police Officer Tippit, which Ruby and the
†Warren Commission denied. Williams told Lane that
in early November 1963, he had been arrested while
working as a chef in an illegal after-hours club. He
said that during the raid on the establishment, he was
"roughed up" by a police officer who then placed him
in the back seat of an unmarked car. Williams studied
the faces of the two men who sat in the front seat of
the car, because he considered complaining about the
way he had been treated and wanted to be sure to
remember who was involved. Williams told Lane that
Tippit was the officer driving the car and that the man
seated next to him was Jack Ruby, whom he
recognized because Ruby had arranged for young
women to work as entertainers at the after-hours club
where Williams worked.

Williams explained that after the assassination,
he began telling people about his experience with
Tippit and Ruby. He said that as a result he was taken

into police custody and threatened with arrest on a trumped-up charge if he did not keep his mouth shut.
📖 *Rush to Judgment*

WILLIAMS, DR. PHILIP

Dr. Williams was a young intern at †Parkland Memorial Hospital when the president was brought in after the shooting. After Kennedy died, Williams was sent to get something in which to wrap the body before it was placed in the coffin. He found a "whitish-gray plastic mattress cover," which he gave to the nursing supervisor, Audrey †Bell. This story obviously conflicts with David S. †Lifton's report that Paul K. †O'Connor claimed to have removed the president's body from a zippered body bag when it arrived at †Bethesda Naval Hospital.
See also BODY BAG CONTROVERSY.
📖 *High Treason 2*

WILLIS, LINDA

Linda Willis accompanied her father, Philip L. †Willis, to †Dealey Plaza on November 22, 1963, to see the president and vice president of the United States. Linda and her younger sister, Rosemary, ran along Elm Street to keep up with the president's limousine. Interviewed by researcher and author Jim †Marrs in 1978, Linda said that the "shots came from some-

where other than the Depository." She then charged that people who claimed they knew otherwise weren't even at the scene, but that she was, "that's what makes the difference."
📖 *Crossfire*

WILLIS, PHILIP L.

Willis, a retired Air Force major, took a dozen photographs of the †Dealey Plaza area immediately before and after the assassination. Two of Willis's pictures are extremely important. Willis claims one of them was taken at the moment of the first bullet's impact to Kennedy's throat and shows the president reaching up to the spot where the bullet hit him.

A second photograph, identified by the †Warren Commission as slide number eight, shows the front of the †Texas School Book Depository Building. Clearly visible in Willis's original picture, but for some inexplicable reason cropped and only partially visible in the copy used by the Commission, is a man wearing dark glasses. Willis claims that FBI agents, when they first looked at the photo, seemed to think the man was Jack †Ruby. When Willis saw Ruby in court, he was struck by his resemblance to the man in the picture. Willis said he pointed out Ruby's apparent presence at the assassination scene to †Secret Service agents and

Commission investigators, but "they weren't concerned." When asked about the ⁺single bullet theory, Willis called it "stupid."

Ruby claimed that at the time of the assassination, he was in the offices of the *Dallas Morning News*. Witnesses at the newspaper cannot account for the full duration of Ruby's presence there. As Willis pointed out, "it wouldn't take five minutes" for someone to walk from the *News* office to Dealey Plaza. *See also* RUBY IN DEALEY PLAZA.
📖 *Crossfire; Rush to Judgment*

WILSON, EUGENE M.
Wilson was a salesman at ⁺Downtown Lincoln-Mercury in Dallas when a man calling himself Lee Harvey ⁺Oswald took a vehicle for a test drive. Never called to testify before the ⁺Warren Commission, Wilson confirmed to the FBI that on November 9, 1963, after being told he was not eligible for credit, Oswald commented, "Maybe I'm going to have to go back to Russia to buy a car."
📖 *Rush to Judgment*

WILSON, STEVEN F.
In 1963, Wilson was vice president of the Southwest division of Allyn & Bacon, a publishing company with

offices in the †Texas School Book Depository Building. He was watching the presidential motorcade from a third-floor window when the assassination took place. On March 25, 1964, he told FBI agents that the shots sounded as if they came from the "west end of the building," the direction of the †Grassy Knoll. He then said they "did not sound like they came from above my head." Frequent and annoying visits from the FBI failed to persuade Wilson to alter his statement. Despite the fact that he told the FBI he had no objection to testifying before the †Warren Commission, he was never called.

Researcher Mark †Lane writes that when he requested that Wilson take part in a filmed interview, Wilson declined because he feared the FBI agents would resume their regular visits to his office, and "my work would suffer and so might my health." We are left to wonder why, if the FBI believed Wilson's information was important enough to subject him to repeated questioning, he was never called before the Commission. *See also* TEXAS SCHOOL BOOK DEPOSITORY BUILDING EMPLOYEES.
📖 *Rush to Judgment*

WILSON, TOM
In 1991, Wilson told a conference on the assassination

that he had been able to break down the Kennedy autopsy photographs using a computer-based scanner that revealed the use of paint to alter areas of the photos. Wilson considered the result of his process evidence that the pictures released to the public were forgeries.

📖 *High Treason 2*

WINBORN, WALTER

Winborn was working along the railroad overpass when the president's motorcade entered †Dealey Plaza. Along with fellow workers, he stopped to watch the president pass below, and thus became an eyewitness to the assassination. In 1966, Winborn told an assassination researcher that he saw †smoke coming from the trees atop the †Grassy Knoll after the shots were fired.

See also OVERPASS WITNESSES.

📖 *Rush to Judgment*

WINDSHIELD DAMAGE

Questions have been raised about whether a bullet pierced the windshield of the president's limousine. Such damage would be proof of yet another shot fired at the president.

While the doctors at †Parkland Memorial Hospital

were attempting to save Kennedy's life, two Dallas police officers, Starvis †Ellis and H. R. †Freeman, were standing watch over the limousine. According to a report by David S. †Lifton, Ellis said there was a bullet hole in the left side of the windshield large enough to "stick a standard writing pencil" through. Officer Freeman corroborated what Ellis found, calling it "a bullet hole. You can tell what it was."

Later accounts of the windshield's condition are contradictory. †Secret Service agent Charles Taylor, Jr., is reported as describing a "small hole just left of center." Secret Service chief James J. †Rowley wrote that other Secret Service agents found the windshield "smooth and unbroken." The FBI lab said the windshield it received for examination had damage on the front surface only. Lifton was left to wonder just how many windshields were examined to produce such contradictory results.

See also BULLETS FIRED, NUMBER OF.

📖 *Best Evidence*

WISE, WES

A reporter for KRLD-TV, and later Mayor of Dallas, Wise was never called to testify before the †Warren Commission, even though Malcolm †Couch had told the Commission that Wise reported seeing Jack †Ruby

walking along the side of the †Texas School Book
Depository Building moments after the assassination.
See also RUBY IN DEALEY PLAZA.
📖 *High Treason; Rush to Judgment*

WITT, LOUIS STEVEN
See "UMBRELLA MAN."

WOOD, WILLIAM
See BOXLEY, BILL.

WOODWARD, MARY E.
A staff writer for the *Dallas Morning News,* Woodward
had walked the few minutes from her office to †Dealey
Plaza to see the president during her lunch break. She
found an advantageous spot near the Stemmons
Freeway sign at the base of the †Grassy Knoll. Just as
the president passed by, she heard a "horrible, ear-
shattering noise" that came from behind her and a little
to her right. The †Texas School Book Depository
Building was to her left. Seconds later, the noise, which
she thought might be a car backfiring, was followed by
two more, and she saw Kennedy slump down.
See also DEALEY PLAZA WITNESSES; GRASSY KNOLL
WITNESSES.
📖 *Crossfire*

WRIGHT, FRANK AND MARY

The Wrights lived at 501 East 10th Street in Dallas, close to the spot where Officer J. D. †Tippit was murdered. The gunshots brought the Wrights from their house. Frank Wright reportedly saw the police officer on the ground and a man standing over him. The man circled the police car, then jumped into an old gray car and sped off. This may be the second participant in the murder as seen by Acquilla †Clemmons.

Despite the fact that the Wrights were so close to the scene when Tippit was gunned down, and that Mary Wright placed the telephone call for the ambulance that took Tippit's body away, the couple was never questioned by the FBI or the †Warren Commission. New Orleans district attorney Jim †Garrison charged that FBI director J. Edgar †Hoover ordered that none of his agents were to question either the Wrights or Clemmons.

See also TIPPIT MURDER SCENE WITNESSES.

📖 *On the Trail of the Assassins; Rush to Judgment*

WRIGHT, O. P.

Wright, a former deputy Dallas police chief, was the director of security at †Parkland Memorial Hospital in 1963. It was to Wright that Darrel C. †Tomlinson gave

the bullet he found on a stretcher—the so-called
†magic bullet, as it came to be known. Wright, in turn,
gave the bullet to a †Secret Service agent. When an
FBI agent later showed him exhibit #399 (which the
†Warren Commission had identified as the bullet that
wounded both President Kennedy and Governor John
†Connally), Wright could not identify it as the same
bullet he had had in his possession at the hospital.
📖 *High Treason*

X-RAY CONTROVERSY

X rays of the president's body have caused considerable controversy, including allegations that some X rays were altered or replaced by forged ones. Differences exist between some of the head X rays and the descriptions of the head wounds reported by the doctors who examined Kennedy at †Parkland Memorial Hospital. Included in these disputes is the possible presence of metal fragments that would indicate the head wound was caused by an unjacketed bullet, instead of the jacketed bullets the †Warren Commission claimed Lee Harvey †Oswald used. There are also differences in the location and size of missing portions of the skull. These differences have led to speculation that the head was surgically altered between the time the body left Parkland and the time the autopsy was performed at †Bethesda Naval Hospital.

At a news conference held in New York City on May 28, 1992, and reported by Reuter the next day,

Jerrol F. ⁺Custer, who took the X rays of the
president's head, said that the official X rays released
to the public were "wrong." He then compared the
wounds he had seen to those shown on the X rays and
insisted, "These are fake X rays."
See also AUTOPSY CONTROVERSY; HEAD WOUND
CONTROVERSY.
📖 *Best Evidence; High Treason*

YARBOROUGH, RALPH

Senator Ralph Yarborough of Texas was riding with Vice President and Mrs. Lyndon B. †Johnson in the motorcade, two cars behind the presidential limousine. He reported that the first shot caused him to wonder whether someone had thrown a bomb. He also commented that he could smell a strong odor of gunpowder in †Dealey Plaza, a perception others reported. The smell of gunpowder resulting from shots fired from six stories above street level would not be detectable on the ground; it would drift away in a breeze like the one blowing across the plaza that afternoon. It could, however, have resulted from a gunshot fired from the †Grassy Knoll area.

Yarborough later expressed surprise at how slowly the †Secret Service responded to the first sound. He said the agents responded "very slowly, with no more than a puzzled look."

📖 *Crossfire; High Treason*

Z

ZAPRUDER FILM

Abraham Zapruder was standing on the concrete monument on the †Grassy Knoll filming the presidential motorcade as it passed. He continued filming as the shots were fired. He testified that the shots "came from back of me," meaning the top portion of the Grassy Knoll where the stockade fence is located. Zapruder sold his film to *Life* magazine, although there are charges that the CIA had possession of the film for a time.

The Zapruder film shows the president reach to his throat at the moment of the first bullet's impact. It also shows his head snap back as the fatal bullet strikes, and the pieces of skull, blood, and tissue fly toward the rear of the car. Abraham Zapruder's film is probably the most closely studied and analyzed piece of film in history.

📖 *Best Evidence*; *Crossfire*; *High Treason*

ZR/RIFLE

This was the code name the †Central Intelligence Agency used for an assassination program that was also called †Executive Action. The program employed criminals who were useful "if you need[ed] somebody to carry out murder," as former CIA director Richard †Helms said. Assassination investigators have used this fact to point out that the CIA had relations with, and even employed people who were, professional assassins. ZR/RIFLE is a link in the chain that appears to tie Lee Harvey †Oswald, the CIA, and the Kennedy assassination together.

📖 *Conspiracy*

A READER'S GUIDE
TO THE ASSASSINATION

Someone recently estimated that more than six hundred books have been published that deal in some way with the assassination of President John F. Kennedy. Many of these books do not actually deal with the assassination directly, but discuss issues that are, at best, peripheral to the subject. In some cases, discussion of the assassination is included in an attempt to boost a book's sales when the book's main subject might be of substantially less interest to those millions of people around the world who buy books on the assassination. For the following Reader's Guide, we have decided to include only books that are about the Kennedy assassination itself or that deal with subjects so closely related that they demand inclusion. We considered the possibility of separating the guide into specific subjects, but we found so many books that would have neatly fit into more than one section that we fell back on the expedient course of making a standard bibliography, listing books alphabetically by author. We have included only books published in English in the United States or Great Britain. Our inclusion of a book on this list is no indication that we recommend it or support its thesis. Since this guide is intended for general readers, we have for the most part excluded books that are self-published (a few do remain on the list) as well as many that are long out of print or otherwise difficult to find.

Adler, Bill (pseud. Jay David). *The Weight of the Evidence: The Warren Report and Its Critics*. New York: Meredith, 1968.

Anson, Robert Sam. *"They've Killed the President!" The Search for the Murderers of John F. Kennedy*. New York: Bantam, 1975.

Ashman, Charles. *The CIA-Mafia Link*. New York: Manor Books, 1975.

Belin, David W. *November 22, 1963: You Are the Jury*. New York: Quadrangle, 1973.

Belin, David W. *Final Disclosure: The Full Truth About the Assassination of President Kennedy*. New York: Scribner's, 1988.

Belli, Melvin, with Maurice Carroll. *Dallas Justice*. New York: David McKay, 1964.

Blakey, G. Robert, and Richard N. Billings. *Fatal Hour: The Assassination of President Kennedy by Organized Crime*. New York: Berkley, 1992. Originally published as *The Plot to Kill the President* (New York: Times Books, 1981).

Bloomgarden, Henry S. *The Gun: A "Biography" of the Gun That Killed John F. Kennedy*. New York: Grossman Publishers, 1975; Bantam, 1976.

Brener, Milton E. *The Garrison Case: A Study in the Abuse of Power*. New York: Clarkson N. Potter, 1969.

Bringuier, Carlos. *Red Friday: Nov. 22, 1963*. Chicago: Charles Hallberg & Co., 1969.

Buchanan, Thomas G. *Who Killed Kennedy?* New York: G. P. Putnam's Sons, 1964.

Canfield, Michael L., and Alan J. Weberman. *Coup d'Etat in America: The CIA and the Assassination of John F. Kennedy*. New York: The Third Press, 1975.

Center for the Analysis of Law Enforcement Practices, Citizens Research and Investigation Committee and Louis E. Tackwood. *The Glass House Tapes*. New York: Avon Books, 1973.

Chapman, Gil, and Ann Chapman. *Was Oswald Alone?* San Diego: Publishers Export Co., 1967.

Crawford, Curtis, et al. *Critical Reactions to the Warren Report*. New York: Marzani and Munsell, 1965 (?).

Crenshaw, Dr. Charles A., with Jens Hansen and Gary Shaw. *JFK: Conspiracy of Silence*. New York: Signet, 1992.

Curry, Jesse E. *JFK Assassination File: Retired Dallas Police Chief Jesse Curry Reveals His Personal File*. Dallas: American Poster and Printing Co., 1969.

Davis, John H. *Mafia Kingfish: Carlos Marcello and the Assassination of John F. Kennedy*. New York: McGraw-Hill, 1989.

Davis, Marc, and Jim Mathews, eds. *Highlights of the Warren Report*. Covina, Cal.: Collectors Publishers, 1967.

Davis, William Hardy. *Aiming for the Jugular in New Orleans*. Port Washington, N.Y.: Ashley Books Co., 1976.

Duffy, James R. *Who Killed JFK? The Net: The Kennedy Assassination Cover-Up*. New York: Shapolsky, 1989.

Eddowes, Michael. *The Oswald File*. New York: Clarkson N. Potter, 1977.

Epstein, Edward J. *Inquest: The Warren Commission and the Establishment of Truth*. New York: Viking Press, 1966; Bantam, 1966.

Epstein, Edward Jay. *Counterplot*. New York: Viking Press, 1969.

Epstein, Edward Jay. *Legend: The Secret World of Lee Harvey Oswald*. New York: Reader's Digest Books, 1978.

Flammonde, Paris. *The Kennedy Conspiracy: An Uncommissioned Report on the Jim Garrison Investigation*. New York: Meredith, 1969.

Ford, Gerald R., with John Stiles. *Portrait of the Assassin*. New York: Simon & Schuster, 1965; Ballantine, 1966.

Fox, Sylvan. *The Unanswered Questions About President Kennedy's Assassination*. New York: 1965; Award Books, 1975.

Garrison, Jim. *Heritage of Stone*. New York: G. P. Putnam's Sons, 1970; Berkley, 1972.

Garrison, Jim. *On the Trail of the Assassins.* New York: Sheridan Square Press, 1988; Warner, 1991.

Gauzer, Bernard, and Sid Moody. *The Lingering Shadow.* Dallas: Dallas Times-Herald, 1967.

Groden, Robert J., and Harrison Edward Livingstone. *High Treason: The Assassination of President Kennedy and the New Evidence of Conspiracy.* New York: Conservatory Press, 1989; Berkley, 1990.

Hartogs, Renatus, and Lucy Freeman. *The Two Assassins.* New York: Crowell, 1965; Zebra Books, 1976.

Hinkle, Warren, and William Turner. *Deadly Secrets: The CIA-Mafia War Against Castro and the Assassination of JFK.* New York: Thunder's Mouth Press, 1992. Previously published as *The Fish is Red: The Story of the Secret War Against Castro.* New York: Harper & Row, 1981.

Hurt, Henry. *Reasonable Doubt: An Investigation into the Assassination of John F. Kennedy.* New York: Henry Holt, 1985.

Joesten, Joachim. *Oswald: Assassin or Fall-guy?* New York: Marzani and Munsell, 1964. Republished as *The Gaps in the Warren Report,* n.d.

Joesten, Joachim. *Oswald: The Truth.* London: Peter Dawney, 1967.

Jones, Penn, Jr. *Forgive My Grief.* Vols. 1, 2: Midlothian, Tex.: Midlothian Mirror. Vols. 3, 4: Midlothian, Tex.: Penn Jones, Jr. 1967-1978.

Kantor, Seth. *The Ruby Cover-up.* New York: Zebra Books, 1978; 2d. printing, 1992.

Lane, Mark. *A Citizen's Dissent: Mark Lane Replies.* New York: Holt, Rinehart & Winston, 1966; Fawcett Crest, 1967; Dell, 1975.

Lane, Mark. *Plausible Denial: Was the CIA Involved in the Assassination of JFK?* New York: Thunder's Mouth Press, 1991.

Lane, Mark. *Rush to Judgment.* New York: Holt, Rinehart & Winston, 1966; Fawcett, 1967; Dell, 1975; Thunder's Mouth Press, 1991.

Lewis, Richard Warren. *The Scavengers and Critics of the Warren Report: The Endless Paradox.* New York: Delacorte Press, 1967; Dell, 1967.

Lifton, David S. *Best Evidence: Disguise and Deception in the Assassination of John F. Kennedy.* New York: Macmillan, 1980; Carroll & Graf, 1988.

Livingstone, Harrison Edward. *High Treason 2: The Great Cover-up: The Assassination of President John F. Kennedy.* New York: Carroll & Graf, 1992.

McBirnie, William Stewart. *What Was Behind Lee Harvey Oswald?* Glendale, Cal.: Acare Publications, n.d.

Manchester, William. *The Death of a President: November 20–November 25, 1963*. 25th anniversary ed. New York: Harper & Row, 1988.

Marcus, Raymond. *The Bastard Bullet: A Search for Legitimacy for Commission Exhibit 399*. Los Angeles: Randall Publications, 1966.

Marrs, Jim. *Crossfire: The Plot That Killed Kennedy*. New York: Carroll & Graf, 1989.

Meagher, Sylvia. *Accessories After the Fact: The Warren Commission, the Authorities, and the Report*. New York: Bobbs-Merrill, 1967; Vintage Books, 1976.

Meagher, Sylvia, in collaboration with Gary Owens. *Master Index to the JFK Assassination Investigation: The Reports and Supporting Documents of the House Select Committee on Assassinations and the Warren Commission*. Metuchen, N.J.: Scarecrow Press, 1980.

Menninger, Bonar. *Mortal Error: The Shot That Killed JFK*. New York: St. Martin's Press, 1992.

Meunier, Robert F. *Shadows of Doubt: The Warren Commission Cover-Up*. Hicksville, N.Y.: Exposition Press, 1976.

Miller, Tom. *The Assassination Please Almanac*. Chicago: Henry Regnery Co., 1977.

Morrow, Robert D. *Betrayal*. Chicago: Henry Regnery Co., 1976.

Nash, H. C. *Citizen's Arrest: The Dissent of Penn Jones, Jr., in the Assassination of JFK.* Austin, Tex.: Latitudes Press, 1977.

Newman, Albert H. *The Assassination of John F. Kennedy: The Reasons Why.* New York: Clarkson N. Potter, 1970.

North, Mark. *Act of Treason: The Role of J. Edgar Hoover in the Assassination of President Kennedy.* New York: Carroll & Graf, 1991.

Oglesby, Carl. *The JFK Assassination: The Facts and the Theories.* New York: Signet, 1992.

Oglesby, Carl. *The Yankee and Cowboy War: Conspiracies from Dallas to Watergate.* Mission, Kan.: Sheed Andrews & McNeel, 1976.

O'Toole, George. *The Assassination Tapes: An Electronic Probe into the Murder of John F. Kennedy and the Dallas Coverup.* New York: Penthouse Press, 1975.

Popkin, Richard H. *The Second Oswald.* New York: Avon Books, 1966.

President's Commission on the Assassination of President John F. Kennedy (Warren Commission). *Report of the President's Commission on the Assassination of President John F. Kennedy* (Warren Report). Washington, D.C.: Government Printing Office, 1964. Reprinted by many publishers.

Prouty, Leroy Fletcher. *The Secret Team: The CIA and Its Allies in Control of the United States and the World*. Englewood Cliffs, N.J.: Prentice-Hall, 1973.

Ringgold, Gene, and Roger La Manna. *Assassin: The Lee Harvey Oswald Biography*. Hollywood, Cal.: Associated Professional Services, 1964.

Roffman, Howard. *Presumed Guilty*. Cranbury, N.J.: Fairleigh Dickinson University Press, 1975; New York: A. S. Barnes, 1976.

Sauvage, Leo. *The Oswald Affair: An Examination of the Contradictions and Omissions of the Warren Report*. Cleveland: World Publishing, 1966.

Scheim, David E. *Contract on America: The Mafia Murder of President John F. Kennedy*. New York: Zebra Books, 1988.

Scott, Peter Dale. *Crime and Cover-up: The CIA, the Mafia, and the Dallas-Watergate Connection*. Berkeley, Cal.: Westworks, 1977.

Scott, Peter Dale, Paul L. Hoch, and Russell Stetler, eds. *The Assassinations: Dallas and Beyond: A Guide to Cover-ups and Investigations*. New York: Random House, 1976.

Sites, Paul. *Lee Harvey Oswald and the American Dream*. Pageant Press, 1967.

Sparrow, John H. A. *After the Assassination: A Positive Appraisal of the Warren Report*. New York: Chilmark Press, 1967.

Summers, Anthony. *Conspiracy*. New York: McGraw-Hill, 1980; Paragon House, 1989.

Thompson, Josiah. *Six Seconds in Dallas: A Microstudy of the Kennedy Assassination*. New York: Bernard Geiss Associates, 1967; rev. ed., Berkley, 1976.

Thornley, Kerry Wendell. *Oswald*. Chicago: New Classics House, 1965.

Warren, Earl. *The Memoirs of Earl Warren*. Garden City, N.Y.: Doubleday, 1977.

Weisburg, Harold. *Whitewash*. Vols 1–4. Hyattstown, Md.: self-published, 1965–1967. Vols. 1, 2 republished in New York by Dell, 1966–1967.

White, Stephen. *Should We Now Believe the Warren Report?* New York: Macmillan, 1968.

Wilber, Charles G. *Medicolegal Investigation of the President John F. Kennedy Murder*. Springfield, Ill.: Charles C. Thomas, Publisher, 1978.

Zirbel, Craig I. *The Texas Connection: The Assassination of President John F. Kennedy*. Scottsdale, Ariz.: The Texas Connection Co., 1991.

A VIEWER'S GUIDE TO THE ASSASSINATION

Best Evidence (1970). Produced by David S. Lifton, this film is based on his book of the same title. Through interviews with witnesses, the film focuses on the differences in testimony concerning the president's wounds and regarding the coffin in which he was transferred from Dallas to Washington.

Declassified: The Plot to Kill Kennedy (1979). This one-hour documentary examines the possible conspiracies behind the assassination.

Executive Action (1973). Based on the novel of the same name, coauthored by Mark Lane, this 90-minute feature stars Robert Ryan and Burt Lancaster as leaders of a group of businessmen who plot to kill the president to protect their business interests.

The Fateful Trip to Texas: The Assassination of a President (1969). Produced by historian Arthur M. Schlesinger, Jr., and Fred Israel, the seven-minute documentary was released by Chelsea House Communications, New York.

Four Days in November (1964). This two-hour documentary was produced by Mel Stuart and released by United Artists.

JFK (1991). Oliver Stone's famous feature starring Kevin Costner as New Orleans district attorney Jim Garrison was widely attacked by establishment press and television commentators for its distortions of history. The movie is based on Jim Marrs's *Crossfire* and Jim Garrison's *On the Trail of the Assassins*.

The Kennedy Assassination: What Do We Know Now That We Didn't Know Then? (1978). This film was produced by Witness Productions and released through Sundicast Services, Inc.

Ruby (1992). This feature film, starring Danny Aiello in the title role, is a fictionalized account of the underworld activities of Jack Ruby. In the film, Ruby is ordered to kill Lee Harvey Oswald to prevent him from talking about the assassination.

Ruby and Oswald (1978). This television film was based on the activities of Jack Ruby and Lee Harvey Oswald before and after the assassination; Frederic Forrest and Michael Lerner starred.

Rush to Judgment (1964). Coproduced by Mark Lane, this two-hour documentary is based on his book of the same title and focuses on the question, Where were the shots fired from? It was released by Impact Films.

The Trial of Lee Harvey Oswald (1977). This TV miniseries cleverly blended fact and fiction; Lorne Greene and John Pleshette starred.

The Trial of Lee Harvey Oswald (1987). This 1987 miniseries created a trial for Lee Harvey Oswald—something he never had in reality. Working without a script and using no professional actors, Vincent Bugliosi attempted to convince a jury of Dallas residents (chosen from voter registration records) of Oswald's guilt. Gerry Spence, a famous trial lawyer, defended the absent accused assassin. The judge was a sitting Texas judge, and the action took place in a real courtroom and followed all the rules and procedures of an actual criminal trial. All the witnesses called to testify were actual witnesses to events surrounding the assassination. The film is a fascinating portrayal of what Oswald's trial might have been like, had he lived.

Two Men in Dallas (1977). Narrated by Mark Lane, this one-hour film focuses on the activities of one of the most important witnesses of the assassination, Deputy Sheriff Roger Craig. It was released by Alpha Productions.

Winter Kill. Jeff Bridges stars in this fictitious account of how the brother of a murdered president discovers that the killing was ordered by Mafia bosses.

PHOTO CREDITS